Table of Contents

Introduction

We are on the brink of a great revelation;
I am not the revealer.

We are on the brink of a great revelation;
This is my role.

We are on the brink of a great revelation;
What is your role?

If you were drawn toread this book, you probably feel no surprise at the assertion that we are on the brink of a great revelation. In fact, many readers of this book have been anticipating this revelation for most of their lives. Bear in mind that with any revelation, any such break*through*, also comes the break*down* of interfering structures, whatever has kept us from seeing and understanding. All of us have these structures, and we have come to depend upon them, even if we haven't realized it.

In this book I offer several distinct writing styles expressly for resolving the blocking structures of our lives. Sometimes the teachings come in through inspiration meant to elevate the reader into the frequencies of consciousness. At other times I introduce certain vital tools that, when practiced regularly, greatly assist in the awakening process. Finally, some teachings are here to elucidate the disharmonious nature of the mind so that we can begin to see it clearly. When we understand more fully how the mind blocks us from realization of the fundamental, unutterable truth throughout all that is, we will find it much easier to tune to the alternative, which is consciousness. The teachings of the mind are quite elaborate, and, unless we have a critical perspective on the nature of the mind, we will be unaware of being tuned exclusively to that channel. In such a case we carry on entrapped in mind, not realizing that we have another option.

One of the primary purposes of this book is to so clarify the differences between consciousness and mind that the reader will immediately begin noticing when they are tuned to mind, which is the source of suffering, and upon so realizing, choose to tune to consciousness instead. As we continually observe the mind and choose to tune in to consciousness, liberation reveals itself. In this work I often use the word "spiritual" for ease of communication.

It is an easily misconstrued word. In truth all things are equally spiritual, so we should be careful not to attach a feeling of specialness to it. "Unfoldment" and "realization" are two other words I commonly employ here as well. "Unfoldment" as I use it indicates radical simplification, while "realization" indicates being aware of something that had previously gone unnoticed. None of these words equate to becoming, growing, or attaining.

In this work, I include many of the visions that have served in my unfoldment process. I have endeavored to record them as accurately as possible, free of personal belief. The value of these visions lies in their service to your unfoldment process, should you choose to explore what they have to offer.

In terms of layout, the book divides into four parts, which you may imagine as spokes on a wheel, all leading to a common center, awareness. The first quarter of the book tells my personal story; I mean it to familiarize the reader with the motivations and the means by which I discovered the teachings that I summarize in parts two, three, and four. Part two lays down the foundational principles and practices to aid readers in an awakening process. Part three discusses ways to keep the body and mind healthy during the spiritual awakening process. Part four explores the soul and the spirit, the fundamental forces that stimulate suffering and drive us toward the awakening process.

This book is written entirely through connection with the unnamable, the Tao. Of course, for the sake of communication, we must have a word: Lao-Tzu used Tao, and I use Isness or Soul. But let's not get caught up in these names, as they mean nothing in particular. This book exists to serve those who are ready for revelation. As this book has the express purpose of revealing what lies beneath, it will bring up hidden disharmonies within the reader. We may feel anxiety and fear. We may feel frustration or anger. We may feel as if something is blocking us from going further. That something is what lurks beneath, not wanting to be seen. These blockages are the internal structures that apocalypse breaks down to reveal the truth within.

I recommend that readers, before engaging with the book, put themselves into as calm and unconditionally loving a space as possible. And only after the dust settles do we read. When the dust rises, we calm again, allowing the dust to settle before we continue. In this way, we can read and receive the true power of this message, a power that goes well beyond words.

Part 1 — My Story

Since my late teens, I have felt compelled to write down all the spiritual visions and insights that I have experienced. I knew it would result in a book that would help to elevate mankind out of unconscious disharmony and into conscious harmony. What I didn't understand at the time I began this was how my personal stories would be of service to anyone else or how those might tie together in a meaningful way that would assist people in their unfoldment process. I did not want a bunch of interesting personal stories that were of no practical service to anyone else. What would be the point of that?

Not until I began teaching weekend intensive meditation retreats did all of the missing information begin to flow in, tying everything together in a harmonious whole to create a deeply practical message to the world. I understood then that I should write the story of my life: I saw how that story wove the tapestry of spiritual unfoldment and how spiritual unfoldment wove the tapestry of my life. One cannot be extricated from the other, because spiritual unfoldment occurs through our lives.

My deepest prayer is that this story be of assistance to others, helping them to understand how spiritual unfoldment and vision flow through their own lives. My life is no more special than anyone else's, but it serves as a workable example of practical daily unfoldment. I pray that your life is an even better example.

Chapter 1 — The Promise

I grew up on a horse ranch in rural Southern California, where sagebrush and chaparral foothills seemed to stretch on forever. During summer months, the neighborhood kids would spend dawn to dusk in those hills. We played cowboys and Indians, hide-and-seek, and war; we built forts, constructing teepees from dill weed and dried grass. We hiked the eucalyptus-strewn hills and valleys and went swimming in the lakes. Life was simple and full of adventure, until one day when everything changed.

After our war game ended one afternoon, an older kid told us that his mother would be teaching Bible study at their house the following evening and that we should all attend. I had no idea what the Bible was, but after he said that we'd burn in Hell for not attending, we all signed up on the spot.

Mrs. Pacetti lived in a beautiful Spanish-style stucco compound at the top of a hill surrounded by four acres of avocado groves. A large garage stood sentry between the narrow driveway and the house, blocking visibility. Mrs. Pacetti kept the palatial house immaculately clean, to the point that just being there made me nervous, for fear of accidentally touching something.

She taught the older children while her daughter taught the younger ones like me. I was only about eight years old, and I couldn't understand much other than Jesus was the heroic Son of God, who used the power of love to save people and perform great miracles. Each of us was given a Bible that we could read as homework. I had a learning disorder, and reading was very difficult for me, but I made time every night before sleep to try to read the Bible. I liked reading the Bible, despite my disdain for reading in school.

All went well until, one night, some months into the classes, when Mrs. Pacetti had us all meet in the main room of the house for a combined study session. She explained that we, as shepherds of the Lord, had a duty to find the lost sheep and lead them to salvation. We were to convert our parents, for if they weren't Born Again then surely they would burn in Hell for eternity. Some of the parents were already Christians of various denominations, but according to Mrs. Pacetti that did not matter, as only Born Again Christians were truly saved. I was terrified. I didn't want them to go to Hell. But how was I, an eight-year-old boy, going to convince my parents to convert?

I went home that night, determined. I had no idea how I was going to convince my parents, but they were going to convert. After dinner, I asked if

I could speak to them about religion. They were surprised but said religion was an adult subject, and that we would have to discuss it as adults. They asked me if I were willing to have this adult discussion. Pride welled up within as I said, "Yes." My father asked me if I had a Bible, which I quickly retrieved from my bedroom while he got his two Bibles. Together we had three different Bible translations.

I told them that Mrs. Pacetti had warned us that our parents would go to Hell if they didn't become Born Again Christians. Gently, my father asked if I believed God to be a loving Being.

"Yes," I said.

He then asked, "Is it loving to send someone to Hell for eternity just because the person wasn't a Born Again Christian?" I was losing confidence, and tears began to well up. He then asked, "If you were God, would you send us to Hell for not being Born Again Christians?"

I said, "Of course not."

He went on: "Would you love or respect a God that would send people to Hell just for being of a different religion?" After thinking about it, I realized I would not respect that God. In fact, I wouldn't even like that God. He told me of the many people in far-off lands who might never even hear of Christianity. He asked if people should be punished if they had no knowledge of Christianity and, therefore, no ability to choose to become Born Again. He then told me about Islam, a religion that teaches that all who worship deities other than the one true God, Allah, go to Hell. Who is right? Who is wrong? Is everyone going to Hell?

We opened our Bibles and began comparing verses. He had me read the text and then compare it to his Bible's translation. They were slightly different, and from even small variations, I saw that the outcome could be quite different understandings. Looking at the resurrection story of Matthew as compared to resurrection stories of Mark, Luke, or John, we could see the accounts were drastically different. After Jesus is removed from the cross, his body is entombed, and the entrance covered over with a large boulder. Because Jesus claimed that he would resurrect in three days, some of his followers went to the tomb to investigate and ritualistically care for the body, if it were there. The stories of each book differ quite dramatically as to what occurred at the tomb. The gospel of Matthew describes an earthquake and an angel descending to roll away the stone and sit on it. In Mark, the stone is already moved away. The text mentions a young man dressed in white, with no indication as to who he is. In Luke, the stone had been rolled away, and inside the tomb are two men in dazzling attire, whereas in John, the stone was moved away from the entrance, and no one went inside to check on Jesus' body. Which story was correct? I had no idea.

At the end of our conversation, my father confided that he didn't presume to know the truth and didn't think anyone else knew, either. He asked me if I really wanted to know the truth about God. I nodded. He said, "Then you must be very honest, keep an open mind, and keep searching."

Later that year I began to have a series of very powerful dreams, wherein I would wake up in a dream state that had far more depth than waking reality to find a man lying on the floor in the middle of my bedroom. The room was filled with a feeling of love and warmth, and I had a strong desire to approach him. When I came close enough to look into his eyes, I could sense compassion and infinite understanding, and instinctively I knew he was Jesus Christ.

His eyes glowed with love, and yet there was also a deep sorrow. I looked at his body and realized something was wrong — it was sagging. I returned my gaze to his eyes, and he pleaded, "Help me." I tried to help him up, but his forearm squished in my hands like a water-balloon. I realized he had no skeleton. Try as I might, I couldn't budge him. I awoke, still hearing "Help me," yet feeling utterly helpless.

How could a child help Jesus Christ, I wondered. This dream repeated many times over a period of months, and each time it ended with the feeling of profound helplessness. The memory seared my soul and replayed itself during my waking hours. I pulled into myself, fearing that no one would understand what I was feeling, or that I would be ridiculed and shunned. I was alone.

In school I would daydream in class, wondering what Jesus wanted, but no answer came. Finally, one night in a dream, I got my answer. The dream was the same — except for the last moment, at the point when I usually awakened. This time an intense energy surged through, anchoring me in the dream. "How can I help you?" I asked.

"Find my bones, for they are the core of my teaching. Most of what is written about me is untrue. Mankind has so twisted my teachings for selfish gain that little of the essence remains. What little remains is largely overlooked in the religious ritual and confusion. Find the essence of my teachings and give it back to the world. That is how you can help. Will you do this?"

Although I had no idea how I would possibly accomplish this task, there was a deep, palpable feeling of Rightness, so I promised that I would. That was my last dream of Jesus and the beginning of a lifelong quest.

Chapter 2 — The Search

My search began with the Bible, but because I had a learning disorder, I couldn't read it well enough to really understand it. I was frustrated by not having the means to understand the sources available to me. I took special education classes in school, but they were not helping me learn to read.

I attended church the few times that my grandparents visited, but always the sermons were negative. I felt that church was not the place for me. Eventually I realized no teachers could give me the answers, and no books held the truth I sought. I was dead in the water from step one. Still, I wanted someone to help me.

At the age of 12 I had a strong desire to practice karate. I wasn't very good at it at the time, but the teacher was a kind and honorable man. In retrospect, his technique probably wasn't particularly special, but his focus on teaching us to build strong character, to have integrity and courage, gave the nourishment that I craved. I became engrossed in karate training. I walked around my parents' ranch, kicking and punching at all manner of imaginary opponents. I must have been a constant source of entertainment for anyone who took the time to notice.

When I was old enough, my mother began paying me for doing such chores as cleaning the horse paddocks. We had usually a dozen to 20 horses on the property at any given time for boarding and training, so cleaning all of the paddocks was very time consuming. And like any kid, I tended to daydream through work.

For safety reasons, my mother demanded that I move the horse out of its corral and into a holding area before I began mucking. One day, I decided to skip this step to save time. I had my back to the horse while cleaning, fading in and out of daydream as usual. Suddenly I felt an intense pressure at the back of my head, and without any conscious decision on my part, my body moved quickly aside as if it had a mind of its own. A horse's hoof flew past me. The horse had tried to kick me in the back of the head. I turned and whacked it with my plastic rake until it was backed into a corner and showing submission. After the horse calmed down, I led it to the holding area as I should have done to begin with, then I returned to my duties.

I felt a tremendous energy in my body, and a profound calm accompanied my work. A few minutes later, I felt a pulling sensation from above. My eyes were drawn to a single cloud, high in the sky, directly overhead. My body filled with light as my consciousness was pulled up into the cloud.

I found myself just inside the entrance of a hotel conference room. I instinctively knew it was a vision of things to come. A man on stage was teaching a standing-room crowd about spirituality, the purpose of life, and how to be truly free. He did not look like a pastor or priest or any other type of clergyman, yet he was altogether holy, not in the way he physically appeared but in the presence that emanated from his very being. An unconditioned love invisibly pervaded the room, giving as great or greater a lesson than the words he spoke. Although people could not see this love, they could feel it. This great teacher had an aura about him which was so true, pure, and powerful that just to be near him was enlightening and healing. At this point I realized that this was my future. Suddenly I was back in my body, filled with bliss. I loved that great teacher, and I knew this was to be my future, but how I would get there I had no idea.

This vision was incredibly inspiring; it reminded me of my promise to Jesus. I was a fairly weak child and not very good at anything apart from running. I could run like the wind, but I knew that running wasn't going to help me keep my promise. I feared that I would disappoint Jesus, myself, and anyone who needed the teachings. If I failed, my life would not be worth living, I thought. In retrospect, I see this was a tremendous pressure for a child to bear.

These were very frustrating times in my life, because I had no spiritual mentors. My only mentor was my karate instructor. I felt he would not understand my situation, though, so I never mentioned it to him. Shortly after that vision, my karate instructor moved away and was replaced by another instructor who was far less noble. I continued with karate for a while, but the entire atmosphere of the dojo changed for the worse once Peter Sensei left, and it was no longer a pleasant place to be, so I quietly dropped out.

Chapter 3 — Personal Apocalypse

Apocalypse is a hot-button word in society, one that most people misunderstand. When we think of apocalypse, we think of total destruction, but what we fail to see is its other aspect, revelation. It entails breaking everything down to such an extent that the only thing remaining is truth. This is exactly what happened to my life as events occurred to destroy my world and bring me to the precipice of suicide.

As I mentioned previously, I had been enrolled in special education in elementary school due to a learning disorder. I and other such students had our classroom in a trailer behind the school. We were not taught how to read but just given busy work. We sensed that the teacher did not believe in us, and I mistakenly took that feeling to heart. Most of the children in that class were frustrated, rebellious, and, of course, troublemakers, and though I was in class with them, they were not my friends.

Fortunately, I had become good friends with an older neighborhood boy who had graduated high school several years early and already had his own computer software company. Tim was a strong reader, able to consume about 100 pages of a typical novel in about an hour. He had an entire closet filled from floor to ceiling, back to front, with books he had read. I was in awe of his intellect.

I received a computer one Christmas, and since no one that I knew, apart from Tim, had any computer experience, he and I became good friends. On Friday nights, Tim would always go to the bookstore and buy three or four books to read over the span of the evening. Sometimes, I would stay over at his place on Friday nights to play games on his computer. The one rule on sleepover nights was no sleeping, so I would play video games while Tim read his books. He'd burn through all of them come breakfast time. I, on the other hand, continued playing video games until it felt like my eyeballs would fall out and roll around on the desk.

Tim often told me of the interesting characters, of the twists and turns in the novels he had read. He read a lot of historical books as well, sharing with me how WWI began with the happenstance assassination of Archduke Franz Ferdinand of Austria, or how the Germans lost WWII thanks to their invasion of Russia as winter set in, and so on. Little by little, I became interested in reading about history, politics, and economics.

Tim, I am sure, knew that I could not read, but he never once mentioned it, which I greatly appreciated. Instead, he ignited my interest by taking me to bookstores, where he would invariably recommend this or that title to me while he made purchases. After repeated bookstore visits, I took the bait. I asked Tim if I could borrow one of his books. He lent one of his favorites, insisting that I keep it for as long as it took me to get through it. I began reading as soon as I got home. I read the first page at least 30 times because by the time I was ready to turn the page, I could no longer remember the content. Nonetheless, I kept trying for the better part of a month, forcing my way through the first 10 pages, unable to retain anything.

Eventually, I admitted my defeat and asked Tim if I could borrow an easier read. This time, he lent me a twisted horror book about vampires. Much less challenging, it also had a lot of sex in it, which is enough to motivate almost any budding teen. I read it a little at a time and slowly became able to understand the story line. This book was the first in a series, so once I finished with it, I borrowed the next and the next until I was done with the series. I was beginning to feel comfortable with reading. As I became more confident, I asked for progressively more challenging books, eventually returning to the first book Tim lent me. This time, I was able to read it comfortably, and my confidence soared.

As I said, Tim had graduated high school several years early. And now that I could read and I had gained some confidence, I became interested in that idea. I was never a very good student, but now that I had some confidence in myself, I wanted a challenge. I wanted to graduate as soon as possible, so I could go to college and thereby pick and choose my own classes and enjoy a more mature student body. I began reading books about war, finding that, in the history of war, we have much to learn about modern civilization.

Human civilization has historically been (and remains) based on war and dominance of resources. Cities are unsustainable, having to acquire resources externally. What happens when people outside a city do not want to give up their resources? Some combination of physical, economic, and/or cultural warfare ensues. Centralization of power creates a resource-hungry situation that inevitably brings about domination and warfare in the name of progress. The studies of governance, law, taxation, politics, geopolitics, economics, energy, technology, and so forth, are all corrupt children of centralized power. School prepares children to be cogs in the machine of centralization, not to question the system. Gradually seeing this connection, I spent less time on my school studies and much more time on my own.

We lived in California, where passing a test called the California High School Proficiency Examination allows students to graduate high school early. All I had to do to get my diploma was pass this test. Tim was sure that I could do it, just as he had a few years earlier, so I gave myself one year to prepare for it. I disregarded my school studies and focused on what really mattered: reading, writing, and to a lesser extent mathematics. During this time, my only social contact was Tim. We'd get together to bowl or play table tennis, billiards, and video games while discussing geopolitics, economics, history, and other such topics.

By and by, Tim moved away, and I found myself alone. During the entire time that I knew Tim, I never once told him of the visions or my promise to Jesus. To him, nothing could exist beyond what the logical mind could define and what science could prove. I knew he would not respect my chosen direction, so I kept quiet. To fill the social void created when Tim moved away, I began training at the dojo again. The new teacher was young and only interested in technique, so I went there more for social purposes than anything else.

About this time my mother hired a new ranch hand, John. Although he was nearly 60 years old, he had a lean, stocky, muscular body. He liked boxing, and I liked the martial arts, so we enjoyed conversation. He was a nice man who often gave me well-meaning if not always wise advice. I really enjoyed having him around. He lived quietly in a trailer behind our barn, his salary a pittance. I assumed he had fallen on hard times and just needed the work even if it didn't pay much. He worked hard and didn't drink, so he was all right by me.

My parents bought me an old Volkswagen Bug on my 16th birthday. One afternoon, I needed to go to the convenience store, and I asked John if he wanted to come along. He agreed, and we enjoyed conversation as we drove. On the way home, I noticed that John had become unusually quiet and that he was paying a little too much attention to the rearview mirror. I looked back and found that a sheriff's squad car was on my tail. Without taking his eyes off the side mirror, John told me to remain calm and drive slowly. The squad car followed us for several long miles, and I was beginning to think that it was nothing when the siren sounded. As I pulled over, John nervously told me that if asked about him I should say that I had just picked him up as a hitchhiker. John was in trouble with the law.

Two deputies came on foot along each side of my car. The one asked for my license and registration while the other took a good look at John. I was informed that I had a taillight out and needed to have it fixed. The officer on my side then leaned in for a long, clear look at John. Surprisingly, he said we were free to go, and they returned to their car.

I pulled away, my head in a spin. I demanded that he tell me what he was in trouble for. He said he would only tell me if I promised not to tell anyone. I said I couldn't make that promise if he was involved in any harmful or violent crimes. He said that I should know he would never hurt anyone. He confided that he was an escaped convict, but he assured me that it was nothing serious. He was busted for selling marijuana. He justified this by saying that it really wasn't dangerous and shouldn't be illegal. He assured me that he didn't do anything unlawful anymore, so I need not worry about it. I promised to keep quiet.

About a month went by without a visit from the sheriff, and I began thinking that they had not recognized John after all. Then one Sunday afternoon, that assumption was shattered when a horde of black cars poured onto our ranch. The property was crawling with what appeared to be thugs, drug dealers, and pimps armed with shotguns, automatic weapons, and pistols. We were terrified. Eventually, several "pimps" addressed us flashing police badges. They calmly told us to remain inside and then peacefully explained the situation.

John was a wanted felon, convicted of cooking up and selling crystal methamphetamine. Crystal is a hard drug and definitely harmful. The police had been monitoring John's criminal activities, through undercover agents, waiting for the right time to spring their trap. He was using the small trailer to cook up the drug and then having a friend come over on occasion to pick up and distribute it.

I asked if I could go to the trailer to confirm his illicit activities for myself. As I neared the trailer, the police were hauling John's girlfriend away. I learned that, earlier, they captured John at a small private airstrip. We never had a chance to see him again, thankfully. I peeked into the trailer and saw his setup. John was a drug dealer. I couldn't believe I fell for his lie.

I was glad they caught John, but I felt guilty for not telling my parents that John was an escaped convict when I should have. I felt that I had been an accomplice to John's illicit activities, enabling him to produce his poison.

Had they wanted to, the police could have legally seized my parents' property, and it would have been my fault. I fell into a silent depression, having lost trust in myself. Unknown to me at that time, an undercover officer posing as a drug dealer had been observing my parents for several months leading up to the sting, so he knew that my parents had no knowledge of the illicit activities.

Just about this time I took the California High School Proficiency Examination, passed it, and earned my diploma. I stopped going to school in the middle of my 11th-grade year. I decided to attend a local college to save money; I could transfer to a university later. While waiting for my first semester to begin, I worked for my mother on the ranch, doing the work that John used to do. Then I changed my college plans from full-time to part-time until we found someone suitable to replace me. Fearful that we would end up with another deadbeat employee, I gave up my plans of transferring quickly to a four-year school. I graduated high school early in hopes of speeding my education, only to find myself back in the slow lane. I had no faith in myself, I had no friends, and my dreams were slipping through my fingers. I told no one.

I continued training at the dojo, where I was to test for the rank of brown belt in karate, the rank just below black belt. Karate tests at that dojo typically lasted four or five hours. The test began in the morning and continued nonstop until about 3 p.m. We did countless pushups, sit-ups, and squats, and we ran to exhaustion, only then to be tested on technique. Finally, we had to spar against the black belt students. After the sparring was finished, the instructor had the students wait in the dressing room while he did the next activity privately with one student at a time. We heard a crackling sound like a Taser and then a scream. After a minute, another student was taken out of the dressing room to be tased. By the time my turn arrived, I had firmly decided not to be fearful. I was going to take the shock without thought or hesitation; I knew that it would not do permanent damage.

I stood in front of my fellow students, the instructor approaching, the blue light of the Taser crackling. He asked me to stand still and prepare to be tased. "Okay, I am ready," I said, not allowing my mind to think about it. He put the Taser toward my arm, but I continued staring into the distance as if he were not there. The crackle sounded, but he did not touch me with it.

It was all an act to test our emotional reactions. He seemed surprised that I didn't flinch or otherwise show any fear. He retrieved a large-caliber revolver from his office. He told me to take the gun, aim it at my head, and pull the trigger. Immediately, without any thought, I took the gun, and without checking to see if it was loaded, aimed it at my head and squeezed what I thought was the trigger – but the trigger would not budge. I released the safety and returned the muzzle to my head. Washed with pallor, the instructor quickly pulled the pistol from my grasp.

He showed me that the trigger had been removed, so there was no way for me to shoot myself. He admonished that we should never blindly follow orders, no matter who gives them, and that I should have checked to see whether the gun was loaded before handling it. Most importantly, he said, I should never try to kill myself. These were all important lessons, but I felt humiliated, I broke down in tears, feeling exposed. You see, secretly, I had hoped that the gun was loaded — or at least I didn't care whether it was. In that moment, I knew I was suicidal, and I felt that everyone else knew it too.

Although I passed the test and received my new rank, I was in no way happy about it. I felt like a total failure. No. I knew I was a total failure. I stopped going to the dojo. I guess I should have known of my suicidal tendencies earlier, but I had been in denial.

I got caught up with a bad element, drinking alcohol and smoking marijuana to escape from myself. My life was a constant performance because I pretended to be what I was not in order to fit in. I couldn't tell anyone of the visions or my true goals, and the further I strayed from my dreams, the more I hated myself. One summer afternoon I locked myself in my bedroom and admitted my suicidal tendencies. I could find nothing of myself worth redeeming. To stay in the world any longer was a waste of resources because I had nothing to offer. I was just another mouth to feed, I thought, and there was no hope for me.

After I finished preparing for my suicide, letter to family written and method set, I sat down on the floor for a moment just to be. Ironically, knowing that I no longer had a future or past to worry about was a huge relief. I had nothing to fear, nothing to become. I no longer had any need to pretend that I was someone else.

I relaxed, and a profound peace enveloped me. My eyes were drawn to the rays of light pouring through the window. I witnessed something that I had never noticed before: the dazzling display as rays of light intersected with particles of dust floating in the air. It appeared as if there were tiny angels of brilliant light. It amazed me that I had lived for 17 years, yet I had never noticed this amazingly divine phenomenon before.

Suddenly, my body surged, and a voice rang through it, my chest feeling like a speaker: "You can change your life. You can stop spending time with those who are selfish and negative, who don't really care about you. You can stop drinking and smoking. You can find friends who are working for something positive, who have a purpose in life that you respect. You can go to college, even if only part-time. Make your life full of positive purpose. You are free to do what you feel is right. Do what you want to do, and be yourself."

It felt as if an angel had spoken through my body. The voice was so clear and full of Rightness that I trusted it completely. Had it been my own thought or the advice of a person, I am sure I would have rejected it. But now I knew I could do whatever I set my mind to if I just kept at it positively.

I experienced a power there that transformed me in an instant. The paralyzing effects of doubt and self-consciousness ended in that moment. It's not that I no longer felt doubt, but doubt no longer held sway over my decisions and actions. My only concern moving forward was doing what felt right. This moment was such a decisive partition in my life that, looking back on it now, I feel as if I have lived two lives, a negative life of self-consciousness, fear, and doubt, and a new life of passion, love, and direction.

I quickly made new friends, but they never seemed to believe the stories I told them of my negative, self-judging, suicidal life before because that was so at odds with the person that they knew. The change was rapid, but it wasn't all glory. Like anyone, I had times of frustration when I regressed a bit into negative attitudes. But regardless of the difficulties, I had decided to live with purpose — fearlessly and passionately, without regret.

Several years went by during which I focused on preparing for a profession. I wanted to be a psychologist so that I could help people the way that angelic voice had helped me. During this time, I experienced occasional spiritual communications, but, for the most part, my life was fairly typical for a college student. I had a girlfriend, and I was learning what it meant to be in love and to have a relationship. I was now living a passionate life and no longer wishing for death.

Chapter 4 — Back on the Path

A few years later I found myself dissatisfied with the direction I was taking in school. Although I had learned a lot from college, I realized that I was spinning my wheels in some respects. I had formulated the plan to be a psychologist in hopes that someday I could do for others what that divine voice had done for me on my day of planned suicide. But after some study I realized, at least for me, that psychology was not the right path, so I put college on hold and began looking for work.

I got a job offer in another state, and I took it as an opportunity to leave everything behind and start anew. I entered my new job with nothing but the passion for working hard and learning something in the process. I was excited about moving to Georgia because I had never been to that part of the country.

I was hired to manage a sprawling warehouse for a publishing company that was just preparing a major new release. As big as the warehouse was, due to extensive preorders of the upcoming release, we had to stack the pallets over six feet high to accommodate all the new books. Due to the high pallets, visibility was very limited, and I realized that I couldn't see where other employees were at any given time unless I happened to be in the exact position to see or hear them. It is my policy to incorporate training into my life in creative ways, so I thought I could use the vast mazelike aspects of the warehouse to train my awareness.

I devised a game to train my awareness throughout the workday. The idea was to expand my awareness over the entire warehouse to keep track of where other people were at all times. In my game, employees were assassins out to get me, so if I noticed someone before they noticed me, then I survived the assassin's attack. But if someone approached or addressed me unnoticed, then I was killed by the assassin. This game kept my attention sharp throughout the day in a job that failed to challenge me otherwise. I hoped training in this way would give me the sort of sixth sense martial arts legends are said to have had.

Over a span of months, my awareness seemed to be improving, but, as I was the only scorekeeper, I had no objective way of verifying my progress. In the back of my mind I was continually searching for ways to verify the quality of my training method. I wondered if my heightened awareness would be there for me when I really needed it.

Within a few months I got my answer. The CEO, prioritizing team building, had our company join a softball league, and I was recruited onto the team. Except for one player, Mark, a former college-league infielder, the rest of us lacked experience, and most were short on athleticism. Mark could throw a ball at terrifying speeds. During one practice session he split a two-by-six fascia board lengthwise with one of his throws. It was intimidating!

After losing our first few games by many runs, some teammates began drinking beer as they played to enhance their enjoyment of losing. Before long the rest of us joined in. Our inebriation caused us to lose by even greater margins.

Once while I was playing drunken pitcher deep into a perfectly losing season, one of my pitches was hit into right field. Our right fielder caught the ball after it hit the ground and threw it to first base. It went high over the first baseman's head, to the catcher at home base. The runner crossed first and headed for second. The inebriated catcher beamed the ball to the right of the second baseman, who missed it by a long shot. It rolled into the outfield where the centerfielder, Mark, retrieved and tossed it to third. By some miracle third caught Mark's speedy throw. The runner was caught in a pickle, so he turned around and sprinted for second. Third flung the ball at second, but it went high over head, into midfield again toward Mark. By the time Mark got it, I was watching the runner cross home base.

I laughed, chugged my beer, and said to myself, "My lord, we suck." Suddenly I felt a piercing pressure drilling into the back of my head, and without a thought, my body spun around 180 degrees to catch the ball inches before it hit me in the face. Mark had thrown the ball at me while I wasn't paying attention. Somehow my body must have sensed the threat and taken action entirely on its own. I can't explain it any other way.

We lost that game by 30 odd points, having failed to turn the score card even once for our team. It was utterly humiliating, but at least something positive happened to lift our spirits a little — the life-saving catch. When asked about it, I credited martial arts training for the small miracle. My palm ached for several days after that catch, so I couldn't help but wonder what might have been had my body not taken action when it did.

I speculated that the awareness game had somehow awakened my body, and I was motivated more than ever to keep working with this active meditation. It felt great and seemed to blend well with my daily life.

Shortly after this occurrence, I was invited to attend a multilevel marketing meeting in Charlotte, North Carolina. The idea of reciprocity, that I had to help others succeed in order to succeed myself, intrigued me, so I accepted the offer.

I didn't have a car, so the couple that invited me agreed to pick me up at the bus station and drive me up from Georgia. A friend dropped me off at the bus station, but after he left, I realized it was the wrong station. The station I needed to be at was over a mile away, and I had to be there in less than 10 minutes. With no other means of transport, I ran, suit and briefcase, on a sweltering summer day.

By the time I arrived at the correct bus station, I was swimming in my suit. I went to the curbside to look for my ride. I was so focused on my search that I hardly noticed the large man who approached me from my right. He asked me if I had any money. Without looking, I answered that I didn't. It was true; I really had no money, only a credit card. He came closer, encroaching on my personal space, and said, "I said, 'Do you have any money?' Give me some money now."

He was in the process of mugging me. I noticed he was holding a knife, tip nearly touching my right rib cage. Due to my martial arts training, I knew that under normal circumstances I could probably handle this guy easily enough, but behind him were two others watching. If I fought them, someone, probably myself, would be seriously injured or killed. I didn't have any energy to fight after my mile jaunt across town. Worse still, I didn't have money to give them, which would have been my ideal choice given the circumstances. I seemed to have no way out of this situation; someone was going to be hurt or killed.

I took a deep breath, expanded my field of vision and relaxed. Suddenly my body filled with energy, and it felt like I was spread over infinity. My mind went totally silent. I turned to him, my left hand very lightly hovering over his arm yet not actually touching him. I positioned myself so that were he to stab, his knife would deflect past me harmlessly. I looked straight through his eyes and repeated, "I said 'I — Have — No — Money.'"

His eyes grew wide as he froze for a few seconds, unable to speak. Shaken, he slowly backed away. "It's cool, man ... it's cool." He turned around and subtly shook his head to his friends, who looked away as if nothing had happened. Just then my ride pulled up to the curb. Calmly, I got in the back seat and we drove off, my chauffeurs not realizing what had just happened. Immediately we struck up a good conversation that ranged from life in Georgia, to family, friends, and so on. About a half hour later the topic changed to the recent crime uptick in Atlanta, Georgia. This reminded me of the attempted mugging, which I somehow forgot about as soon as we drove away from the bus station. Seeing as we were discussing crime, I used this opportunity to tell them about the mugging attempt, but they clearly didn't believe me, so rather than arguing with them, I let it drop.

As it turned out the attempted mugging was only the beginning of the adventures in store for that weekend. The multilevel marketing meeting was so popular that it took place in a sports stadium. When we entered the stadium, I noticed that off to the right, raffle tickets were for sale. I have never liked lotteries or raffles, so I just ignored it and walked past. But as I passed I had the sensation of a very strong feeling coming from the raffle area, as if someone were pulling on the back of my collar.

Whenever this feeling arose, it always meant something miraculous was about to happen. In the past, if I ignored it, invariably, I had a deep sense of regret, so I surrendered and bought a raffle ticket for a free phone, which I didn't need. I got my ticket, and we took our seats in the bleachers to listen to the day's many speakers talk about "The Business." Nothing else out of the ordinary happened that day.

The next day opened with a prayer session led by a Christian minister. This struck me as odd, as it was immediately followed by prayers to Mammon by top-level sales people. Thousands of people occupied the stands, and the speakers, all millionaires, without exception discussed owning big houses, having luxury and sports cars, and being worth lots of money. The audience seemed to worship these people. I was dumbfounded that they could start out this event with a prayer service about love and light, and then in the next moment be worshiping greed. It was shameless. The speeches went on for hours, and the audience as a whole treated these speakers as if they were saints.

The level of sheer greed was beyond my comprehension. I just couldn't understand why anyone would spend so much time and energy trying to acquire so much stuff. Humans have a limited amount of time and energy, and how we invest that energy determines everything about us, our families, our communities, and ultimately our world. Considering that upon death all of those riches are naught, what is the point? Of course, in order to sustain our physical bodies and put a roof over our heads, we must be mindful of money, but beyond that ... well, I just didn't get the appeal.

Looking around, I felt that these people were missing something in their hearts. Immediately, I was moved to prayer, a prayer from my soul to theirs. I imagined unconditioned love pouring into their hearts. It was so clear that I could actually see it with my eyes — love displacing the greed and causing it to drain away. The whole stadium was filled with the light of love. I must have been immersed in this prayer for a long time because several speeches took place while I was praying, and a popular 1980s rock band had come onstage and played some of its hit songs — I paid no attention to any of it, so engrossed in prayer was I.

The concert ended with a standing ovation. I stood up too, to remain incognito. The momentum of my physical body stopped when it reached its full six feet, two inches, but my spirit just kept on rising. It rose halfway out of my body. I looked around, and it was as if I were seeing through eyes that were several feet above my head.

The spiritual "eyes" gave me much more information than my physical eyes ever could. Everything glowed with a white light — the floor, the bleachers, even people's clothes. I knew that everything was alive and intelligent in a way that people can't see. Time seemed different, too. From this perspective, I was able to experience a much greater depth than normal. As the band left the stage, we sat down, and although my spirit descended back into my body, it remained my window of perception.

Onstage, probably 70 yards from me, came the raffle announcer. I looked at him as if through a telescope. I could see inside his right front pants pocket, which contained a folded piece of paper. Just then, a bullet of pure white light shot from the paper and hit me in the forehead, and I saw that my name was written on the paper. He reached into his pocket, took out the paper, opened it, and with a strong southern accent said, "The winner of the MCI cordless phone raffle is—" I stood up before he said the name, "— Richard Haight." I had won the raffle, yet I didn't care about the phone. All I cared about was the depth of spirit that had touched me through prayer and what it might imply.

I don't remember anything else of the meeting nor the ride home, so totally engrossed was I in trying to understand the incredible spiritual experiences of that weekend. All I wanted was understanding, and I was going to do whatever it took, go wherever I had to go, in order to get it, so long as it was right by my conscience and led by spirit.

Chapter 5 — Isness

I knew I had received what it was that brought me to Georgia and that the time had come to move on. The urge to go back to California then grew so powerful that I gave my notice at work immediately and left as soon as I could. I drove 52 hours straight, meditating the entire time, consuming neither caffeine nor stimulant. I was fueled by spirit.

Almost immediately upon my return to California, I found a group of Spiritualists who were doing healings, readings, channelings, and so on. I wanted to understand the things that were happening to me, so I joined them in hopes that they had something to teach me. I met and worked with many psychics of the Spiritualist community, but there was always something about this work that didn't quite sit right for my life. It wasn't until I broke my ankle while preparing for a karate tournament that everything became clear.

As I was helping some friends prepare for a black belt division tournament, I fractured my ankle by checking a kick incorrectly. It didn't hurt, and there was no swelling, so I had no idea that it was broken. We just continued sparring until the tournament contestants were clear on their strategies and tactics. After practice, I drove to the home of a friend, Michaela, who was studying to be a medium — someone who channels spirits and reads people's futures, and so forth. We went out to dinner at our favorite Chinese restaurant to talk. Shortly after sitting down, I felt a growing pain in my right ankle. I looked down to see that it had swollen to twice its normal size. Moving it brought excruciating pain, and I was unable to put any weight on it. I had previously fractured that same ankle, and it looked and felt exactly the same way it had then.

I went to the doctor's office only to be told that it was a hairline fracture. He explained that it is fairly common for people not to feel a broken bone until hours later. As it was just a slight break, and casting it would not help much, I decided to wrap it and use crutches. Little by little, however, the pain got worse, so I visited Jane, a mentor of mine. She had taken me under her wing to protect me from some of the darker elements within the psychic community. Her healing energy was rather powerful, so I was hoping that it would take away the pain enough that I could at least sleep.

Jane, upon seeing my ankle, agreed to help out, so I lay down on her healing table and she began sending energy with her hands. To my surprise, this made the pain much, much worse. I respected her so much that I felt I couldn't ask her to stop, for fear of insulting her. Instead, I decided I would try to meditate myself beyond the pain.

As I meditated, I cleared myself of all disharmony. Little by little, I felt as if my spirit was rising up, not out of my body, but rising through spiritual dimensions. I would float up to a certain extent, and, invariably, some negativity within would prevent me from going further. I had to identify and release it to continue rising. I entered the consciousness of the sun, the solar system, the galaxy, the universe, and beyond. Each has its own identity, feeling, responsibility, knowledge, wisdom, and so on.

I went through spirit worlds and what felt like Heaven. Finally I encountered a great void, and just beyond it a presence, intelligence, and power so perfect and loving that there are no human words to describe it satisfactorily. It was utterly whole — holy. We humans have a very limited idea of what love is and of what God is, and at that moment my limited perception of both evaporated.

This limitless presence began communicating with me, not in words but in direct understanding. It seemed as if it put knowledge and experience directly into my consciousness, so information came through purely, beyond the filter of the mind and limitations of words. I inquired, "What are you?" Its answer as best as I can put it into words was, "There is no other."

Indeed, this presence felt to be exactly as it described itself, but I just could not wrap my mind around the next logical implication, that we were one and the same. The all-loving presence was unmistakable, yet what it was saying just did not make sense to my logical mind. How was it possible that it was me if I did not perceive myself as being it?

If I was it, then I would be equally aware, and since I had no such awareness, this seemed proof that what it was saying could not be true. So I decided to question this presence further hoping to resolve the ultimate Gordian knot. I started out by asking, "What am I?"

It replied, "No other than I." I was shown how it was always aware of me, even though I was entirely unaware of it up until that moment.

I had read the assertion of Jesus that God is the alpha and the omega (all that is), and the words of Buddha that ultimate reality is Oneness, but words are not actuality. The experience is so difficult to adequately explain that words feel like lead dropping from my lips, heavy and out of place.

My mind partially resisted this new understanding, yet somehow I knew it was true. A power resided in this presence that was incomprehensible, yet utterly palpable. If this was God, it was entirely beyond the God that I imagined when reading the Bible.

The portrayal of God in most accounts reminds me of a violent, racist, jealous, wrathful, insecure, judgmental man. But I found absolutely no condemnation in this presence, nor is there wrath, jealousy, or negativity of any sort. This presence is perfectly forgiving (knowing that there is nothing to forgive), nonjudgmental, and unconditionally loving. Its perfection and love are so enlightening that although it did not judge me, by stark contrast, I could not help but see the imbalance in myself. The light of this presence is so pure that anything seeming less than total purity stands glaringly forth, out of place, although my mind was not aware of this until several months later.

My conscience greatly amplified, and I understood that no thought, feeling, or deed of inequity goes unresolved. Until the resolution, the individual cannot truly be at peace, and will continue to experience separation. The soul within constantly draws to the individual the perfect opportunity for balancing through the situations, events, and relationships of life. Our attitude toward these things either binds or frees us.

Because the word "God" carries with it so many negative associations, and since this presence is beyond the binds of all definition, the word "God" just felt inadequate to me. I tried to come up with a term to more accurately portray its limitlessness. The best one I could come up with was the least defined. It simply is with no qualifiers, and so I began calling it "Isness" for lack of a better term.

Isness unconditionally forgives all things instantly. Even the most evil individual is fully and completely loved by this presence. Able to perceive all universes, bound by nothing, it knows no fear, only total harmony and oneness.

To feel one with Isness became my goal. The feeling is summed up well in the New Testament: "Therefore you shall be perfect, just as your Father in heaven is perfect." I felt that this was possible for all, but I wondered how my mind could create such a convincing sense of separation, negativity, and disharmony. I asked, "How is it that I perceive myself as different from you? How is it that I perceive myself as being imperfect? How is it that I can perceive imperfection at all?" My attention was directed to what appeared as a giant nebula, or star-forming region of space. When I focused on that region, I saw that it was really a clouded mind surrounded by darkness. It had a curious, playful nature, yet it seemed ignorant of its identity and was immersed in the undirected play of self-discovery like that of a young child. From this curiosity countless universes arise, expand, and extinguish, only to birth again and repeat the process with a slightly different angle on things. I understood that there were uncountable universes of many different natures, some similar to our own and many not, seeming to be of different dimensionality.

I was shown countless billions or trillions of years in an instant. Across these universes, ignorance of Isness and the desire to define the self is common. But as deeply engrossed as this clouded mind seemed in its play, it was never for a moment actually outside of or separated from Isness. Otherness was merely a playful dream. The idea of the individual self is, according to Isness, not ultimately true.

I remained consciously aware of Isness for several days. I understood that I and others like myself serve as ambassadors helping those who are ready to wake from the dream of self-identification/otherness to the realization of Isness. It also became clear to me that those who are not palpably aware of and fully tuned to Isness are bound to experience great disharmony.

After the Isness experience, I tried my best to put the experience into words, but I found that certain words were very misleading. One of the most misleading words is "experience," which according to the Merriam-Webster Dictionary, means direct observation of or participation in events as a basis of knowledge. Knowledge means the accumulation of learning, but the effect of an Isness experience is neither knowledge nor learning, but rather an *unlearning* of all that blocks us from awareness of Isness in every moment.

In my attempts to communicate the Isness experience as honestly as possible, I felt a new word was necessary. Therefore I coined "inspirience" – a substitute for experience. Inspirience is my word for any experience of total unity; its roots are *inspire* and *experience*. I understand that you might not appreciate this word initially. Once you have had a true Isness inspirience, though, I suspect its value will be clearer, as it will serve as a reminder not to turn the memory of Isness into knowledge or philosophy. The mind wants to encapsulate everything into the known, but Isness is beyond all definitions, so the very attempt to encapsulate it is to miss it. Just remember, if you are truly seeking the transcendent, knowledge will not long satisfy you.

After the Isness inspirience I found myself in a depression for several years. I realized how selfish, judgmental, prideful, arrogant, small-minded, and hypocritical I was compared to Isness. All of my darkness was so obvious that I couldn't hide it away anymore, as I had been doing unconsciously to some extent all of my life. Since I didn't know how to cleanse myself, I could do nothing about this depression until it wore away with time. This may be one reason that very few people have consciously encountered Isness. Could it be that we are unconsciously avoiding realization of Isness for fear of what will be exposed?

Understanding the Isness inspirience became my sole purpose in life. I spent the next few months living with my parents in the mountains while my leg healed. I used this time to begin digesting what Isness had shown me. Mostly I just ached to return to that consciousness, but I couldn't. This longing haunted me for years but I didn't know how to bridge the gap between the concept of the self and Isness, even though intellectually I understood that there is no real separation. Unable to reconcile the perceived self with what I knew to be true, I felt frustration beyond measure. So I prayed for an answer.

Several years later, the answer came in a dream. I was in an elevator with a group of strangers going up a skyscraper. About halfway up the building, between floors, the elevator suddenly jolted to a halt. All the passengers were surprised, their eyes betraying their nervousness. Something snapped, and the elevator jolted again. Another snap, and we were in freefall, the floor numbers counting down in a blur as we sped toward the ground. Everyone was in a blind panic, screaming. Although I knew this was the end of my life, I had no fear. Instead, a great appreciation for life, the good and the bad, welled up within, for I had learned from all of it. I prayed from my heart, "Thank You," and I stretched out my arms to embrace my last moment on Earth. At that moment the elevator began to slow, and just before hitting the ground floor, it smoothly stopped.

I awoke in deep thankfulness, knowing that this was the way to live with Isness. Freed of my fear of death and my desire to escape "the prison of the body," I would embrace the present moment fully and with passion, because only through the present moment do we truly live.

All of which is a lot easier said than done. Living in the present is an ongoing process wherein relaxed persistence pays dividends. We will have our ups and downs, regardless of who we are. When we fall, we peel ourselves off the asphalt and get back up. If we need to cry, then we cry. And when we're ready, we get back up and move forward again.

Chapter 6 — Land of the Rising Sun

While digesting the teachings of Isness over the next few years, I got a stable job and worked a regular schedule. I met a woman from the Spiritualist community, Kate, who was interested in learning about the Isness inspirience to discover what wisdom might be hidden there. She supported my search with her interest, which helped me to feel more comfortable with sharing the information. I loved the opportunity to elucidate on Isness and its implications. Although I cannot say that I was very successful in my attempts then to pass on the information, Kate was a wonderful cheerleader and supporter, which helped me in ways beyond description.

One day another martial artist asked which martial art I thought the most effective, a question I normally would not answer, but before I knew it out of my mouth came, "Aiki." It was not my opinion, but my mouth said it anyway. It was not me speaking, but it felt right. I didn't really know the meaning of the word, but I was familiar with aikido. I went in search of an instructor but was unable to find one who felt right for me. I saw a video of a martial arts instructor from Japan who taught a style called Daito-ryu Aikijujutsu, the predecessor of aikido. In his Daito-ryu school, the training focused on aiki, a core principle of his art. In the video, that man could throw people effortlessly and with almost no movement whatsoever. It looked fake, but his movement had a flow and stability that was undeniable. Listening to this instructor explain his art, I could feel no deceit. I felt pulled to go to Japan to meet this man, so I quit my job and was on a plane within a few weeks.

I arrived early with a translator at the training hall, a local sports center similar to the YMCA but with mats for martial arts training. We met with the instructor before class, and over a light meal, he told us that his art had a long tradition and that he was one of the few instructors teaching it openly. He welcomed us to observe training that night; if I were interested after observing, I was welcome to become a member.

After the meal, he changed into his training attire, and the lesson began. We watched from the edge of the mats as this master threw students of all sizes around effortlessly. We were not the only incredulous observers that night. It just so happened that a reporter from a Japanese martial arts magazine had come to take photos for an article. Judging by the quizzical look on his face, he too was not sure what he was seeing.

Later he politely told the instructor that he could not understand why the students were falling down so easily. He confided that he was not sure that the techniques were real. He said that he was a sixth-degree judo black belt and that he wanted to feel the techniques for himself to verify the art. He did not want to write an article on something that was not authentic.

What happened next absolutely astounded all of the observers. The instructor held out his right arm and told the man to grab him hard in an arresting fashion. The judo man latched onto the old man's arm and cranked down, causing the instructor to bend at the waist. The instructor asked if the man was ready, and in reply he was given the okay. The next moment the judo black belt lay flat on his back while the old man stood upright, as relaxed as if he had just consumed a glass of wine.

The judo man got up, shook his head in disbelief, and asked if he could try again, saying that he was not ready the first time. The old man smiled and extended his arm again, allowing for the exact same hold and telling the judoist not to hold back. The judoist bore down on the arm and fixed his stance for stability. The old man said, "On the count of three I will start the technique. Are you ready? One ... two ... three ...." Instantly the younger man was flattened, hitting the back of his head firmly on the mat. A little dazed, he got up slowly, bowed deeply, and thanked the instructor.

Not realizing that the instructor did not normally allow outsiders to test him in this way, I asked if I might be allowed to try. A confident, strong, young man, I was not going to allow myself to be fooled. The instructor agreed to demonstrate the exact same technique with me. I also was flattened. Once I got up, he held out his index finger and told me to grab it. As soon as I latched on, I was sent flipping, heels over head. As I was getting up, he walked briskly back to his changing room.

I joined the dojo that night, attending every training session thereafter, but before long an old back injury re-emerged, interrupting my ability to train. When I was 17, I had been struck by a runaway horse, the collision compressing my spine like an accordion. After the injury, I wasn't able to train in martial arts as energetically as I had in the past. I wanted to fight in full-contact tournaments, but hard training would always cause my back to go out, preventing further training for at least several weeks. Strength training became impossible. I hoped aiki training wouldn't bother my back, but after taking a bad fall, I found myself unable to walk without severe pain. I was no longer able to train, so although I continued to attend class, I did so only as an observer.

One day, while observing training, my eyes were pulled to the entrance of the dojo as another student came through the door. He seemed to be glowing with a faint light. I went to him and asked what he had been doing to cause such a glow. Surprised at my comment, he told me that he had just received a type of physical therapy called sotai-ho. He gave me the business card of the practitioner, and I called immediately to set up an appointment.

Although that therapy didn't fix my back problem, it did relieve the pain a great deal and gave me a much greater range of motion. I was able to train again, which was my main goal. I also knew that I needed to take lessons from that man, so I became a private student.

A few years later I received my practitioner's license in sotai-ho and opened up my own clinic, operating out of my house in Tokyo. Through my practice, I found that this therapy could help a great many things, and I decided I wanted to find a way to expand its effects to help with an even greater range of ailments. I prayed for wisdom, but I had to wait for the answer.

Chapter 7 — The Quest

While studying Daito-ryu, a Samurai art, I learned that in ancient Japan survival training was a vital element of all warrior studies. During times of war, the reasoning went, a warrior might encounter survival situations in the deep forests of Japan during missions. I became curious about survival training, but was disappointed to discover that it had long ago been dropped from the curriculum. I began searching for survival classes in America and participated in such classes whenever I returned to visit family.

About a year into this process, I felt a strong pull to vision quest, something I learned about during wilderness awareness and survival training. Nearly every indigenous culture from antiquity consciously recognizes the value of spiritual training and traditionally incorporates some form of vision quest. The ancient Japanese, for example, would go into caves and sit alone while fasting in the dark, seeking understanding. The Aborigines of Australia would set out alone for a month, walking in the wilderness in hopes of gaining understanding. The native peoples of North America sat alone in the wilderness without food or water for a certain period of days to await revelation. The New Testament relates that Jesus spent 40 days fasting alone in the desert. The forms may vary, but the intent is the same.

My first vision quest took place deep in the Pine Barrens, a flat, sandy forest of pine, oak, and blueberry on the east coast of the United States. A group of more than 70 people from all over the country had assembled for questing. We spent a few days tenting there to be instructed on the vision quest process and to prepare our personal quest locations.

We all spread out from a long, main trail to find our individual quest locations. I was pulled quite far away from the trail into a thickly brushed area that was not logically "ideal" as it had no substantial shade trees to ward off the hot August sun. Also, with no clear path leading to it and being located so far out, after several days without food and becoming lightheaded, I might have trouble finding my way back to the main trail. I didn't want any distractions, though, and the spot was about as bland a place as could be found. One of the quest helpers advised against this location due to its remoteness and rough terrain, but the feeling of rightness was so strong that I sided with the feeling, accepting whatever difficulties it might entail. I marked the center of my vision quest circle and then used a string connected to the center, pulled taut to walk around while scuffing the ground to mark the perimeter. Then I cleared out the brush and leaves from the circle. Finally, I dug a small hole a short distance from the circle to use as a latrine. I would spend the next four days and nights inside the larger circle, leaving only to use the latrine and to mark the main trail every morning, thus letting the vision quest helpers know all was well. This circle was to be my life.

The first day of the vision quest proved exceedingly hot, with direct sun beating down on me relentlessly. I had one little pine tree that stood not much taller than I for shade. I spent the day like the hand of a clock following the small shadow of that little tree. To make matters worse, the sunshine on my water jugs made the water taste like plastic. No particularly exciting revelations arrived that day, which I found somewhat disappointing; nevertheless, almost all 20 of the pressing questions that I had prepared for myself were resolved by midday. Most of the things that I had thought important turned out not to be, so the majority of my questions were rendered irrelevant. I realized that many of my priorities had been askew. With that insight, I had much less to worry about.

Despite the correction in my priorities, I still had a lot to challenge me. The same annoying thoughts and feelings went round and round, like flies that just won't stop landing on your face. In modern society, a person wouldn't even notice these thoughts because we unconsciously avoid them by turning on the TV, listening to music, surfing the Internet, striking up a conversation, or otherwise keeping ourselves busied. Always there is something to distract oneself from the fly.

The night sky was full of stars, and I spent many hours gazing at the universe as I tried to quiet my mind. Even the mosquitoes that swarmed and harassed me I found less bothersome than the buzzing of my own thoughts. I had a tarp with me for protection in the event of rain. I rolled myself up in the tarp and tried to seal off any entryways to keep the mosquitoes at bay. It more or less worked, but nothing would stop my head from buzzing on.

The next morning's greeting was drizzle, and it continued, nonstop, for two days and nights. Because of the lack of variety, I found myself hoping for the scorching sun again. The sheer monotony of the constant drizzle was mind-numbingly dull, but the chatter in my mind never missed a beat.

Around noon the third day, my mind began to quiet. Long periods of silence were followed by more noise. That afternoon the clouds began to clear, making way for a beautifully rejuvenating sunset. I climbed that poor little shade tree, causing it to bend over sideways, just so I could get a clear view of the sun setting. Having all forms of entertainment and distraction removed from one's life, one really starts to appreciate the simple things. I could fully understand how a person kept in solitary confinement aches for the opportunity to walk outside and see the sky. I promised myself that I would take the time to notice simple beauty every day.

By that evening my mind had quieted, and I thought I was over the hump, but after the sun went down a wave of frustration and annoyance came over me. I was boiling over with a disharmonious feeling in my body that had no apparent cause. I asked myself, "Why am I so pissed off!?!" To my surprise, I yelled, "Because I am fucking hungry." And with that the frustration faded away, as did the hunger.

That night I slept sporadically, waking to the feeling of a dark presence watching me from just outside my circle. I had a flashlight with me which I shone in the direction of the presence, but nothing was there. I knew it was not physical. After I observed the area for a while, the feeling receded, but it returned as soon as I fell asleep. I went into a meditation and projected a feeling of love and warmth to the entire area. It felt right, so I expanded the feeling to the entire forest, and then the state, the entire country, and the planet. It just grew and grew, and nothing was excluded from it. Even Satan, if he existed, I welcomed into this light. I fell into a deep sleep, feeling safe and secure.

The next day I experienced undulation between the light and dark sides of the spirit. I would be in a loving, clear space where it felt as if a light shone through me to the universe, which would then fade into a feeling of tension and anxiety. The anxiety became so intense that I had to stomp it out while walking around my circle, and when the anxiety disappeared, I'd be back in the light once more. Again and again this cycle repeated as I purged. I slept in short, seemingly random spurts throughout the day and night without any dreams.

I awoke early to a beautiful sunrise on the last day. This morning we were supposed to leave our quest circles — the quest was over. I had spent four days wishing it to be finished, but once it was actually over, I didn't want to leave. I had finally reached a point of sublime silence, where I felt totally connected to my environment. It felt as if the earth, the plants, and the animals were my family, for they had supported me through an important spiritual endeavor. After hanging out with my new family for another hour, I decided to leave before someone came looking for me (as was the policy).

The vision quest was officially over, but it never really ends. I stayed in the forest, camping for several more weeks before heading back to the hustle and bustle of Tokyo. I knew I needed to find a new teacher for my path to continue unfolding properly. I was pulled to another instructor of Daito-ryu who also taught use of the sword and short staff. I took up the training in earnest, embracing all of the arts he taught. This instructor taught very conscientiously, giving a little private time to each student every lesson, which I felt was extremely beneficial.

I was a bit frustrated that none of my techniques worked on his students. I was already a second-degree black belt, but my training was useless. I decided I needed to completely give up any ideas about the art and start afresh. I knew nothing.

Chapter 8 — The Amazon

As a result of the vision quest, I knew I needed to take a trip into the jungle and spend some time with a tribe. I didn't know when, where, or why, but I knew at some point I needed to learn directly from people living close to the earth. I did not know what I should be taught; I only knew I needed to go. Four years later I joined an eco-tour to Ecuador. This 10-day tour started in the Andes, going through the mystical cloud forests and descending to the Amazon Basin for a five-day immersion into a small village. I landed in Quito in late July and met with the tour group, 13 wonderful people from all over the world. We spent several days in the Andes, where we met a Quechuan shaman who lived in a valley between two huge volcanoes. He invited us to take part in a cleansing ceremony before heading down the Andes to enter the jungle.

For the ceremony we took off our clothes and stood in a dungeonlike room beneath a brick house. The shaman and his son wiped our bodies and hair with various herbs. They used stones and eggs to remove darkness from us. They even blew flames from their rum-filled mouths at us from a safe distance; the energy and warmth felt surprisingly good. Despite the strangeness of it all, every single one of us said we felt a lot better for having participated. Unanimously, we agreed that our bodies felt lighter and clearer.

After the ceremony we were famished, so we headed to a restaurant. We had been warned not to drink nonbottled water in Ecuador due to diarrhea-causing bacteria in the country's water supply. Not thinking, I ate the salad. In retrospect, I realized, it was certainly washed in tap water. By the next day, I was exploding out both ends, and for three days I was unable to eat anything. Despite my intestinal plight, I still felt excited about what was to come.

We wound our way down the Andes to a town called Shell (after the company that built it) that stood at the edge of the rain forest. The Achuar tribe owned a hangar there with several small, prop-driven planes used to transport people to their jungle village. We boarded our respective planes, piloted by trained Achuar tribesmen, and within minutes began our adventure in the sky.

Our pilot flew high over the forest, following a meandering river east, the jungle below us stretching to the horizon in every direction. As we neared the pilot's tribal runway, he looked back at us with a grin, then suddenly, we were in a sharp dive for the river. He leveled off just above the river, the wingtips nearly skimming as he banked to follow the water's flow. My neighbor, a gregarious Australian woman, reached over and grabbed my arm stiffly as I smiled from ear to ear.

Finally, off to our left, a muddy airstrip running parallel to the river appeared. Achuar children who came to watch us land lined both sides of the runway. The moment we splashed onto the runway, the windows streaked with mud. The little boys ran and hid, leaving behind only little girls, the mighty warriors. We climbed out of the plane, scampered off the runway, and blessed the earth.

The second plane came in, and we lined up along the runway like the Achuar children to watch. After the new arrivals reacquainted themselves with the earth, we were led down to the riverbank, where a couple of motored canoes awaited us. We boarded them and headed down the river to our final destination, a small lake surrounded by Achuar-style huts for eco-tourists. Each hut was equipped with a bed, a shower, and mosquito netting.

Over the next several days we took hikes through the forest to learn about its ecosystem, the Achuar guide teaching us about various flora and fauna and how each had its place. We learned what was edible and what was medicinal. While the rain forest holds untold potential for beneficial medicines yet to be discovered, many plants and trees there are inedible to humans. We were also surprised to learn that living in the jungle required some degree of farming, which was the responsibility of women. Men were responsible for fishing, hunting, and building structures as well as protecting the tribe. Women worked harder on a daily basis, but the men had a much more dangerous life.

On the second morning we hiked deep into the jungle; we used the river to come back in the afternoon. We floated for hours on a slow, meandering tributary that fed into the Amazon River. There were kayaks for those who wanted them, but many of us just swam. We saw a variety of wildlife: river dolphins, red monkeys, large turtles, and sloth. Anacondas, caimans, and piranha inhabit the river, but we weren't worried much about them with our Achuar guides keeping a lookout. We had heard stories of a little fish that swims up the urethra of unwary individuals who urinate while in the water. Its fin-bones can't bend backward, and once it enters the urethra, the bones get lodged in the passage's walls, leaving the tiny fish stuck in there. It's supposed to be extremely painful and to require surgery to remove. We didn't know whether the stories were true, but we held it.

By the time we returned to our host village that evening, we were famished and exhausted. As we enjoyed our Achuar meal of piranha and mashed cassava, we learned that we had been invited to join in a traditional ceremony by a neighboring tribal shaman. The Achuar and many other tribes typically practice the consumption of an herbal concoction for the purpose of having visions. As I had once used substances to escape from myself, I did not consider them to be of any positive use on a spiritual path. Despite these reservations I felt strongly pulled to take part in the ceremony, and I knew I was about to have an extremely important revelation.

Our group leader instructed us on what this ceremony entails. We would be offered a medicine called *natem*, a concoction of visionary plants that, ingested, would send us on a spiritual journey. Each individual would glean their own personal lessons during their journey. We would receive what we needed, which is often not what we want. We were admonished not to fear or resist, as that could cause a very negative experience. The *natem*, they said, would not alter our sense of self or our thinking. It would tune us to the Godhead, which would instruct us. We were free to accept or reject any teaching after the journey was over, but during the experience we should remain open. After the ceremony we would have time to journal, consider, and make our own decisions regarding the lessons received. At this point everyone who wished to imbibe the medicine began fasting. The ceremony would take place the following evening.

We left the next afternoon for a silent, prayerful, three-hour hike to the shaman's village. As we neared the village, we took about 30 minutes for solo meditation. We spread out, finding sit-spots to meditate and privately construct a list of questions to be answered through the ceremony. I planned my questions and knew that this vision would give me guidance for my life's mission.

After the meditation we continued our trek, and soon we came to a creek with deep walls and a steady flow. A felled tree lay across the waterway and gave access to the far banks, where an apparently amused Achuar man in a loincloth stood and silently watched us. One by one, our guide led us across the creek. Once across, we continued through a small valley and up a hill to a village atop a plateau overlooking a vast Amazon tributary.

The locals greeted us and told us we could set up our tents near their gardens, a bit away from the main tribal huts. By the time we were done setting up, we had another meeting to prepare us for the approaching ceremony. We decided who was going to receive the *natem* and who was going to help. The helpers would assist journeyers to a secure place at the edge of the forest, ensuring safety during the ceremony as well as a safe return.

From a high cliff we looked out over the vast forest, beyond a river that was easily several hundred yards wide, to the horizon where the sun bade us farewell for the night. We remained in silent reverence, awaiting the onset of the ceremony. About a half hour later, when it grew dark enough, we were led to the shaman's hut and asked to sit on the benches around the rim of the room. Achuar huts are palm-leaf-covered, open-sided structures. They do not have walls, so our backs were to the open air.

The leader of our expedition asked if I were willing to be the first to take the *natem*. I agreed and sat at the front of the bench closest to the shaman, who wore traditional attire with an orange, parrot-feathered headband. He was engrossed in a whispering song-prayer, sending his blessings into a neon-orange brew that had simmered for most of the day. He stirred the *natem* with affection, and when it was just right he turned and greeted us.

He directed me to sit on a stool in front of him, and he blessed me with a feather. He gazed at me, then filled a large decorated clay bowl with the orange liquid. He handed it to me, telling the translator that I was to drink it down to the last drop without pause.

Receiving the bowl, I had to be careful not to spill it, as it was filled to the brim. We were told that *natem* is a bitter drink and that we might have trouble getting it down. Finding it really not so bad, I drank it down as quickly as I could, but my stomach had shrunk thanks to the unexpected four-day fast, which made it a struggle. After emptying the bowl, I received water to wash out my mouth. I returned to my bench to await my journey.

From my perch at the front of the bench, I was able to observe the portions that the shaman doled out to everyone. It made no logical sense that most people received considerably less than I had been given, despite the fact that almost everyone outweighed me and had fasted for fewer days. I was pretty sure I was in for a heck of a ride.

After everyone finished receiving a portion, our guides said that we should expect the effects to start in about an hour and that the effect would last just about as long. Once the effect began the helpers would take us out into the forest where we could purge and have our vision.

Within fifteen minutes my entire vascular system began to vibrate, my blood feeling like static electricity. Dizziness overtook me, and I told my helper, Larry. He assured me, "You're imagining things. Fifteen minutes is way too quick for effects to begin." I told him I was about to puke, and without further debate he helped me out of the tent. He guided me toward the forest, my arm over his shoulder. My mind spinning and stomach rebelling before we got halfway there, my legs became too wobbly to walk in a straight line. There was no way I could have made that walk without help; I had never been so dizzy and disoriented in my life.

Once at the edge of the forest, I got on my hands and knees to purge. After several powerful contractions I lay down on my back, appreciative of the stable ground cradling my body. I felt a mosquito land on my forehead and spear my third eye, and with that the journey began.

I heard an undulating vibration like that of millions of cicada in chorus. The sound rose and fell in rhythm, increasing in intensity and tempo as the gap between the peaks narrowed. I could feel the energy rising from the base of my body up to the top of my head. By the time the energy reached the crown of my skull, it was a screaming, high-pitched, frenzy of building pressure, and finally it exploded out of the top of my head as if from a volcano.

The first thing I saw was a small, light-blue butterfly with a dot on each wing that looked like eyes. Then a boldly colored fluorescent lizard flashed before me. Then I found my mind no longer in the forest, but in the heart of the earth. A frighteningly powerful voice addressed me. My lesson had begun.

It began by teaching me the purpose of life on Earth. I learned of the destruction and renewal to come in the near future. It instructed about the coming spiritual awakening and about how this will lead to a cascading shift in consciousness throughout humanity. I received my mission and direction with regard to that mission. Humanity is on the verge of an incredible enlightenment, but first the corruption of humanity must be fully exposed.

Conscious light from the center of the galaxy will bathe the solar system with ever-increasing intensity. And with this light, corruption, greed, and selfishness will collapse upon themselves, consuming everything they touch. Within short order the three pillars of humanity — economy, ecology, and society — will fail. Everything based on lies and selfishness will crumble with exposure.

I was shown two possible futures, the outcome to be determined by the attitude humanity takes when things begin to collapse. If people maintain selfish, negative attitudes and resist positive change, the suffering will be an immeasurable Hell on Earth. The human population, as well as most of the flora and fauna of the planet, will be reduced to near-extinction levels. The unbearable suffering of humanity rushed in on me; the horror was beyond words. If, on the other hand, we choose a positive, loving attitude that honors all life and embrace the changes as much as possible, things won't be quite as difficult. Even with this attitude, the suffering will be beyond comprehension just because there is already so much negative momentum. In either case, the population of humans will shrink, after which the remaining population will transition into a truly inspiring, consciousness-affirming way of life. Life on Earth will become much richer after these changes occur. People will live positive, inspired lives in communion with all things.

Earth is a school and a teacher. Here, we are receiving training the way an athlete receives training. In sports, does the coach baby us in hopes that we will gain skill and ability? No, of course not. The coach puts us in difficult situations, knowing that through hard training we will gain ability and strength. The only question is whether we are coachable. In the same way, the earth experience is training—training that seeks not to add but instead to strip away all that is false, until nothing remains to veil realization.

There is no escaping the physical experience until one consciously awakens. The death of the body offers no escape; we will return in a new body and experience repeatedly until we awaken. In the event that this planet becomes uninhabitable to us, we will incarnate on another planet that serves the same function.

I was shown that we have created the world into which we are born through past incarnations, just as we are creating the world we will be born into in future incarnations.

For the awakening individual it is wise to live as if experience is earned by the individual; which is to say, there are no accidents. We get the experiences that we need for growth. Eventually, the endless striving for pleasure, power, safety, comfort, approval and distraction will no longer satisfy, and that is when we will begin to make optimum use of the training opportunity and thereby realize our true nature, which is harmonious.

We have more people on the planet now who are ready to awaken than have ever been at any one time in the history of the world. I was shown that first one person would "graduate" and light the way for many. We would see a great enlightenment on Earth.

I learned that people with negative, selfish minds, who are unwilling to change perspective will die off and reincarnate elsewhere, and for roughly the next thousand years, this planet will be in a high state of consciousness, where many will awaken. Can you imagine a world in which everyone lives positively, seeking understanding, where spiritual awakening is seen as a possibility for all? What a beautiful world it would be.

The proper attitude is the key to unfoldment, and an awakened individual has mastered right attitude. We must not expect someone else to change us or save us. Each individual needs to walk their own path mindfully and decisively with the intent of opening to Isness at their very core. Walking your own path does not mean that you do not learn from others or that others cannot assist in your process, for this is as it should be. Teachers and guides are beneficial and extremely valuable, depending upon the attitudes of all involved. Learn from them, but do not assume anything; avoid over-reliance on them, and do not worship them.

With right attitude, one will learn a great deal from others while questioning and testing everything within oneself. Most importantly, we will open our hearts to direct learning from Isness. Humans will no longer view the people, other creatures, and things of the world as utilities and resources to be exploited, but will instead tune directly with everything and see the intrinsic value and beauty that is and has always been. We will understand that the harvest is important to the health of the ecosystem if done with the right attitude and in the right way.

I received instructions as to what I needed to do to prepare for my mission on Earth. By combining the aiki and sotai-ho principles and practicing them together as one, my martial arts instructor and I would discover a new art: at once a path to enlightenment, a therapy art, and a self-defense art. Through this path, a great multitude will awaken.

After the vision was over, Larry led me back to the shaman's hut. He had me lie down on a table where the shaman cleansed my body with a feather and his breath. I was taken outside, where blankets were laid out under the stars. I laid myself down there and gazed up at the stars for hours, until the disorienting effects of *natem* wore off. I got up, went back to my tent, and slept until morning.

At 4 a.m. I awoke to laughter outside. I climbed out of my tent to see what was going on. Near the shaman's hut was the tribe of Achuar, young and old, in a circle to share their dreams. The Achuar believe that their dreams are not for themselves but are messages from the spirit world to be shared with others. So, every morning they all gather and drink a purging tea, and each person has time to share dreams with the tribe. This tea causes the stomach to bring up anything remaining, so that any undigested matter is purged, which the Achuar say prevents many health issues.

Wanting to be a part of a sharing community like that, I felt a strong desire to join them. But it felt inappropriate, so I went back into my tent and just listened as they laughed and told stories in their local language between purges. I wondered if my ancient ancestors had dream-sharing rituals like this one, and, if so, when and why those rituals were discarded. It seemed to me that this sharing community spirit would help a lot of people who suffer from depression and loneliness.

By mid-morning we returned to our village via canoe, and we used the rest of the day to journal and reflect. That night our group visited another Achuar family living in a different area of the forest to enjoy a meal and be shown their traditional lifestyle and skills. I was still so overwhelmed with the vision that I opted out, remaining in my hut and trying to get a grip on the enormity of what I was shown. What I had seen of the destruction to come and the things I needed to do to prepare for my mission was totally beyond my ability to comprehend. I just didn't know how to handle all of the pressure, and my mind was in overdrive. For the rest of the trip, though I was physically present, I was pulled into myself and out of touch. Many of the group members kindly showed concern, but I was unable to share anything with them because doing so felt inappropriate.

After years of digesting, I now see that we must be willing to give up falsehoods before any truth can be accepted fully. And I can see that, in our society, few are willing to give up the falsehoods to which we cling. Indeed, we may be in for a rough ride. But I no longer concern myself too much with that, as I can't control other people's attitudes. My main focus is fulfilling my part in the story. I am confident that many others out there have also received important teachings and are doing all they can to fulfill their path in this epic adventure of life.

Chapter 9 — Discovering the Path

After returning to Japan I visited my martial arts instructor, Shizen Osaki Sensei, and told him of the vision as it pertained to him and the homework I had been given. Of course, he could have thought me crazy and turned me down, but despite my fear, I told him anyway. I told him that I wanted to combine martial and therapy training, and that through this combination something new would be born, a simple and clear path to enlightenment. I asked him if he would be willing to go down this path of exploration with me.

To my surprise, he responded with excitement about the idea. Before I left for my Amazon trip, he had a problem knee that was making training difficult. I had used sotai-ho to help him recover, so as a result he too became interested in bodywork.

In the Amazon vision I saw that when I had gone far enough down the path of enlightenment an energetic field would serve to protect against malicious intent. I told Sensei about this effect and also that, at a sufficient level of enlightenment, we would be able to execute the entirety of our martial arts skills without any effort or thought. What this really meant was that meditation would become the core of our training.

We began first with uncovering the meditation by way of practicing sotai-ho on each other. There was a feeling in the body that we discovered after receiving therapy. Eventually we were able to tune to this feeling purely through meditation, and then by using this feeling we could apply therapy to each other without using techniques. In this way, the therapy became technically liberated. We could easily detect areas of heaviness in the body and use the energetic touch that we had discovered to free up the energy in that area.

We discovered that we could go into this meditation, search our own bodies for low-frequency places, and, merely by lightly intending toward that spot, we found that our bodies would begin to move on their own. It is a spooky experience at first because the body will move quite dramatically as it naturally stretches itself out and opens up energetic pathways. Previously, my body had moved on its own out of self-defense, but that movement occurred only in extreme situations, such as when the horse tried to kick my head. Now that response was happening easily and in nonthreatening situations.

We paid attention to the feeling in the body during these sessions, fed that feeling back into our meditations, and soon a protective field began to emerge around our bodies when in meditation. I noticed only because after meditation, Sensei's body felt to me like it was radiant, and when he asked me to attack him, I couldn't, no matter how I tried; it seemed as if an invisible wall stood between us. The phenomenon was so strange that at first I wondered whether I was just imagining it. He remained in that state, standing there relaxed in front of me, for quite a long time before the effect wore off. This effect confirmed for me one of the points from the Amazon vision.

The next day, we began our training session with meditation, again trying to find that feeling. After some time, Sensei again found it, and I could not attack. I was able to move effortlessly when grabbed and execute many techniques that I previously could not do, but the protective field was not there for me. With persistence, we kept at this for several weeks; not once was I able to get it right. Many times Osaki Sensei succeeded, though. At this point about a year had already passed since the Amazon trip, and the therapy method had evolved tremendously, as did the martial art and the meditation.

We needed to test the field thoroughly but safely, so we used a hard-hat. One of us would put on the helmet and sit on the floor in meditation, and the other would try to hit him on the head with a leather-padded bamboo sword. Sensei was often successful in reaching the meditative state that produced the protective field, yet I did not have a single success until a session some weeks later, when Sensei came in to hit me as hard as he could. He got halfway through his swing, and his foot slammed into the ground, propelling his body backward, his sword frozen in midair. He looked like he was in pain. Slowly he put the sword down and sat cross-legged in front of me.

"You know," he confided, "I have been thinking you were only stopping your swings because you had brainwashed yourself into believing that you could not hit me. I was getting tired of this useless training and wanted to make you give up, so I swung as hard as I could to discourage you from this kind of training. I wanted to work on something real, but to my amazement this time, when I swung, it was as if I hit a brick wall. My foot hit the ground so hard that my heel hurts. It really worked. I have to admit, it really worked. Let's break for tea. I want to consider this for a bit."

After this success, we practiced more enthusiastically than ever. I started to get a better feel for the meditation and, gradually, had more success with the protective field as well. Session after session brought new discoveries and realizations that kept us busy for hours. We poured our new understanding back into the traditional martial arts as Sensei introduced me to advanced skills in the sword, staff, and open-hand, using the feeling from meditation and therapy as the engine for the traditional forms. My martial arts improved dramatically, and within a few years I was given instructor licenses in the four Samurai arts that Sensei had taught at that time.

During my last year in Japan, I stopped work entirely and focused solely on training with Sensei privately. At this time I came every day with some new insight as to how the training needed to go that day for progress. I didn't know how I knew, I just knew. We would start at 1 p.m. and continue training until 6 p.m., break for dinner, and then continue with the regular group classes from 7 p.m. until 9 or 10 p.m. I was training five days a week for at least six hours a day and making rapid progress.

Still, I was often unable to get the protective field effect because I really did not understand what was occurring to cause it, and the more I thought about it the further from it I was. During this training, both Sensei and I regularly became quite exhausted, and after just a few hours, we had to break for rest. It seemed to me that we were using too much willpower to produce this effect. The Amazon vision showed me that this would eventually be an effortless, constant field, but we had yet to discover how. Also, the time and effort we took to activate this field made it highly impractical for a real situation that required immediate response.

I knew we still had more to discover, but I also knew that I needed to return to America. It was not logical, but I saw clearly that it was time for the next step in my journey and that step had to occur in America. In my last six months in Japan I received the Master's License and, with Sensei's blessing, was sent out to teach. I asked Sensei to help me find a name for this new training method and he suggested shinkaido, which means "open-heart path." Shinkaido is more of a description of the method than a name, because through the process of opening the heart our unfoldment occurs.

I moved to a small town in southern Oregon and began teaching a few dedicated individuals. I was new at teaching and quite nervous about it, so I taught only technically and did not get into the meditation until well over a year after I left Japan. Due to my identification as a teacher, I just could not relax enough to make use of the shinkaido method. Of course, I harbored a fear of failure and being embarrassed if I were unsuccessful. I also feared that the effects would be so startling to people that it might scare them off.

Eventually, I began to relax into the teaching role and introduced a basic meditation that my students could practice for just 10 minutes before each class. My students really seemed to enjoy this meditation, so I incorporated it into regular training. They had been working on a challenging beginning technique and for six months and had not been having much success, but after the meditation, they could do the technique easily and without any thought. They were very surprised by this, and from that point they requested that I make the meditation a primary part of training. Around that time a woman from whom I had been renting space for therapy in a neighboring town became very interested in having me teach meditation classes there. A small group of individuals met there every Tuesday night, and I led them through a basic meditation for an hour, assisting them to move toward greater and greater harmony in their lives. The goal was to have a little more relaxation and awareness each week. They made rapid progress.

About this time, I began mentoring private students several times per week for three hours each session. I found that they gained much more from the concentrated three hours than they would gain from three hours spread over three weeks. So, we set up a full Saturday of training as an experiment. They advanced tremendously from that one day. Whereas before a tiny distraction would cause them to collapse out of meditation, I was then able to use more intense stimulus to test them, but their meditation would hold strong.

I had been away from Japan for two years, and I suddenly felt strongly pulled to visit my teacher there. Three months later I was knocking at my teacher's door. I lived in his dojo for ten days, during which time we practiced from 7 a.m. until 2 the next morning, living on meditation and coffee. During this time, both Sensei and I regained our footing in the advanced shinkaido method of martial training, as neither of us had been working with it since I left Japan. This intensely concentrated time proved incredibly powerful for me. I gained a deeper awareness of intention, the mind, consciousness and Isness, plus a new confidence to practice in this method and even to teach it.

When I returned to the United States, I began holding weekend intensives to help students reach deep awareness of inner harmony and remain there for extended periods of time. Their rate of progress became truly impressive as the presence of each student deepened at an astounding rate. When students had questions for me about the process, I turned the questions back at them, and they were often able to answer themselves through direct insight. A teacher could not have been more pleased.

Before the first intensive I was not sure what I was going to teach, so I prepared a detailed schedule of activities and teachings. As soon as the students sat down in front of me, my hand reached over and put the plan behind me. All teachings emerged spontaneously, and many of the things I taught were new to me as well as to the students. I found it exhilarating to realize that I did not need to plan anything, and answers would just flow out of my mouth.

Little by little, the students were able to tune more accurately to consciousness, allowing it to flow. Their lives were becoming more enriched and stable. Their minds and emotions became more transparent and mild.

When they lost stability, they realized it quickly and recovered harmony. In only a year's time, they went from near-total energetic instability to a point where they were ready to teach introductory meditation themselves. I could not have hoped for quicker progress.

I firmly believe that tuning to consciousness will end violence on the planet. When individuals understand and prove in their own bodies that love is more powerful than violence, then violence has had its last breath. My hope is that the reader joins us in taking this leap of consciousness as we move out of reactive mind and into conscious unfoldment.

Part 2 — The Path

The path of spiritual unfoldment is first and foremost a process of resolving to Isness by way of intentional tuning to consciousness. Through the tuning process, identifications that we hold slough away, little by little, like dead skin. We can consider these identifications to be like a dark field surrounding us. With each release of darkness, a little more light is able to shine through, allowing further insight into our true nature.

For this reason the path of unfoldment is unlike any other path in life. It's not a building up of skills and structures but instead is a resolution or dissolution of structure. It's not a becoming but an unbecoming. It's not a complication but a simplification and purification process removing all that we hold onto, for what we hold binds us.

Isness is not something we create or hold on to but instead is most fundamental and, therefore, the default. Thus, even belief systems must be discarded at some point, for all belief systems are of the mind, and it's the mind that veils us from Isness. Through the process of unfoldment the disharmonious structures of mind are unbound, revealing what is most fundamental, and only when the most fundamental is revealed can we embrace everything without holding on to anything.

In Part 2 we'll look at the essential nature of the universe and its fundamental relationship to the human experience. Then, we will discuss the differences between mind and consciousness, so that we may become aware of when we are tuned to mind and thereby choose to tune to consciousness more often. I'll also introduce unconditioned forms of meditation, prayer, and chanting that will serve as fundamental tools for tuning to consciousness. Finally, we will go over potential pitfalls regarding the practice of meditation, as well as discover powerful methods for resolving inner disharmony.

Chapter 10 — Genesis

Imagine you are a formless, curious deity blowing imaginary soap bubbles. A single bubble would represent our universe. Other bubbles would represent other universes. Sometimes an entire clump of connected bubbles floats out together. This clump of bubbles would represent the multiverse, the sum-total of all universal bubbles combined. The multiverse has more bubbles than could be counted by a supercomputer. And each of its bubbles represents a different reality. Many only slightly differ from one another, but others are so drastically different in content and dimensionality as to be unrecognizable to individuals in other universes.

The source of the multiverse is no different than the source of a human being. The ongoing processes of both are identical, so by understanding the multiverse we can understand the human being, and by understanding the human being we can also understand the multiverse.

"The Eternal Buddha has a three-fold body. There is the aspect of Essence. There is the aspect of Potentiality. There is the aspect of Manifestation."

— *The Teachings of Buddha*

For practical purposes I name the aspects as Soul/Isness, as spirit/potentiality, and as mind/manifestation. These three are actually one when viewed holistically, but when viewed individually they appear to be separate, unrelated, or even contradictory.

To understand the nature of the multiverse, it's important to rid ourselves of notions of time, place, form, and the sense of self and otherness. Avoid initiating cause-and-effect relationships; instead, consider only the formless moment and all that is occurring within the moment.

An easy way to get yourself into the right perspective to digest what I am about to teach is to imagine that you have just arrived in the body that you now inhabit, and that you have absolutely no memory or knowledge. Without an idea of who or what you are, you also lack the idea that you should know such things. Because you have no memory, there is no fear, for you have not learned to fear. In utter innocence you do not even know that the body needs to eat and drink, and therefore you have absolutely no reason to worry or do anything in particular.

With no knowledge or memory, you have no ability to recall the past or imagine the future. There is only the vibrant aliveness of this moment through unbiased perception and feeling. Relax into innocence and enjoy being.

Take as long as you like before reading on. Once you start reading, you might notice that at times the mind struggles or becomes agitated. Whenever the mind tightens in this way, go back to innocence for a little while.

In all likelihood, perception will shift between mind and being and back again as you read. These shifts of perception will afford you a direct experience of what this chapter is really about, and that experience will help to reveal the underlying message of this book as you read on.

When I was 22 years old, I had what I call the Isness inspirience. During that inspirience, Isness indicated that I was in no way different from it. I felt at a deep level that Isness was indicating truth, but I could not understand how it was possible for me to be Isness and also be ignorant of that fact. Isness is not ignorant, as Isness is aware of all things. Therefore, it seemed to me that my ignorance proved that I was not Isness.

I asked Isness to show me how it was possible that I could have a separate identity and not be aware of my true nature as Isness. When I questioned how I could be ignorant and still be Isness, I was given the answer. However, I did not understand it until almost two decades later.

Isness directed my attention to a clouded mind that looked to me like a star-forming region of space called a nebula. I will describe the wordless mental processes of the clouded mind through words to show the commonality with what is happening in the human mind, for they are one and the same in their desire to identify who and what they are.

Imagine there is neither time nor form, but only the undifferentiated, unbound, vibrant awareness of precisely this instant. Awareness notes, "I don't know what I am." Curiosity wonders, "What am I?" The assumption that is built into the question (that there *is* an "I") perturbs and clouds awareness. Curiosity searches into its nature, unaware that there is no true answer to this question, no final conclusion.

As curiosity wonders, "What am I?" attention narrows, imagination posits, and assumption concludes: "I am X." Each theory is the basis of an entire universe. Curiosity is never satisfied through this search because each theory is inevitably incomplete, but like a child it plays on in its excitement. Through this play of self-definition, countless universes bubble out into what is called the multiverse. Remember, all of these universes represent potentiality, and because there is no time from the holistic perspective of Isness, all possibilities are in the very same moment, yet the clouded mind frames these potentialities in a moment-by-moment progression in order to grasp them, which is the effect of time. Thus time both is and is not dependent upon perspective, which is to say within the clouded mind time is real, but outside it time is not.

Some core commonalities exist among all universes, namely the desire to define the self, as well as the instability and disharmony that this desire causes. Another commonality is the unconscious desire to find balance within an inherently imbalanced system. These two primary desires stimulate a great game of musical chairs throughout the multiverse, where everything is vying for a permanent, safe position but never able to find one through the effort because all theories of self are inherently untrue, and, therefore, unstable.

The multiverse is a projection of the desire for self-definition, which is an illusion, so the multiverse itself is not ultimately true. We could look at the multiverse as the pearl that forms around a grain of sand which represents the sense of otherness. The physics of any particular universe depend upon the nature of that grain of sand — the specific theory of self that the clouded mind collapsed upon.

To restate this slightly differently: in the ongoing process of the clouded mind, "What am I?" does not yet represent as a universe, although it does stimulate speculation. When speculation creates a premise to answer the question, "What am I?" that premise of self necessarily projects a sense of other to contrast with the premise of self. As soon as an answer to the question "What am I?" is formed, a mind-bubble of manifestation, a universe, expands in order to fully explore that conclusion. From elementary particles, to subatomic particles, to atoms, to molecules, to structures such as stars, planets, galaxies, and solar systems — and ultimately to organisms — the premise of self is explored to get as many perspectives on the premise as possible. At the moment the bubble begins to expand, time is present, and things begin to appear in relativistic, linear cause-and-effect relationships — i.e., experience.

The nature of the clouded mind is found in the attempt to define the self. The first conclusion is "I am." But because there is no actual self or form to clearly define "I," assumption willfully projects form through imagination in the attempt to understand "I." The form must always exist in opposition because we need the illusion of other to sustain the illusion of self. For example, strength can be understood only in contrast to weakness. Therefore, everything that stems from otherness we perceive through contrasting opposites: masculine versus feminine, high versus low, near versus far, good versus evil, and so on. Because definition and opposition are the origins of the clouded mind, definition and opposition are what a clouded mind naturally does. So long as there is desire to identify self, which is to define it, the mind has no choice. It defines, it contrasts, and it suffers.

In actuality, only the timeless moment of being is real, and there truly is no self to identify; so, whatever is projected is inherently unstable. Whatever is unstable suffers change and decay, which elicits the sense of time in the multiverse. Therefore, all that is bound in the multiverse must break down and/or change. Disharmony is the inevitable outcome of the conclusions of mind, as is the effect of becoming.

Yet through and beyond the clouded mind exists Isness, and, therefore, disharmony is not the only possible perception open to us. We always have the chance for clarity when the mind is not clouded by ignorance and speculation. What would this perspective look like? It's the unconditioned acceptance of being, without any further attempt to define the self, while lovingly observing the totality, including mental activity, with clarity.

This perspective relaxes into and enjoys being without trying to define itself. Isness observes and accepts formless nonduality, and, therefore, it's not divided or bound in any way. Buddhism indicates it as the Eternal Buddha. The New Testament figures it as the Holy Father. Taoism indicates it as the

Tao. Different cultures may employ other terms that indicate the same thing. But no matter the term, rightly understood, what we are talking about is not really a name but just an indication or hint.

The possibility of unconditioned consciousness does not name, describe, or define itself so long as it is unconditioned. The possibility that names or describes itself, attaching to an identity, is conditioned and bound in suffering. Remember, any attempt to define the self creates a mental bubble, which is disharmony, change, decay, and time — the multiverse.

Consider that a developing human embryo goes from undifferentiated being to greater and greater differentiation. A newborn baby doesn't know the difference between its body and the surrounding environment. It develops a sense of self and other to navigate the environment that surrounds its body. As the sensory definitions refine, the baby gains greater function within the universe. But in the process of self-development, the individual forgets the undifferentiated awareness of being. And once fully bound in identification, the person's greatest fear is utter loss of identity, which represents in the unconscious as falling into the infinite dark abyss of the unknown. This unconscious fear keeps the mind swirling in its attempt to hold onto a sense of self.

Fortunately, once we realize that we are suffering from the compulsion to identify, we are able to unbind awareness from the cloud of self and regain conscious awareness of Soul. Awareness of Soul begins when we embrace non-defining, unconditioned acceptance of being.

The wonderful thing about the possibility of nondefining, unconditioned acceptance of being is that it observes the projecting process without judgment, for it understands that the multiverse is purely the natural outcome of defining the self; it's not a mistake, it's a possibility. Consciousness and mind are potential perspectives: the former, all inclusive; the latter, exclusive, and existing within the smallest, most fundamental building blocks, elementary particles, as well as the largest celestial objects of the multiverse, and even within you.

Chapter 11 — Frequencies of Mind and Consciousness

When a superior man hears of the Tao,
he immediately begins to embody it.

When an average man hears of the Tao,
he half believes it, half doubts it.

When a foolish man hears of the Tao,
he laughs out loud.

If he didn't laugh,
it wouldn't be the Tao.

— Tao Te Ching

With each bubble created in seeking self-definition, the individual's conscious awareness grows further veiled, making it more and more challenging to maintain the holistic perspective of consciousness. Each mental bubble we have, such as "I am a doctor" or "I am smart," becomes an identification that must be fed to survive. Each time we associate ourselves with or react to disharmony, we are feeding an identification unconsciously.

These identifications swarm, parasitizing Soul energy. This swarm of chaotic disharmony blocks the individual from realizing Isness at the very core. Because the individual identifies with these definitions and limitations, the very sense of self is on the line whenever we illuminate the phenomenon. Because of the tendency for identifications to fight back and to protect themselves, the reader may experience difficulties when reading this book as the light of consciousness begins to shine through identifications that do not want to be seen.

If we look at this situation as a chance to see behind the curtain of our own mind, then resistance affords us an incredible opportunity, depending on our attitude. It's wise, when resistance comes up, to patiently observe it and let the dust settle within before reading on. Otherwise, we will be moving through a cloud of dust that will reduce visibility. Because we are going to be learning to observe the mind, we will find it helpful to have a common understanding of typical mental activities such as thought, imagination, memory, emotion, and the senses, with which to work. Minus a common language to work with, we leave too much room for misunderstanding. So let's use the Merriam-Webster Online Dictionary to draw our definitions.

Thought: an idea, plan, opinion, picture, and so forth, formed in your mind: something that you think of.

Imagination: the ability to imagine things not real: the ability to form a picture in your mind of something that you have not seen or experienced.

Memory: the power or process of remembering what has been learned.

Emotion: a strong feeling (such as love, anger, joy, hate, or fear); feelings.

Senses: the five natural powers (touch, taste, smell, sight, and hearing) through which you receive information about the world around you.

Are we always thinking? Almost always, yes. With regard to thinking, consider driving down the road in a car. You see all the other cars on the road in front of you, and you are able to drive well without thinking about it, assuming you are a competent driver. You'd recognize the brands of cars around you without having a labeling process occur in your mind like, "Ford," "Toyota," "Chevy," etc. If you are a skilled driver, you might have no particular noise in your head actively making such identifications as you are driving, right? Instead, you know by association. You see a Ford, and you know it's a Ford. You see this book, and you know what it is without mentally saying to yourself, "This is a book." To say to yourself, "This is a book" is a thought.

When we have become competent at something such as driving, we are not thinking about driving. Instead we are often thinking about other things as the mind meanders to this topic or that, or we might be trying to solve a problem that we are having at work, for example. Constant thinking does not have to be the case, though, which we will get to in a bit.

Speculating is thinking. For example, "I wonder what kind of animal just crossed the road in front of me? It was too big to be a cat. The movement was not really like a dog's. It had stripes on its bushy tail. It must have been a raccoon." This is thinking that leads to the conclusion in the thought, "I saw a raccoon."

How do senses reinforce the clouded mind? Observing how you use your senses, you will notice that you perceive something that stimulates an associated meaning within you. For example, while driving along you see a raccoon cross the road, and before you know it your mind has gone into a memory of when you were a boy and your father took you raccoon hunting. The next thing you know, your mind leaps into imagination as you think about what that meat might have tasted like if you had killed one and had to eat it. You might have an emotional response to the thought of eating a raccoon. Next, you notice that you are a little hungry, so you think about what you might have for lunch. You decide on a fast food drive-through, then you remember that the last time you ate in the car, you spilled soda on the crotch of your pants and then were too embarrassed to go to work, so you had to go home and change pants, which made you late. Your face actually reddens at the memory of it as you feel the emotion of embarrassment in your body.

The content of thinking and imagination is sourced from memory, fueled by emotion, and often stimulated by associated meanings connected to what the senses pick up in the environment. Overt emotion may pop up here and there throughout the process. Can you imagine what it would be like to drive down the road in a totally relaxed, yet alert silence, feeling as if you were vastly and lovingly connected to everything? This is a taste of the consciousness of which I speak. Of course, you may just be imagining it, which is not consciousness, but you get the idea – again, not consciousness.

For most people, thoughts, imagination, memories, and emotions move almost constantly around in the mind, stimulated by associations the senses trigger, and the only times of respite come when the moment is so intense and exhilarating that one has no time for thought, such as when we are bungee jumping or playing a fast-paced competitive game. In such a moment, we haven't enough time for the movement of thought; thinking would cause us to lose if the opponent were truly competent. At such an intense moment, we experience heightened mental silence. Unfortunately, these moments also involve a lot of focused intention, which tires us and eventually leads into dullness. By far the most common cause of mental silence, though, is being too tired or dulled from poor health to have much mental activity. This is not a healthy situation.

So how do we step out of the mind and into consciousness? First, we need to become more aware of the distinctions between mind and consciousness. We can use the idea of frequencies as a good model to explain those differences. Scientific research in biomagnetism by David Cohen at MIT has verified that human beings have an energetic field resonating in proximity to the body, constituting the magnetic field we sometimes call the aura. The energy of this field comes, primarily, from biological processes of the body and mind, such as ion current flow through the muscles and nerves. You may view some of that material here:

https://engineering.dartmouth.edu/events/biomagnetism-magnetic-fields-produced-by-the-human-body

Through the unfoldment process, I have developed the capacity to perceive energy fields to some degree. While I can't be sure that what I perceive is the same as what David Cohen measures, his studies provide verification that energy fields do surround the body, which is an important step in the right direction. I have noticed that an aspect of the field that I perceive contracts when the mind is highly active or the body is sick or tired. For healthy, relaxed individuals this aspect of the field usually extends out from the skin about 12 inches, but as the body tires through the day, the field may recede to as low as six inches. A person with a bad cold or flu will typically have an aura that extends only four to eight inches, depending on the severity of the ailment and the time of day or night. The energetic field is usually at its lowest between 2am and 5am. Having an energy field measuring six inches or less for an extended time indicates a potentially serious health issue. I urge people to see their health practitioner when the field is four inches or less even for only a short duration. When the aura drops to skin level or less, sudden death is a very real possibility.

The first time I saw an aura drop to skin level was with a fellow middle school teacher. At work one day he said he was not feeling very well and that he thought he had a cold. I felt drawn to look at his energy field and was shocked to see that it was at skin level. To my surprise, I blurted, "You need to get to the hospital right now, or you might die." He looked at me incredulously and said, "No, I just need some sleep. I'll take the rest of the day off and go home." He lived quite near the school, and during his bicycle ride home he became dizzy and stopped for a moment to stabilize himself. As soon as he got off the bike, he fainted. Fortunately, someone on the street immediately called the paramedics. My friend spent the next few months in the hospital. As it turned out, he had a previously undiagnosed autoimmune disease. According to the doctors, the disease would probably have killed him that day had he not been rushed to the hospital.

Although being able to perceive energy fields has clear health related benefits, for me, the biggest benefit has been in being able to perceive the differences between mind and consciousness as those differences reflect in the field around the body.

Mind reflects in the electromagnetic field, but during meditation another field emerges that is similar to but distinct from the electromagnetic field. During deep meditation, you may feel a clear, harmonious field radiating out well beyond the aura. Although I suspect the field of consciousness is not electromagnetic, I teach it using the electromagnetic model. Thus for instructional purposes we will say that the mind resonates at lower frequencies than consciousness on the electromagnetic continuum.

An easy way to conceptualize these fields for communication purposes is to imagine them radiating like the electromagnetic spectrum. We could break up the different frequencies into classes or bands similar to the bands of color in the rainbow. Let's take a look at the frequencies of mind as if they exist along the electromagnetic spectrum, which is commonly divided into seven classes of waves.

Electromagnetic Spectrum Classes:
1 - Radio
2 - Microwave
3 - Infrared
4 - Visible
5 - Ultraviolet

6 - X-ray
7 - Gamma ray

Mental Spectrum Classes:
8 - Emotion, Feelings, Will
9 - Thought, Imagination, Memory

Beyond the mental classes, higher frequency classes exist that bridge to or are of consciousness. These spectra include the harmonious fields that lead to resolution of the self when activated by intention. I have given several associated descriptions that resonate with each frequency class, but these are not the only descriptions that we could use. For example, we might extend our scale to include the following.

Frequency Classes that Bridge Mind and Consciousness:
10 - Curiosity, Relaxation, Innocence

Conscious Frequency Classes:
11 - Observation, Sharing, Compassion
12 - Silence, Acceptance, Appreciation
13+ - Unconditioned Love
[For quick reference to frequency classes, see the Appendix or download a pdf file at _www.richardlhaight.com/links_]

Note: The terms I use to represent conscious frequencies are not to be confused with mental/emotional frequencies. Conscious frequency classes are experientially distinct from the mental/emotional experiences that are represented by the same words.

The use of the mind is always a double-edged sword. Although using the mind can serve practical purposes within the multiverse, each time that we use it, energy is expended and some degree of agitation occurs. For this reason, I indicate the frequencies of mind as being disharmonious. I do not mean this as a judgment against the mind, but simply as an observation of the price we pay for using it.

As I run through various scenarios of mind and consciousness, I will use parentheses to indicate the frequencies being attuned to. For example, fear would be followed by (8) and would be written "fear(8)" in the text. As a sentence, it might appear this way: "Fear(8) is in the frequency of emotion(8), so it carries disharmony(8-9)." I recommend the reader observe their own mind while reading and frequently refer to the lists above to note the frequencies being reached.

Through the process of intentional unfoldment, we tune to consciousness(11+), the transformative frequencies that purify and remove divisions.

Curiosity(10) and innocence(10), are natural portals to consciousness(11+). When we begin to question(10) all assumptions about the self(8-9), we then have the opening through which resolution can begin to occur. Curiosity is not to be confused with thinking(9), for they are distinct fields. Curiosity leaves the door open for inspirience and insight, whereas thinking is biased(9) by one's assumptions(9) about what is real. Such paradigms are entirely of the self, whereas questioning innocently offers an open portal to consciousness(11+) as long as it does not turn to speculation(9). Therefore I strongly encourage my students to be playfully curious. Adults have such difficulty with curiosity, but for young children it comes naturally because innocence is not yet blocked by knowledge(9) or ignorance(8).

We should not confuse innocence(10) with ignorance(8). Innocence is open, whereas ignorance is closed. Look closely at the word "ignor-ance" to get a sense of how I am using it. To ignore is a willful(8) act, so ignorance is disharmonious(8-9). Innocence, on the other hand, is open and, therefore, harmonious(10+). Consider that innocence is defined as being blameless and as lacking the knowledge(9) of right and wrong. It's not willful because it's open.

Consider Genesis to develop another metaphor: "And out of the ground the Lord God made every tree grow that is pleasant to the sight and good for food. The tree of life was also in the midst of the garden, and the tree of the knowledge of good and evil." If we were to say that the tree of the knowledge of good and evil represents self-consciousness(8-9), then the tree of life represents Christ-consciousness. The allegory continues with a warning that Adam and Eve may eat freely of all trees in the garden except the tree of the knowledge of good and evil, which is located at the center of the garden.

Should they eat of the tree of the knowledge of good and evil, they are warned that they will surely die.

Adam and Eve ultimately ignore the warning and eat the forbidden fruit in hopes of gaining the power of God. From this allegory, we can see that the desire(8) of knowledge(9) for the sake of selfish power causes great disharmony(8-9). Then there is the concept that knowledge brings about a sense of opposing contrasts(otherness), which are represented as good and evil, judgments of the self-conscious mind(8-9). Could this be a warning that using the mind thus births disharmony?

After eating of the fruit of this tree, Adam and Eve know that they are naked, and so they sew fig leaves together to cover their shame. Before eating the forbidden fruit, Adam and Eve are similar to small children or animals in that they are not self-conscious. Eating of that tree births self-consciousness(8-9), which covers over innocence(10).

Later, when they hear the sound of God walking in the garden, Adam and Eve hide themselves among the trees of the garden in fear because they are naked. When God questions them, Adam justifies himself by indirectly blaming God, saying that Eve, whom God made for him, persuaded him to eat the fruit. When God questions Eve, she blames the serpent for deceiving her. Clearly, we can see fear, blame, and justification expressing for the first time through Adam and Eve. All three of these energies are corrupt children of self-consciousness.

The allegory continues with the birth of enmity between humans and serpents, with the beginnings of suffering through pain, and the need to toil for food. Humankind now begins to experience death.

God then drives Adam and Eve out of the garden, and he places cherubim east of the garden of Eden, and a flaming sword which turned every way, to guard the way to the tree of life. Cherubim are angels with no fixed form, like heavenly signposts that beckon us to the gate. The flaming sword totally blocks all inappropriate access into the garden to eat of the tree of life, Christ-consciousness, which is identity-transcendent consciousness. Because the flaming sword blocks access in every direction, nothing can enter, which is to say, no thing can enter. Only when totally free of content of the self can we reenter the garden to eat of the tree of life and thereby end suffering(8-9).

At first glance, the beginnings of self-consciousness would thus appear to be a mistake, but it is not. After the development of self-consciousness, quite naturally, content of the self accumulates via emotions of fear and shame and subsequent thoughts of self-definition, such as "I am afraid" and "I am naked and ashamed." Fundamentally, we are speaking of a sense of vulnerability.

At some point, the individual becomes self-aware to the point of noticing that content of the self is a millstone around the neck. Then the individual begins to question the very sense of self and the sense of separation, at which time content of the self can be observed and resolved through the frequencies of consciousness (11+). These harmonious frequencies allow for resolution of this out-of-sync content through removing all feeling-level associations as well as intellectual definitions of the self. As content of the self resolves, disharmonies dissipate, and remaining consciousness naturally gravitates ever closer to the gates of Eden. Ego caused Adam and Eve's disharmony(8-9), and, therefore, innocence(10) is the first step to reentering Eden.

The desire(8) for knowledge(9), which is erroneously perceived as power, smothers innocence(10) and then bars reentry into Eden. Therefore, we must revitalize innocence, but in order to do so we must begin to see through the illusion of the self(8-9), and for that we must also revitalize curiosity(10). Curiosity through innocence is what begins the process of resolving the self. Consider these sayings attributed to Jesus: "Truly I tell you, unless you change and become like little children, you will never enter the kingdom of Heaven," and "Truly I tell you, anyone who will not receive the kingdom of God like a little child will never enter it."

There is an innocence(10) to young children that allows for curiosity(10). The knowledge(9) of "wise" elders jades(8) and biases(9) all perspective, thereby closing the door of innocence and curiosity. Adults typically lack curiosity, and this is a true blockage because the natural doorway to consciousness(11+) is innocent curiosity.

We must be careful with curiosity, though, because curiosity can easily be corrupted by ego-based motivations. Many criminals are very curious, but that curiosity is directed toward personal gain, not toward unfoldment. In such a case, curiosity becomes the boot that kicks one out of the garden. Motivation is essential in the unfoldment process, which is why curiosity through innocence is an essential distinction.

So innocent curiosity(10) assists us in tuning to conscious(11+) frequencies that begin the process of resolving identifications (8-9). The higher the frequency of harmony, the more transformative is the field. The potential for these harmonious frequencies is always there, but remains inaccessible unless activated by intent. The frequencies of consciousness automatically represent our intent so long as that is not blocked by identifications(8-9), a dark band that veils the light within.

Curiosity used rightly is a vital tool in the process of unfoldment, but it's not our only tool. We also have meditation, which greatly speeds the process. Using meditation, we tune to observation(11), and then, little by little, as disharmony(8-9) sloughs off, we become able to tune to higher frequencies without using willpower(8). Unconditioned love(13+) is what we are ultimately moving toward, but having it as an idea(9) or philosophy(9) is not the same thing as actually tuning in to that frequency in the body. The thought(9) of unconditioned love, in those cases, still exercises the mind(8-9), which incorporates disharmonious frequencies.

Many individuals I have met who embrace the philosophy(9) of unconditioned love(13+) are actually emitting the frequencies of thought(9) and emotion(8). They are in love(8) with the idea(9) of love, which is not unconditioned love. The frequency of love in the class of emotion is a personal love(8), which, albeit high compared with other emotion, is not unconditioned(11+). Personal love and unconditioned love remain distinct.

To prime students and guide them up to the higher frequencies without going into willfulness(8) or stimulating the thought(9) of love(8) or the emotion(8) of love, which are of the self(8-9), we practice the Warrior's Meditation, which I detail in the next chapter. The Warrior's Meditation quickly tunes us to the frequency of the 11th class of the conscious(11+) spectrum, where disharmony can be addressed productively.

It sounds to me as if you are suggesting that thinking is wrong. That I should be thoughtless. Wouldn't that make me a very foolish person?

I find it very interesting how we call foolish people thoughtless. Foolish people are not thoughtless and may have a lot of thoughts, but those thoughts may not be sharp or skillful. Sometimes a foolish person may indeed have few thoughts, usually because they are tuned to a frequency below thought, which creates the effect of dullness. If you reflect on your thinking and thoughts over a normal week, what percentage of your thinking and thoughts, do you think, are necessary?

I see where you're going with this. You are saying I do a lot of unnecessary thinking, which is true. But I do a lot of necessary thinking as well, especially for my job.

Be aware that the structures of our society are of mind, which means our economic system, governments, politics, businesses, education system, buildings, jobs, relationships — all structure, really, is designed through mind, which means that working in them tends to pull us into mind if we are not careful. You may find that a lot of what you currently believe to be necessary thinking becomes less and less so as you tune more to consciousness.

You have said that using the mind causes agitation. Can you explain a little more about the agitation?

When I was a child, we had a flea infestation in our house. In the process of taking care of the fleas, we discovered that mice had taken over a storage room, and the fleas were coming from there. They had made home of the many boxes that were stored down there. The mice brought in the fleas, so to get rid of the fleas, we had to remove the mice.

While cleaning out the room, we let the cats in to catch the scurrying mice. The hunt was a frenzy of cat and mouse chase. It didn't take long before most of the mice were gone, but due to a gap under the door, new mice would come in from time to time. We converted that room to a game room, and installed a pool table and a dartboard. Knowing that mice would come back, sometimes while playing pool, I would let a cat into the room to hunt. Tom was our best hunter, so I would let him in for best results. I began taking keen interest in Tom's hunting process. I noticed that when he spotted a mouse, he would sink down low and focus keenly on the mouse as he slowly stalked the mouse. His focus was extraordinary, and he almost always got his mouse.

One day, I played a trick on Tom. As he stalked the mouse, I approached

Tom from the side. I was in his visual and auditory field, but he seemed to be oblivious to my approach, even though I was not making any attempt to disguise my movement and the sound of my footsteps were clear enough. I walked right up to Tom, and he didn't even notice me until I touched him. In that moment, he shrieked in surprise, and he leaped away from me and hissed before slinking off to the other side of the room in apparent frustration.

The exclusive activities of the mind cause attention to be more or less exclusive, and the more intensely we rely on the mind, the more exclusive our attention becomes. When the aim of the mind is interrupted, we experience agitation. To see what I mean, you only need to observe your own frustration when interrupted.

As we live our lives, our sense of self and our personality mold around the emotions arising from agitation, through associative identification. Thereby we fold disharmonies even more into our sense of who we are. Over time, this form of identification takes on many sub-personalities, which I also call identifications.

Identifications keep the mind in an exclusive state most of the time, which means that perception is conditioned, habitual, and out of context with life. When life brings the unexpected, agitation follows, to the extent that we identify with habits. This in turn reinforces and breeds still more identification through feeling association.

The next question is how we can live productively through consciousness, because to live productively, we need aims and goals. The trick is to learn to take aim in a different way than does my cat. Instead of focusing awareness to exclusion, one keeps awareness broad, with the goal in the center of awareness. An easy way to explain what I mean can be found in the use of the eyes. To get a comparison between exclusive and inclusive vision, try this experiment. Stand up, and for a minute, focus your vision tightly on something specific. After a minute, defocus the eyes, but, instead, keep the target in the center of vision while being aware of the entire visual field.

Practicing these two ways of seeing reveals subtle, or not so subtle, differences depending upon your awareness at energetic, feeling, and physiological levels. When I observe someone who is highly focused, what I see is that the energetic field rises up in the body and pushes forward out the forehead, making the person top-heavy and unstable. On a subtle level the same thing is happening physiologically that causes undue tension in the body. A clouded mind exhibits similar energetic and physiological instability as occurs with hyper focused vision.

When we relax into the entire visual field while keeping the target in the center, the energy of the body remains even, which represents in the body as better balance and less stress.

Focused vision and common mental activity are by nature exclusive, while unfocused, centered vision and consciousness are inclusive. Practicing inclusive awareness is essential to living a productive life through consciousness.

I can't perceive energy fields, so how do I know when I am tuned to mind versus consciousness?

We need not perceive energy fields to make clear progress. Energy field perception helped me to find the differences between mind and consciousness. But now that I see those differences, I realize that other ways to develop discernment do not require energy field awareness initially. There is another route.

We are caught in mind when our attention is captured by any accumulated information. Setting aside all accumulation reveals consciousness. The less tethered perception is to the content of memory and the senses, the higher the active frequency of consciousness. Can you witness, then set aside the content of self to reveal what else is present? This practice sharpens discernment. To develop clarity about the distinction between the "noise" of the self and essential consciousness, take time to regularly perceive directly without avoiding, resisting, latching onto, interpreting, or attempting to explain anything.

Feeling the difference between mind and consciousness repeatedly, one eventually becomes sensitive to energy fields, energetic atmospheres, and presence(s), which can help to further our unfoldment process so long as we do not get distracted or put off by the whoo-whoo factor.

In the next chapter, I provide tools for practicing direct perception in daily life. These tools reveal the direct inspirience of consciousness, so that you can step beyond the limits of words. Reading alone is insufficient. The value of these teachings cannot be assessed until one has practiced sufficiently with pure intentions. What is sufficient practice? To be sure, it will take sincere dedication. I have put in well over 10,000 hours of dedicated study. That said, if your mind is focused on how long it will take to make progress, you will be blocked from the outset.

Chapter 12 — Tuning to Consciousness

Words of warning before we begin the tuning process, it is vital to recognize that the tuning process, although pleasurable and inspiring, will bring up unconscious darkness to be observed and resolved, sometimes during the process but usually afterward. The things that come up may be that which we have not wanted to see. The process of unfoldment is for those who are tired of deceiving themselves and who are willing to slog through seemingly endless amounts of muck in order to reach the shores of enlightenment.

In this chapter, I will provide several tools for tuning to consciousness: unconditioned meditation, unconditioned prayer, and unconditioned chanting. To establish a principled foundation, we will begin with a form of unconditioned meditation that I call the Warrior's Meditation before moving onto prayer and chanting.

This meditation was inspired by the Amazon vision and ultimately realized through the combined training of both martial and therapy arts during my time in Japan. Through training in the martial arts, I gained appreciation for the power of fluid stability under pressure. A good instructor gradually exposes us to increasing levels of pressure and difficulty until we are able to handle real attacks with grace. In much the same way, we want to find fluid stability in our meditation so that grace can shine through the disharmony of everyday life. If we are not being challenged, then we are probably not making much progress.

The Warrior's Meditation is a fundamental and highly refined tool that I use to guide individuals through the unfoldment process. As you may not have personal access to meditation coaching, we will start with a sedentary meditation and work on what we can without a coach. Although we will start out seated, we will quickly progress into more activity and greater challenge. It will feel like a baby learning to see, then crawl, then walk, run, and so on.

We will initially use the senses in an unconditioned way to springboard into a more pure meditation. I use this form of meditation because it does not incorporate any religious symbolism, and all that is necessary for its practice is readily available to you through your physical body. Its greatest value is in its natural simplicity. For anyone who lacks in any of the physical senses, just skip them and work with what you have. As your system will have compensated for any missing senses, you should still reach the same energetic place as anyone with full access to all their senses. Also, remember that we will quickly progress beyond the senses, as we do not want to have any crutches.

Set a timer to 15 minutes for your first session and add a few minutes to each session thereafter. The more time that we grant to this meditation, the more stability we will achieve. Find a comfortable place to sit, but do not rest your back against anything unless you must do so for such circumstances as injury or pain.

Sit comfortably on the floor or in a chair to begin, gaze straight ahead, and extend your arms out to your sides (palms forward) so that they are just outside your visual field. Bend your wrists so that your palms are facing the sides of your face and wiggle your fingers. Slowly bring your arms forward until you can just barely see the tips of your wiggling fingers while gazing straight ahead. This is the horizontal range of your visual field. Generally it will be nearly 180 degrees for most people.

Next, move one hand down, below your abdomen, and one hand up, high above your head, until they are outside your visual field. Wiggling your fingers, slowly move them forward until you can find the vertical range of your visual field. Once you are aware of the vertical limits of the field, move your hands circularly to find the entire outer edge of the visual field.

This is the field that your eyes pick up at all times but that your mind selectively and unconsciously edits to the point where more often than not you perceive only a small portion of what comes into the field. An example of this selective awareness is what happens when we read. As we read we are almost entirely unaware of what occurs outside the page unless we try to be aware of what's happening around us as readers.

Once familiar and comfortable with the total visual field, rest your arms, and we'll move on to the next step in the meditation, sound. Pay attention to the total auditory field. Allow yourself to become unconditionally aware of all sounds around you. Just allow all sound to enter the body unfettered, and do not allow your attention to latch onto individual sounds.

Relax into unconditioned awareness of both the visual and auditory fields for several minutes to become accustomed to them from an unconditioned perspective. We want to be as relaxed as possible in this process, but at the same time not allow the physical body to be too slack, as that may cause drowsiness and lead to inattentiveness or sleep. Continue with your attention on the visual and auditory fields for several minutes before moving on to the next step.

Next, become aware of the entire surface area of the body. Pay attention to the feeling of the clothing and air touching your skin, the feeling of gravity pulling on the body, the floor beneath you, and so on. Do not allow your attention to focus on any particular point on or in the body. If you have aches and pains, allow the attention to spread out and not condense at these points. Remain aware of the body in this way for several minutes before moving on to the next step.

Next, become aware of the olfactory sense, the sense of smell. You may notice the smells in the room, the smell of your own body and the smell of the food that you have eaten earlier in the day. Do not allow yourself to get caught up in the process of labeling individual smells, however. Just smell purely and unconditionally without labeling anything.

In warmer temperatures, smells are easier to detect than in cold environs. Also, when the nostrils are moist, they will pick up smells better than when dry. So, do not be concerned if, on some days, you are able to notice smells better than on other days. Moreover, some people have a much better sense of smell than others. Do not be concerned with how much you can smell, but instead pay attention to the sense itself and the feeling inside the nostrils as the air moves through them. Again, relaxation is essential.

Finally, we move on to the sense of taste and the feeling within the mouth. You will probably be able to taste some or many of the things that you have eaten throughout the day, but in the event that you do not, have no concern. Just relax into the sense of taste and the feeling within the mouth. Give yourself a few minutes to acclimate to the sense of taste while remaining unconditionally aware.

At this stage of the meditation, our awareness is extended much more than it would typically be. Although the extent of our awareness is important, it's not the only thing we are looking for here. The natural habit for most people new to this form of meditation is to rely on eyesight for most of their awareness, creating an egg-shaped field of awareness. Because modern humans have the tendency to be visually focused, attention is almost entirely to the front, which causes physiological imbalance and stress.

What we are working toward is a perfect, spherical awareness that extends equally in every direction from the center of perception. The way to tune to this sphericality is to start giving some attention to all directions through feeling, but do not be too willful; instead, relax into it. Gradually our addiction to the visual sense will break, and, little by little, we will be more functionally attentive to the total space around us.

To get an image of the Warrior's Meditation, imagine a master samurai surrounded by opponents intent on killing him. A novice's attention will jump from opponent to opponent in an anxious attempt to defend himself. He will soon tire and be defeated. An expert warrior will spread his attention evenly in all directions but will still experience anxiety as he mentally plans his strategy. His thought and anxiety may be his downfall if his opponents are truly skilled. A master's attention, like the expert's, is spread evenly, but he is as calm as a cat resting in the peonies, with no thought of what his actions might be.

Once relaxed and fully into the meditation, begin moving a little while maintaining unconditioned awareness. You might move an arm or a leg, for example, or look around. From my experience coaching people, their energy fields tend to collapse while moving in the early stages until they acclimate and gain more stability in the process. This indicates the unconscious use of the mind. It's good to challenge oneself, moving arms and legs, getting up and sitting down, and so forth. The point of the practice is not to perceive energy fields, but you should notice silent spaciousness, and when that spaciousness grows, shrinks, wavers, or collapses entirely. Furthermore, you will notice when avoidance, resistance, interpretation, mental explanation, or selective interest arise within the mind. Once we notice these things, we calmly return to unconditioned awareness.

Start out using the senses as I have instructed, but quickly wean yourself of this technique. Within a few meditation sessions, you should no longer need to use your arms to find the visual field, and gradually you will be more able to feel the total space through and around you.

There will be days on which the meditation practice seems flat and other days on which it's truly inspiring. Do not be concerned at all with outcomes, as this perspective is egoic. Just make time to meditate and allow each session to be unique. Sometimes we may be highly distracted and have the strong temptation to quit, feeling it's a waste of time. The last thing we should do in this case is quit. Instead lightly and gently look into what it is that is distracting you. When you see that something within does not want you meditating, then you realize that the worst thing you could do is to quit. Stay the course even if that means just sitting there for the allotted time. But rather than sitting I advise incorporating meditation into daily life and a great way to do that is to meditate while doing daily chores. Meditating in this way will never feel like a waste of time.

When we consider any noteworthy accomplishment in the world, the person or persons who achieved it were unfailingly persistent. I once enjoyed a conversation with a retired Navy Seal, who told me that the Seal selection process is very simple. They put the potential recruits through Hell and see who gives up. If the individual gets through the tests, even if they do not look spectacular, then they are accepted into Seal training. But the vast majority of people quit.

The quitter is an identification that people feed during the small activities of their lives. They quit at things that they consider insignificant first, and in this way they start feeding the quitter. With each quitting experience the quitter gets stronger and stronger, and pretty soon its voice is overwhelming. "It's boring. It takes too long. It's too much work. It's too troublesome. It hurts. I can't. It's impossible. Someone let me out of this, please." These are some of its seductive utterances.

If we have fed the quitter, then we can start to resolve it through meditation and through the smaller activities of our lives. Little by little, we will face challenges without quitting. With regard to unfoldment, it's not necessary to be a tremendous athlete or to be incredibly academic, but it's exceedingly important to be persistent over the long term, as this process can take years or lifetimes, depending on the individual and the specific path we are walking.

In any case, in the mind there must never be a finish line. Sometimes people ask me when I will stop practicing martial arts. To me this question is like asking when I will quit breathing. There is no end as far as my intention is concerned. Just keep moving forward.

There is a lot more to be understood in this process than I have been able to explain in this section, much of which we will realize through continued meditation practice. I cannot state enough how important the Warrior's Meditation is. Remember to keep it simple and keep your eyes open. Do not allow into this process any crutches, such as the use of spiritual symbols, spiritual items, or anything else; keep it pure. We are already born with all we need to unfold, and the more crutches we use, the less applicable the meditation will be to our daily lives. We are now at a point in the consciousness of this planet when spirituality needs to be more than just a hobby, sideshow, or weekend activity; instead, it needs to be lived. Have faith in your unfoldment process, and abandon all that is nonessential.

Consistency is the key to this meditation. The more we practice the easier it is to remain tuned to consciousness. We will also find, with consistent practice, that the things which used to easily knock us out of consciousness no longer have much impact on us. Immerse yourself whenever you can, but remember that even a moment here or a second there is greatly beneficial. It would be much better to meditate even for a few seconds than to not meditate at all. Set a meditation regimen that you know you will actually do every day. All that we need to do is get some momentum going with regard to meditation.

Ultimately we want to develop a life-pattern that supports meditation over the long-run. As it gets easier and easier to remain in the frequencies of consciousness, we will have time to incorporate it into our life and make necessary structural changes that support the unfoldment process. Many of our blockages are structural, which is to say the blockages are found in our life-patterns — habits, addictions, and varieties of codependence. We want this process to become a part of our daily life so that meditation and life are one and the same. There simply is no substitute for daily meditation in this regard.

If you would like support with your path of meditation and awareness, *you can get free 30-day access to my daily guided meditation service by clicking here.*

Deconditioning Meditation

There are many types of meditations in the world, each with unique features and differing aims. Some of these methods are very good for relaxation, for religious practice, or for healing the body. Some of these meditations make use of rituals, symbols, sound devices, music, or chanting. While almost any meditation is highly beneficial, some methods are more applicable to unfoldment through daily life than others. Because a human being's life experience is nothing like the conditions of these meditations, I have found that they do not translate well into our daily lives, which are active and chaotic by comparison to the meditation methods being practiced. The specific conditions of these meditations have become obstacles to functional silence in daily life, and since it's through our daily life that unfoldment occurs, conditioned meditation is not very applicable.

I have also found that the more austere forms of meditation are in general not very beneficial to initiates in daily life because the individual is highly unstable, thanks to emotion, thought, and sensation. As such, the individual's amount of mental chatter and unconscious reactivity is tremendous. Because of the magnitude and intensity of unconscious disharmony, it's easy to be distracted, or bored, or disturbed, or use force of will to push through the meditation time. The result is that many who are eager for unfoldment find these types of meditations to be boring, impractical, and/or prohibitively difficult, which is why so few individuals are able to stick with the process over the long term.

Within a few months of Warrior's Meditation practice — which is a dynamic, unconditioned method, one's awareness would be more spherical and would extend farther out in daily life, indicative of a less conditioned self. I have seen no other form of meditation that produces such rapid, stable results. The reason for the rapid progress through the Warrior's Meditation is that it's designed to embrace what would normally disturb others. By expanding awareness, it naturally provides more conscious and physical stability. I quickly have students up and moving to challenge their stability and to find applicable expansion for daily life.

First, they practice listening and speaking until they develop enough stability to maintain expansive awareness. One would think that listening and talking during meditation would be simple, but it's surprisingly difficult for newcomers and even those who have practiced sedentary meditations for years. Once they gain some stability with conversation, they then practice standing and walking without collapsing. Continuing with this expansion into daily activities, this process eventually enables the individual to fully function under high pressure and not collapse back into mind. Because this form of meditation is so dynamic, people find it to be extremely soothing yet also challenging and inspiring.

Through the Warrior's Meditation, people are able to gain more stability and functionality while remaining rooted in a more loving and connected way through their actual lives. Little by little, through observation, individuals root their lives in consciousness. Many students who are somewhat new to the process ask me what it feels like to be tuned in this way, and the best way I can describe it is as a constant, clear, loving, vastness. A person bound in the spectrums of emotion, thought, and the conditioned senses would feel finite, small, stagnant, and turbulent.

Sometimes you might wonder whether your meditation sessions are productive. If you've made the time and gone through the process, it was productive. Making the time and space for the meditation process is really the key, especially early in the effort. If we are too busy to set aside much time, then do it while on break, on the toilet, or while walking. Even a minute here or a minute there is good. Meditate while driving, while on trains, and in any spare moment. Just keep at it and, eventually, it's constant. Doing so, I was able to maintain higher frequencies through all activities of my life and find sublime silence. It's no longer meditation; it's life.

Initially we will be using all of our senses to go into meditation, which will require a lot of intent, so we will look like zombies. This is natural because we are completely retuning our awareness away from the conditioning of the self toward unconditionality. Once we retune fully through our daily life, we will always have stability through Isness, and there will be no need for us to meditate to be in harmony.

Remember that the Warrior's Meditation as I have described it is a powerful step in the process of spiritual unfoldment, so no matter how far along the path we go, the fundamentals that we find through this method will serve to illuminate the path. Keep it simple, and allow it to purify your life.

You have said using the senses reinforces the mind, yet you are using senses in your introductory meditation. Why is that?

When we use some senses to the exclusion of the other senses, which is what people habitually do, it leads us back into the mind. But when the senses all work together in an unconditioned fashion, there is a harmonic effect that tunes us to the 11th frequency class, which is harmonious.

I am a very low-energy person. It's very difficult for me to remain alert and even sit up straight because I just feel dull all the time. How do I meditate if I don't have energy?

I also found this to be a real challenge on days of dullness. I chose not to fight the dullness but instead to flow with it. Lie down on your back and bend your knees so that the bottoms of your feet are flat on the floor to keep the lower back from arching too much. Put your arms out to your sides on the floor, bending them at the elbow 90 degrees while keeping your lightly clenched fists up in the air. The goal is to keep the knees and hands up through the meditation process while being as relaxed as possible. If you start to doze off, then the knees and hands will begin to fall and that is likely to awaken you enough to correct the posture and remain in the meditation. With this method do not concern yourself with the senses, as you may not have enough energy for that. Instead, just direct enough awareness to keep your knees and fists upright.

Often I found I would enter a kind of twilight state just between being asleep and being awake, but still able to observe. That's a fine meditation that I came out of clear and refreshed. If you lose circulation to your hands, put them down for a time until the blood flows back and rejuvenates them, then put them back up. If you find that keeping your knees up is enough to keep you alert, then you can just use your legs and relax your arms. Play with it to find what works for you.

For some people, lying on the back is uncomfortable, so we can modify this process if we look at the principles. Find a position that is comfortable and create a light focal point with the body to stimulate alertness. For example, if lying on our right side, we could place our left hand on our left hip with the elbow bent and pointed at the ceiling. The key in this example is to keep the elbow pointed at the ceiling. When you become more proficient, you can sit with tension in your outstretched fingers preventing the fingertips from touching your lap. All of these methods serve to keep just enough attention to be successful but not so much that it becomes uncomfortable or willful.

If this tension method does not work, take a cold bath or shower just before meditating, and consider getting a little more sleep if you are sleep deprived. If that still does not help, see your health practitioner as there may be some health issues that need addressing. We do not want to build an unconscious association with sleep during this process because once that association begins then meditations will put you to sleep consistently, which is counterproductive.

For some reason, I have tremendous difficulty meditating. Is there another way to reach the frequencies of consciousness?

Yes. We have many ways to tune to consciousness, with prayer and chanting being most obvious. Early on some people have an easier time with prayer or mantra than they do with meditation due to religious upbringing, so for such individuals, we can make use of these tools to tune to the frequencies of consciousness, and then little by little, move toward deconditioning these tools by removing the cultural biases, unhelpful feeling associations, and form-based limitations, so that they naturally grow into dynamic meditations with practice.

Prayer as a Tool of Awakening

Let's say for example, you were Christian. You could use the idea of the Holy Spirit coming into the body as your prayer. Be sure to select a prayer that you feel drawn to utter in your mind. For example, in your mind, you might say, "I pray that the Holy Spirit shines through my body and into the world as Christ instructed." As you repeat this or some similar prayer, notice the feeling in the body. Open your eyes and share that feeling with the environment around you. As you practice this prayer over a period of days, weeks, or months, move gradually away from words and toward more feeling, and from closed eyes to open eyes throughout the process.

The reason we want to move away from words, is that we want to continually reduce the impediments to the expression of consciousness in our daily life as much as possible. If the goal is to be an inexhaustible light to the world, which is the real teaching of Jesus Christ, then you must transcend words, because you can't function in the world while uttering a mental prayer constantly.

If you have an associated image with God or The Holy Spirit, be aware that forming attachments to that associated image is a form of idol worship. As Jesus stated, "God is the Alpha and the Omega." Alpha is a counterpart to our letter *A*, while Omega is equivalent to Z. The essential meaning is that God is the beginning and the end, and all that is between – *All That Is*.

Also, be aware that Hebrew is grammatically gendered, so all nouns and pronouns have gender. Due to the limitations of the language and the choices of translators over time, God is gendered male. But *All That Is* includes and transcends gender. Through the practice of prayer, begin resolving the limitations of language and culture, so that consciousness can flow through unimpeded in every moment of life.

Early in the process, be sure to pray while lying down, on your knees, seated, standing, and walking. Unclasp your hands and pray unconditionally wherever you are. Be a light unto the world!

Chanting as a Tool of Awakening

Many religious and spiritual practices include chanting or mantra. Chants are often tonal utterances of specific religious or spiritual doctrine. A common Buddhist chant is as follows, "Ananda, be dependent on yourself, take refuge in yourself and not in others, by this means be dependent on the Dharma — the righteous principles." It matters little which chant you choose, so long as it resonates with you.

The key to chanting toward consciousness lies in feeling the vibration of the voice travel through the entire body during the chant with each extended consonant and vowel. Once you feel the vibrations traveling evenly through the body, intend the vibrations to move through the entire universe.

Be sure that you can chant with eyes open or closed, while seated, while standing, and even while walking. Do not allow the body to develop a specific association that will limit your chanting process. Allow feeling to move with the sound vibrations, as they extend through and beyond the body. At some point during the chant, a clear vibrant space in and around the body will develop. Stop the chant and notice the clear vibrancy everywhere. Move around while maintaining this clear, powerful frequency for as long as possible.

As you practice chanting toward consciousness, gradually set aside the specific words and use only one tone, such as "Ah" from the first word in the chant, "Ah-na-nn-da," and feel it travel the body and the universe. The next step is to reduce the volume of the voice, while still feeling the vibrations travel evenly through the body to the whole universe. At some point, you will arrive at pure breathing absent voice. When done right, it will feel as if the universe is breathing you — but don't stop there. Move toward pure feeling and intention, absent breath technique. Going further, make unconditioned awareness your very being even while sleeping.

Chapter 13 — Potential Pitfalls

In pursuit of knowledge, every day something is added.
In the practice of the Tao, every day something is dropped.
Less and less do you need to force things,
until finally you arrive at non-action.
When nothing is done, nothing is left undone.

— Tao Te Ching

As I have stated, the process of unfoldment is a revelation of what is and always has been, therefore we must be very careful about adding to this process. Techniques, modalities, skills, and so on, are all potentially dangerous distractions taking us away from unfoldment as we become dependent upon these things. What we are looking for in this process is to discover the core and the fundamental, so we strip away all that is unnecessary as we go.

All techniques and tools that I teach are only temporary and are meant to be discarded as the individual discovers the principles behind the techniques. Therefore, although we do respect the tools and techniques so far as they assist us to move beyond them, we do not allow ourselves to become reliant upon them. The self will most certainly do its best to turn each and everything into a crutch, so we must be "careful as a warrior in enemy territory" as Lao-Tzu puts it.

Eventually, we will find that nothing other than unconditioned love is necessary, and that will be the natural effect of your very being, not something that you do. Until then, we do what we can to strip away and find the purity within, while tuning to the frequencies of consciousness as often as possible.

Techniques and Comfort Zones

Many people will have a technique or visualization that makes it seem easier to meditate, but such things invariably lead to imbalance and become crutches upon which dependence quickly develops. Remember, we are looking to strip away all nonessentials so that we have clarity in our high-speed, high-pressure lives.

Keep it simple and pure even if it seems a little more difficult initially that way. You will come to appreciate this advice in short order. Also, be careful not to meditate in the same comfortable place and position. Little by little, expose yourself to potential distractions and new locations while also sitting in different positions, facing in different directions. At my first training center, which was in town, we had a dance studio just above our space. The building was more than 100 years old, and there was no insulation between their floor and our ceiling, so effectively their hardwood floor and our false ceiling made a giant speaker. When they danced, it sounded like a buffalo ballet. Throw in the music, and you have a herd of disco-dancing water buffalo.

Initially there was the thought that it would be a bad place to meditate, but I challenged that assumption and had my beginning students meditate through the racket. What they found was they were distracted only if they held a negative attitude toward the music. If we just allow for the "distraction" it quickly ceases to have any power over us. If we practice accepting attitudes in our lives we will find that a lot of "distractions" lose power over us.

Force of Will

Modern people around the world hail willpower as being a virtue since all that we do in modern culture is based on force. But willpower is firmly in the frequency of disharmony, so it's not an effective vehicle for tuning to harmony. Pay attention to what happens in your mind when experiencing willpower. Everything closes in to exclusion as the mind focuses on what it's going to forcefully accomplish. At this moment there is strength in only one direction and weakness in every other direction. This is not the way of consciousness; it's of the mind. The power of consciousness is distributed equally in all directions because it's unconditioned and unbiased.

Be aware of willpower as it arises in the meditation process, and instead of feeding willfulness, try relaxing into the process. We set a goal of using no more than 10 percent of our attention to do anything in particular. The more time given to this process, the less effort will be required to do it. Initially, you may look like a zombie, but as you acclimate and incorporate it into your daily life, it will be more and more natural and, of course, beneficial.

How can we accomplish anything without willpower? Lao-Tzu gives us a hint: "Do you have the patience to wait until your mud settles and the water is clear? Can you remain unmoving until the right action arises by itself?" Instead of using force and willfulness to accomplish, we need to find another avenue, which is consciousness. There will come a point at which the body will just accomplish things on its own. When this first happens it will be quite astounding, but eventually it will feel normal. No matter how often it happens, it will always be inspiring because it does not come from the mind.

Until it begins to occur, practice the 10 percent rule that we use during meditation. The rule goes this way: Never use more than 10 percent of your focus on any particular thing; instead, keep awareness spread out evenly. In this manner we are able to accomplish without feeding willfulness and force. Keep some awareness spread out and open to the environment within and around the body. This is sure to be difficult at first, especially during very challenging tasks, but eventually we are able to do things in this way, which ultimately leads into the body moving on its own to accomplish tasks.

Artifacts

In meditation, especially in the early stages, one may experience what I call artifacts. Artifacts are strange visual phenomena that sometimes show up during meditation. The frequencies of consciousness will initially be beyond the brain's ability to work with, which will create odd effects such as the appearance of a funny haze over the floor. The walls or ceilings may appear to be undulating. The room may appear to brighten and darken repeatedly, or suddenly the whole visual field may collapse entirely and leave you in total darkness, even though your eyes are open.

The mistake would be to assume that there is some important meaning in these effects and then allow yourself to become fearful, distracted, or entertained by these things. These tendencies are perfectly exemplified by the experience of an acquaintance who had ingested some peyote, a hallucinogenic cactus, for fun.

He found himself surrounded by a troop of young, naked, dancing women.

He quite enjoyed this hallucination, but after a few minutes of it, the scene vanished, and he was confronted by the powerful spirit of the cactus. The power and intensity of this spirit was such that the individual was knocked out of his sexual haze and into total rapt attention. The spirit demanded to know what his question was. My friend felt like he needed to have a worthy question quickly or he would feel the wrath of this spirit for wasting its time. Suddenly and without thought, he asked, "What is the purpose of life?" The spirit was pleased with this question and gave him an undeniably valuable answer.

This spirit did my friend a great service by slapping him out of his distraction while still offering him a chance to learn further. In most cases, getting distracted is the end of any learning as the motivation becomes entertainment, not spiritual unfoldment.

Memory

After the Isness inspirience (Chapter 5), all I wanted to do was to get back to that divine place that I called Isness. The memory was always on my mind, constantly being compared to my daily life. The effect of holding this memory was extremely negative. It caused stress and did not allow for the least bit of enjoyment because my experiences just could not compare to Isness. The memory of Isness had become a millstone around my neck.

One day, while taking a therapy lesson from my instructor in Japan, I told him about the Isness inspirience and how it was constantly on my mind. I hoped that he would have some good advice. Because of arrogance, I was also expecting that he would be impressed by the inspirience, but contrary to my expectation he told me, "I recommend that you forget it." I was stunned. That was the last thing I thought he'd say. It felt like blasphemy. Honestly, I was a little insulted because he did not appear to value something that I held in such high esteem. I did not want to be rude or argue with him, so I let it drop. It's my policy, however, to be open to any criticism or advice, so for the next several months, I allowed his comment to simmer within, being open to the possibility that there was something of value in what he said. Little by little, the memory of the Isness inspirience slipped out of the forefront of my mind and stopped tainting everything. Life became beautiful again, and I was able to be more present.

My mistake was equating memory with actuality. Most students do this very same thing early on in their meditation practice, I find. They have a great session, and then, for a number of sessions afterward, try to remake the prior experience. This is attachment, not observing without judgment. The memory of the previous experience which they have decided needs to be repeated blocks them from being present, and the conscious energy field does not expand, indicating mental captivation. They may believe that they are in a harmonious frequency, but anyone who has the eyes to see knows that they are actually tuned to the mind. Let memories be memories, and do not try to relive them. Toss out all expectation, and be open to all possibilities at all times. This is true inspirience in the moment.

Psychic Senses

Words of warning: we are not trying to develop psychic senses here. We are merely resolving inner darkness and revealing what is innate once the veil of conditionality is removed. Psychic senses do not help reveal Isness because Isness is not localized in any specific realm, nor has it an image or a definition, so there is no way to sense it. In the event that a psychic sense opens up, do not feed it with attention. Instead, keep attention spread evenly in a relaxed fashion.

Sometimes an individual will inadvertently open up a psychic doorway by focusing on a specific sense and then be unable to close it again. One such student opened up clairaudience by paying too much attention to the sense of hearing in the meditation because of the ease with which he thought he could meditate if he focused exclusively on sound.

Since his attention was focused on sound as opposed to all senses globally, and because he was predisposed to clairaudience, he quickly opened up that psychic sense and found that he could not stop it during that meditation. It surprised him that he found he could hear the sounds of a party that had taken place in that room many years earlier, glasses clinking, drunken people chatting at full volume. As a meditator he became totally distracted by something completely useless for his goal of tuning to consciousness.

We tested him and found that he was unable to do basic movements that one can do effortlessly in a balanced meditation, so his over-focus on sound had imbalanced him and allowed disharmony to settle in the body. Feeding psychic senses will tune one in the direction of disharmony due to conditioned focus upon a certain direction, sense, place, or thing rather than toward the whole of all that is.

Fortunately, after getting this student back to total awareness, he could feel the difference and chose to continue tuning toward Isness rather than playing psychically. The next session, he did not have any problem with clairaudience.

Many new students mistakenly assume that my awareness of their energy field is a psychic ability, but in reality it's nothing of the sort. It's purely through tuning to Isness that I perceive it. I am convinced that anyone who resolves their divisions can do the very same thing.

Final thoughts on psychic senses. It is often the case that "extra" senses open up naturally through the awakening process and that is perfectly fine so long as our primary focus is not on developing special abilities, but instead, on finding the clarity within.

Psychotropics

Warning: Consumption of psychotropics is potentially dangerous because of the possibility that someone with an allergy or illness could be harmed or even killed via the use of these substances. The author is in no way recommending that anyone take hallucinogenic substances of any kind.

I generally caution against taking any psychotropics (hallucinogenic substances) unless one feels deeply pulled to do so. The natem experience in the Amazon was extremely valuable to me, and were it not for that ceremony I might not yet be at a point where this book could be written. The natem ceremony sped up my unfoldment process dramatically — not because the medicine did the work for me, but instead because it helped guide me in a direction that allowed me to work out the hints received through the vision.

I have heard of many people who have had profound spiritual understandings from the use of other psychotropic plants, so clearly psychotropics can be an extremely valuable tool in the process of spiritual unfoldment. And for some individuals who are extremely caught up in themselves, and who simply need a plant intervention to break a negative cycle and give them some insight into their state of mind, psychotropics may be an important tool, because a lot of individuals who are in such negative, self-absorbed states will not be able to meditate or will be unwilling even to try.

That said, there is a danger to using any substance for revelation. What I have noticed and warn against is that because the information comes easily, it often stops there. What I mean is that we may gain a very interesting story and some spiritual information from the experience, but often it does not significantly alter the structures and choices of our lives. If one gains useful guidance through any vehicle, that is only the beginning. Do the homework of incorporating the guidance into daily life in order to complete the circle. If this critical step is omitted, then how was the ceremony different from using any other type of drug for entertainment or escape?

The most dangerous aspect of using psychotropics is that, almost without exception, we begin to feel that we need them in order to have spiritual insight. This means that in our daily lives we feel disconnected, and therefore we start to rely on a hallucinogen to get that spiritual feeling. This is a crutch if there ever was one. Instead of realizing that human beings are born with all they need to tune to consciousness, we may begin to feel that we need the hallucinogen in order to make a connection. This idea is not much different from that of needing a priest to be the mediator between us and God, a crippling limitation.

It all comes down to motivations and intentions. If one feels pulled to take a psychotropic, and it feels right to do so, if the intentions are purely for gaining insight and healing, and there is a firm determination to follow through with the process by incorporating any valuable lessons into one's life, then it's probably going to be an incredible learning opportunity. That said, if we make space for the meditation practice as outlined above and have the right intentions, we will probably have no need for psychotropic substances to gain spiritual insight, and with persistence the meditations will harmonize our daily lives. Even meditation is a tool that we must not allow to become a crutch. Eventually we will transcend all tools.

The Savior

Throughout human culture the savior archetype is ubiquitous. We can see this tendency in ancient cultures through such stories as King Arthur and his sword Excalibur, and through religions including Buddhism and Christianity. In modern culture, we have added greatly to this archetype through movie characters such as Superman, Luke Skywalker in *Star Wars*, Gandalf from *The Lord of the Rings*, and Neo from *The Matrix*. Add to these all the video games in which we play the role of the savior, such as *The Elder Scrolls*, *Half-Life*, *Final Fantasy*, and *Deus Ex*, to name but a few.

I commonly hear people say, "I am a very spiritual person," or "I'm not a very spiritual person." Both of these statements come from a fundamental misunderstanding that anyone can be any more or less spiritual than anyone else. Everyone and everything is equally spiritual because everything is of Isness. The difference between people is merely their degree of realization of what lies at the core. But everyone has the potential to realize Isness. Consider this statement: "I am very spiritual." What frequency does this statement arise from? Mind, of course, because it is comparative to other people, whom the speaker sees as being less spiritual. What about: "I am the chosen one"; "I am the Savior"; "I am the Christ" — what is the root that gives expression to these statements? Mind, right? These statements stem from identifications. If we pay attention, we will realize that there is a feeling in the body that goes with these statements. Resolve the feeling in the body, tune to consciousness, and be at peace. It's profoundly simple. But thanks to its simplicity, it is elusive to the mind.

The truth is we are all here to realize Isness. It's not a race, so some of us may appear to realize before others, but if we truly have realized, we also realize that time is an illusion of the multiverse. From the perspective of Isness there is only potentiality expressing in the eternal moment as the multiverse. From this perspective, are not all of us fully realized in the eternal moment? Tune to the timeless, and make it your abode.

Imagine having a vision wherein you are declared to be anointed to teach a path of unfoldment that would help humanity to tune to consciousness. How might you feel after this? After the Isness inspirience, I was clearly reminded that I had a mission on Earth to help bring the awareness of Isness within to the people of the world. I began to feel as though I were somehow special in the world even though, paradoxically, I could see that Isness is throughout all that is and in the heart of everyone. After being shown the specifics of my purpose on Earth through the Amazon vision, the feeling of "I'm the chosen one" was even more palpable. Although I could see that each person has the very same core, which is Isness, somehow hearing that I was anointed for the purpose of revealing that to humanity made me feel even more "special."

There was a great struggle within me, as two voices waged war. One said, "You are no different than anyone else." The other said, "You are special". Whenever I heard that second voice, a feeling of superiority and arrogance began to flood my body. This identification brought about a feeling of great separation because it meant that I was superior to others in some unseen way; I was the authority. Thankfully, there was also the feeling that all people had this same potential, so I worked to resolve "special" whenever it arose. It was an identification, and a powerful one at that. Through teaching I have clearly seen that each person not only has the core of Isness within, but they are able to access and express it to an astonishing degree in a very short period of time.

One individual told me, "I feel such divine states of love. It is truly amazing. Why me?" This question, of course, is covering over a deeper question, which is "Am I special? Am I chosen?" In reply to this student I simply answered, "Why not you?" The seed which was planted in this person hopefully grows into a different question: "Why not everyone?" Be ever watchful of spiritual arrogance. It is an identification that knocks a great many spiritual leaders off the path. Remember, we are all of Isness with the very same potentiality. Some may realize Isness before others from a timeline perspective, but ultimately all potentiality is actuality in the eternal moment. So, why not everyone?

Chapter 14 — Resolving Disharmony

Just as two legs help a human to walk, so do two tools help us to move in balance in the initial stages of unfoldment. The first tool is the meditation that I have already outlined. The second tool is the releasing process, which is called Dance of the Self. I teach here something learned many years ago; it has proven essential in the unfoldment process.

The Warrior's Meditation as taught is extremely powerful, and it will bring up darkness to be consciously experienced and resolved. Ideally, when bound emotion rises up in our life, we will simply experience it purely, with great curiosity, until the energy resolves to harmony on its own. But to be honest, at times the rising energy is so utterly overwhelming that it knocks you into an unconscious state, rendering you unable to be with it purely. During such times, Dance of the Self will prove an invaluable tool.

If you meditate but do not have a tool to resolve the overwhelming darkness that arises, it's akin to closing all the windows in your house and then sweeping the floor. You're going to kick up all that dust and not be able to breathe. Dance of the Self is a method to open the main windows of the self — the physical window, the emotional window, and the mental window — to allow the uplifted dust to exit while experiencing it consciously.

Dance of the Self

Every day set aside 10 to 15 minutes of time to use consistently for Dance of the Self. Go into a private space such as your bedroom or bathroom, where you know you will not be disturbed. Reflect on your day and notice any disharmony within yourself during interactions with other people or related to any events. What we are working with in this exercise is recognizing disharmony within ourselves, not in other people; for example, you might have felt annoyed when speaking with the person in the adjacent cubicle at work. All mental disharmony resides within the body, so when you remember the interaction with that individual, feel where the disharmony is in the body. Once you find it, forget the story, and focus lightly and lovingly on the feeling in the body.

Once in touch with the feeling, allow the body to move it out. You might find that the body wants to shake and the fists want to clench, or it might feel like dry heaving — or any number of other things. Let the body do whatever is necessary to channel that disharmony out. To amplify the flow, we can add vocalization as well. As your attention focuses on the disharmonious feeling within the body, the voice will also be tuned to that feeling; therefore, it may not be a beautiful voice. However, it should not use words; instead, just keep to basic sounds. The key to a powerful release is really feeling the energy from your very being as it flows out.

Let this process continue until the feeling is totally drained. When it's finished, you will often feel extremely clear, as if you just meditated. This is good. If there is more to release, go back, locate the emotion in the body, and release some more.

An easy and effective way to test whether more negative energy needs to be released is to go back to the memory of the day on which you noticed the original disharmony. If, when remembering the story, disharmony remains, then more is available for release. As soon as you find the energy in the body, set aside the story again, and just "dance" and "sing" out the darkness.

Dance of the Self is an extremely effective method of releasing negative feelings that we would otherwise unconsciously allow to spill into our daily life. Such spillage can cause tremendous relationship strife, but we are able to circumvent that through intentional release in a private, safe place. Just remember not to become overfocused or willful in this process. It's all about flow.

After I learned Dance of the Self, I did it religiously every night. I began in the shower because I was self-conscious of any noises that I might make while vocalizing. I didn't want my wife to hear it and think I was crazy. Only about a month into the process I started to see the positive effects of Dance of the Self.

Through this new process of self-reflection, I became aware of an issue that I had previously not recognized. For years, probably all the way back to my childhood, I had experienced a tremendous anxiety that would flood my body and leave me unable to relax while walking. It felt like an engine revving up in my chest, and anxiety radiated out to the rest of my body. The feeling drove me to constant movement. My foot would tap constantly. I felt like I had to fast-walk everywhere I went. Sometimes the anxiety would grow so intense that I had the overwhelming and unconscious desire to run, which is to say that, even if I tried to walk calmly, within a minute or two I would be fast-pacing, then running. I would realize it only after the fact. If I had no way to burn out that anxiety by running, then it erupted at people through general grumpiness and emotional reactivity.

About a month after I had done Dance of the Self consistently, that anxiety disappeared. I found myself able to enjoy a nice stroll home in the evening, and my foot stopped tapping constantly. I was able to relax, an entirely new thing for me, and this benefit taught me the profound value of Dance of the Self.

I had many days when only minor darkness found release in my dancing, but I continued Dance of the Self regardless. Other times I found a release so powerful that it felt as if my body was possessed because of the overwhelming intensity of the energy. After dancing, I always had more clarity.

This kind of dogged persistence is vital to finding success in any endeavor worth doing. It's like drilling for oil. The drill may have to go down quite a ways before it hits a major pocket of oil. In the same way, you must go through the dirt days of minor oil to eventually hit a large pocket. When you hit a big pocket of darkness, you may feel as if you are possessed, so powerful is the energy coming through. Just let it come, without interfering or judging.

If we find that we suffer from self-consciousness that prevents us from releasing, then that is the first thing to dance out. Notice the location in the body where the energy of self-consciousness hides, and then drop the story and dance it out.

After a dramatic release you may feel as if no disharmony remains, and it may be true for that day. But rest assured so much more is stowed away down there than we imagine. Just keep at it, day in and day out, without skipping. The only mistake we can make here is the mistake of not practicing Dance of the Self.

I just can't bring myself to do Dance of the Self. It feels strange, and sometimes I get fearful just before I start.

It's not you who feels it's strange, nor is it you who is fearful, but those are both things that can be danced out. When those feelings of disharmony come up, meditate and then inquire into them, and you will see that they are not you. Many people will feel embarrassed to do Dance of the Self even in a totally private space. This embarrassment is not really them; it's an identification to which we have given power, and it has taken the pilot's seat of our mind. Feel into this embarrassment. When you are ready, dance out embarrassment first.

What do you mean, it's not me who feels it's strange?

When I say "you," I am not referring to your personality or to the self, but instead to the unconditioned, eternal, undefined you. This actual you never changes, never ages, and does not suffer. This is the being realized through the process of unfoldment.

It sounds so mysterious — unbelievable, really.

To the contrary, what I am teaching is so simple that people overlook it. Simply set aside all accumulated content. Forget all that you know. Set aside all assumptions and biases, including any ideas of who or what you are, and your identification with the body as being you or yours.

This inspirience is a glimpse of what I am referring to as "you." Everything that the mind thinks of as you causes suffering, and the longer you remain stuck in identification, the longer you suffer. Oppositely, the longer that you remain unconditionally aware, the more full is the inspirience, which resolves suffering. That said, be aware that mind does what it does. It will likely spin itself into a tizzy trying to identify "you" even after you have had a deep inspirience. Mind is like a woodpecker on a concrete pole. It will continue bouncing its brain around until it tires of pecking. Forgive it, and revisit unconditioned awareness as often as possible.

I get so angry sometimes that I am unable to stop it. What should I do?

At times we are so identified and overwhelmed that we lose all perspective. If anger is such a volatile identification for us that it immediately takes over and controls us, then we need to become very proactive with regard to anger. Don't wait until you become wildly angry to try to resolve it. Assume it is there on a simmer, always, and spend time each evening dancing out anger proactively so that this identification is not so highly pressurized.

We also want to look into the feeling of anger in the body with curiosity, treating it as a completely new experience to explore. When we do this, we may come to see that it's not really our true being becoming angry, although we may have believed this story for a long time. Couple that with proactive dancing, and we may find that anger does not develop into rage so quickly. Hence we may be able to make calm, productive choices later, even under pressures that would usually stimulate the identification of anger. We can choose not to allow the identification to express at an inappropriate time. We separate ourselves from the situation and do Dance of the Self to release the energy and return to unconditioned awareness.

In most cases of extreme anger, I have found that the emotion just covers over a deeper hurt. Often, anger conceals shame or a feeling of vulnerability due to being violated in some very emotionally painful way when we were children. It may be confusingly combined with pride. That said, we never want to assume anything, so we look into anger with curiosity, to open the door for insight. Who knows what lies beneath?

You have said that we should not try to push away or escape from identifications or darkness. But it seems to me that Dance of the Self is just another way of pushing away.

Well, being honest, that boiling-over energy is going to come out one way or another, but better that it comes out at a time of our choosing rather than unconsciously affecting other people. Ideally we would be able to remain in unconditioned love, which resolves darkness directly. However, that requires a level of clarity that a person new to this process does not usually have. Dance of the Self offers a way to help get us to the level of clarity at which unconditioned awareness does the work.

I can't bring myself to do the vocal aspect of Dance of the Self. It's just not me.

The statement "It's just not me" raises the question, "what is you?" This statement provides a perfect example of self-identification, in which we have put a definition on the self and allowed that definition to become the limiting factor. As you define, so you limit. Any more than "I am," and we get into trouble. We all have to work from where we are, which is usually in self-definition, whether we realize it or not. We do not wish to become willful, so we'll just do what we can with Dance of the Self and move forward one step at a time. So, in this case, I advise to omit the vocal release until the sense of self has softened to the point at which the voice can be added.

I tried Dance of the Self a few times, and I am not yet free of my issue. I don't think it's helping.

We must be careful that our motivation is not reactive or stemming from a desire to escape an issue. If the actual motivation is a commitment to self-study and unfoldment, then positivity can bring us to peace; but if the desire is to escape an issue, then darkness is the guiding force. The desire to escape is also an identification that leads us into more disharmony. Take some time to meditate on both your conscious and unconscious motivations. You may find that observing resolves the desire to escape. We didn't get to our current condition overnight. Therefore reaching a greater level of clarity and self-understanding requires us to make regular investment into the process.

Are you suggesting that we should live our lives without knowledge? How would we function in the world?

No, I am suggesting that you do not connect knowledge to a sense of self. Allow knowledge to aid in survival, but keep awareness unconditioned. In this way, we can experience life purely and directly.

Negative Atmospheres

One night I was sleeping over at the home of a friend, Jane, on the living room floor. Earlier in the evening a healing session had occurred, with a dozen or so people present. Gatherings like this commonly took place in the living room. Around six o'clock in the morning, I was startled awake by a presence right next to me. I looked to my left and saw a man sitting with his knees folded beneath him, gazing into my chest.

He had the exact appearance of a trusted friend. I found it strange that he would be there, not only because of the early hour, but also because he did not know Jane. I looked into his eyes, and a current of dread ran through my body. This was not my friend; it was pure evil. I tried to move away from this spirit, but my body was totally frozen. He smiled maliciously at me and began to pull energy from my torso. I was being drained. But worse than being drained was the feeling of helplessness.

During this paralysis I could move my eyes, and I noticed that the woman whose house this was had walked right past me into the kitchen to prepare breakfast. She was a professional psychic, so I tried to call out to her in hopes that she would be able to help me, but no sound passed my lips.

Suddenly I realized that my fear was empowering this spirit. The more fear I felt, the more powerful it became. With that, my fear turned to determination, and I was able to summon enough clarity to break the binds. The spirit's face betrayed his surprise as my body was freed. He immediately disappeared, and I could no longer feel his presence. Free of the paralysis, I got up and told the story to Jane, who was in the kitchen.

This could simply have been a dream, some might assert. Some may interpret this experience as being of an evil spirit, then assume that this spirit came to be there because the work being done in the room was evil, but that would be an incorrect assumption. This experience came from a crucial oversight and lack of awareness. It wasn't until many years later that I understood the dynamics of what happened that evening.

After some months of doing Dance of the Self, I awoke suddenly in the middle of the night, feeling an evil presence in the room. I looked up and saw, just above my face, a dark form staring down at me. I awakened just before the paralysis I had felt before, and the spirit immediately disappeared. I was a bit surprised by this encounter, but the earlier experience had taught me that fear was not a valuable response.

Again, about a month later, the same thing happened. Then several weeks later, then a week, then several times a week, and finally five times in one night, each spirit progressively more powerful than the last. I was utterly exhausted. I knew without a doubt that this was a serious problem that needed to be dealt with right away. No matter how aware we are, if we awaken enough times during the night, eventually we will fail to wake due to exhaustion.

Clearly, I thought, the strategy was to exhaust me and take my energy while I was asleep. I didn't think I had enough disharmony within me to draw darkness in this way, so I was somewhat confused. I thought about the issue all day while at work, searching for a solution. Many teachings say we should put up spiritual protection, but I felt that shielding is a crutch that compensates for our inner corruption, the fuel that actually attracts "negative spirits." We could liken these spirits to flies; if you take out the garbage, you don't have many flies around.

That night when I got home, I went into the bedroom and meditated on the issue. My awareness shifted, and I found myself scanning the room, looking for disharmony. My eyes stopped at the spot where I always did Dance of the Self. I had been sloughing off darkness night after night for months on that spot, and, I realized now, it just sat there like so much garbage. And like garbage, it was attracting flies. That spot had become a beacon of disharmony in the house. I had put the energy there, so I was responsible for it, and that had caused these negative experiences.

I understood that I needed to clean up that energy. Since I could feel the dark energy with my eyes and hands, I started sending it love and transforming it into positive, light energy. Little by little that darkness resolved to positivity. I understood that one of the laws of consciousness is that what comes through our minds, we are responsible for, and until every last bit of it is resolved to Isness, we are not free. I made a habit of going through this healing process after every Dance of the Self session. The negative visitations ceased.

The more we walk the spiritual path, the more identifications will come up within us, causing inner disharmony, unless we have a method to release and resolve this darkness. If we release identifications without resolving that energy to purity, then we will create a negative environment wherever we have been sloughing off that disharmony.

Certain spiritual techniques prompt us to transfer inner darkness to items or onto paper and then burn them. Burning separates us from that disharmony, dispersing it over a large range, but it does not resolve the energy back to purity. Since we have not taken the important step of resolving the energy, we are still responsible for it. Thus, burning increases the amount of time that the energy is separated from us, but it will return because we are, at an unconscious level, identified with it. Taking personal responsibility is the key to resolving disharmony.

Resolution Process

Once your dancing is finished, step out of the room and spend a few minutes to acclimate to being without that disharmony. Because we have carried and identified ourselves with that energy over time, it is effectively camouflaged as us. It's as if it carries our scent, and, therefore, we can't smell it. Other sensitive people may be able to, but we cannot. So, by separating from it for a bit, we increase the odds that we can perceive it as if it were not our own.

After a few minutes, go back into the room as if you were a totally innocent and pure child, and clean up the place where the energy was released. Because the energy is negative, it will be heavy and naturally fall to the floor. It may extend up from the floor several feet or higher depending on how much and how powerful the release was. Direct loving attention to that area and feel that energy becoming light and clear, rising up to "Heaven". Now, in truth, "Heaven" is in no one particular place, but we understand that light things float up and heavy things drop down, so we can use this associated understanding as a way to communicate spiritually that we want this darkness to resolve to unconditioned purity. Keep directing love to that spot until the area has a light, fresh atmosphere.

It won't take very long before you find your own personal way of resolving energy, but the key point is to keep it simple and pure without adding unnecessary steps to the process. Most importantly, do not condemn, fear, or push away the energy. All energy, even that which has been tainted with darkness, ultimately comes from Isness, and it's not our place to condemn it. Our job is only to resolve it and to remain loving and peaceful.

Clean up after Dance of the Self every day, without fail if at all possible. If you skip a day, make sure to do it the next day or the disharmony that sloughed off will start to create a dark atmosphere in that space. Eventually, you may end up with an intensely dark spot that attracts disharmonious experiences. The law is that we are responsible for the energy that we put out. If we do not resolve it, it lingers and will create disharmony. Releasing and resolving darkness to Isness is the way to make consistent progress.

Many people who suffer from sleep paralysis experience an evil presence in the room, similar to what you describe. Maybe it's just a dream...

Yes, that could be the case. Studies have shown that the phenomenon, sometimes called "night terrors," has occurred in all cultures around the world, and some reports of it date back to antiquity. People experience these "dreams" whether or not they believe in evil spirits. While people who do not believe in evil spirits don't report experiencing the phenomenon as often as people who confess to believing in the supernatural, non-believers still suffer from the phenomenon. We have no real way to know whether or to what extent belief plays a role in such experiences, although I suspect that it does. What we can see through the research is that stress and negative states of mind correlate with the phenomenon. Belief in the phenomenon could certainly create a fearful atmosphere, which could increase the chances of having the experience. I would recommend not believing in the phenomenon, while also cleaning up one's inner space.

Yes, but you make it seem like the phenomenon is real. I don't believe it is real.

Have you ever experienced the visitations that I referred to?

Yes. But I think they are just dreams.

Tell me, during the experience, did you think it was just a dream?

No, during the dream it seemed totally real, actually.

Were you fearful?

Yes, it was terrifying.

Was the you in that dream the same as the you now?

Yes, I seemed to be completely myself. I was awake, except that I could not move my body at all. So I think that part of my brain was awake and part of it was asleep, and that may account for the phenomenon.

So during the experience you believed it to be perfectly real, but now that a demon is not staring you in the face, you don't believe it. If the demon were staring in the face right now, could you disbelieve it?

I don't know, as I have not had that experience.

You see, the visceral fear runs deeper than logic, and when you were in the dream, you believed fully that your life was in danger. You are not threatened by that "demon" right now, so you find that conclusion easy to disbelieve.

When you get to a point where you are awake enough in the "dream" to dispel the fear, then you will also be awake enough in your daily life to dispel identifications and expedite the spiritual awakening process. In many ways the sense of self is much like a dream which stimulates visceral emotion.

Clean up the inner and outer atmospheres, reconnect with unconditioned awareness, and you can't help but dispel the dream of self, the source of "demons."

Part 3 — Daily Unfoldment

The process of spiritual unfoldment is first and foremost a process of tuning to Isness, the truest you. Gradually, through this process, impedimentary perspectives that we have held slough away like dead skin, and with each layer released and resolved, a little more light can shine through, allowing further insight into our true natures. In this way, unfoldment is an undoing and unbinding process that reveals the very core, which is Isness.

In this section, I discuss many of the challenges that the unfolding individual will likely resolve in the process. As most of us will be drawn to a teacher at some point, we discuss the student/teacher relationship thoroughly, as well as some of the fundamental, insightful teachings of my teachers. This section also covers the various ways in which Isness may provide hints that serve to awaken us, so that we may best take advantage of them when they occur. Then we look at methods for improving the health of the body, for without a healthy, vibrant body, the conscious unfoldment process becomes far more challenging. We explore our relationship with the body itself, with food, with exercise, and with the elements. Next, we look at various aspects of caring for the mind, for with the mind out of balance, our lives spiral out of control, potentially derailing the active unfoldment process and causing a great deal of disharmony. Finally we address common difficulties with purpose, forgiveness, and prayer, and we shed new light on these vital human processes. This section also includes some basic advice on the unfoldment process, as well as things to consider releasing. This is your process, so you are welcome to hang on to anything for as long as you want. When you are ready to release something, it will begin to happen. Until then, play with what you are willing to release and resolve. In this way we unfold without using much willpower.

Chapter 15 — Teachers

I have been blessed to train with some of the very best teachers in Japan, carriers of ancient traditions into the modern world. Their level of experience is deep, and much of what they pass on largely goes unrecognized and unvalued in the world, as modern people have largely relegated these practices to the bygone days of the samurai.

Although these ancient traditions emerge from martial training — focused on fighting with swords, staves, and knives, as well as the unarmed body — we have much to learn from them. The ability to quiet the body and the mind under the pressure of potential injury or death has much broader applications. The depth and intricacies of these arts require the practitioner to explore deeply the workings of the mind and the body. When we train genuinely to discover the gaps of the mind and the weaknesses of the body and to eliminate those gaps and weaknesses, we may begin to open a path to realization.

I learned countless things from such training, but most of them can be understood only through direct physical contact and experience with the body. To speak or write of them would trivialize the teachings. For that reason I have not dealt much in this book with these training methods, even though they were pivotal to my unfoldment process. That said, some core teachings are absolutely vital to the unfoldment process, and they can be conveyed through the medium of a book.

A certain wisdom comes from cutting away all that is unnecessary to maximize effortless efficiency. I'd like to share some of the wisdom of my teachers, who have spent most of their lives studying the mind and the body and refining their arts to as near perfection as is humanly possible.

The Student/Teacher Relationship

In much of the world these days people have very little respect for teachers, which causes a negative environment in most schools. Teachers receive little pay and are often overlooked or undervalued by society. An unfortunate saying that sums up the attitude goes, "Those who cannot do, teach." As a result of the low status of teachers, the forceful nature of school, the factory model that schools embrace, and the focus on testing, most individuals develop very unhealthy associations with learning and with teachers.

The relationship between a teacher and the student on the path of unfoldment differs distinctly from comparable relationships on other paths. In old-world countries, some traditions of discipleship and apprenticeship remain intact. We can see this demonstrated in certain schools of ancient martial arts and certain monasteries. These schools focus on transmitting certain traditions and skill sets, many of which incorporate spiritual training methods, but as these schools are focused primarily on quantifiable deliverables, they necessarily create a different environment than that of a school specific to spiritual unfoldment. We must bear this difference in mind when we study any tradition.

Very often, individuals on the path of unfoldment will feel moved to study under teachers and mentors of a variety of traditions and skills. The teachers serve not only to pass on information and bring out the very best in their students, but also to inspire students to surpass their level. If such teachers have journeyed far along the path of unfoldment, just being in their presence helps to raise us out of mind and into consciousness.

Regarding formalities, students should address a teacher by title to show respect, unless the teacher specifies otherwise. The student needs to have a deep interest in the teacher, to the point of being captivated, because everything about that teacher offers meaningful information to students. However, the student must not worship the teacher, nor must the student be blind to the teacher's shortcomings. Instead, the student observes and learns, conscientiously seeking to discern what is of value as well as what is not, while showing deep respect.

The student and the teacher decide on a training schedule, and both abide by it, arriving on time and practicing with enthusiasm. Although the student deeply respects the teacher, he or she must never act against conscience, even at the direction of the teacher. If the teacher does not accept this stance, then the student in search of unfoldment may be better off finding a new teacher. A student is polite, listens carefully, and practices what the teacher teaches without trying to demonstrate outside methods or otherwise show off. After training, the student cleans and tidies up the training space.

Students who fail to show respect, who repeatedly arrive late, or who cannot keep to a training schedule might want to consider looking into their own motivations because they are, in all likelihood, wasting everyone's time and energy. The student pays all required fees in a timely manner so as not to unnecessarily burden the teacher. Individuals unable to attend a scheduled class or who know they must be late need to contact their teacher in a timely manner. If the student wishes to take a prolonged break, it is proper to inform the teacher. If the student intends to withdraw, they should let the teacher know this respectfully, either personally or in writing. If one fails to do these simple things, one is unready to study anything of depth.

Senior students intending to become teachers of a path must meet higher standards. They need to be willing to enthusiastically support the teacher in training activities and seminars and with matters of the school or organization. They may be asked to handle some aspects of training lower-level students. This prepares them for becoming independent teachers. In such a case, they must always defer to the main teacher and not demonstrate things they have not been encouraged to teach. They must never seek to bolster their position or ego.

The important thing to remember is that the school often serves to represent an entire lineage of hard-earned wisdom that stretches back many generations, possibly hundreds or thousands of years. Students who join such a school become part of that lineage and therefore should be aware that they represent all of those individuals. Such a student should use the high standards of the lineage as a motivation to improve and find the internal dignity.

Blame

For one fellow student at the dojo, I had much difficulty applying aiki techniques, even after I already had my master's license. I remember that one night after training with this student, I mumbled privately to Sensei that I didn't think this student was attacking honestly. He looked down for a moment thoughtfully and replied, "I think maybe it's something that you are projecting which is causing this person to attack in ways that feel strange to you." After letting that message sink in for a moment, he continued: "I have come to understand that I can't improve if I blame other people. I try to remember that whatever happens could be a reflection of the energy that I am projecting."

I find it fascinating to see what happens to the mind when we are tuned to a high frequency of harmony. During this time, we will wonder why we get upset when our spouse does this or says that. A frequency of consciousness enables us to see how petty we are about many things when we are tuned to mind. Believe it or not, we can attain such a high frequency of consciousness that there can be no abuse. But we may not be tuned to this high frequency all the time, so there can be vulnerability.

We should realize that any frequency of mind lies open to abuse, so even "good" people become susceptible to error if they put themselves in a position for it to occur. Years ago many a wife was blamed when her husband beat her. People would say, "It takes two to argue" or "You must have done something to anger him." But really, she was just tuned to mind, not consciousness, while he was expressing an abuse-identification on her. If a spouse identifies with abusiveness and acts it out, and we are unable to tune to a frequency beyond this level, then we may ask ourselves whether maintaining the relationship is actually beneficial for all involved. If it's not, then separating may be the best option. To remain in a toxic relationship is not really a sane choice, is it? The desire to remain in such a relationship may indicate some strong identifications of our own. To remain in the relationship will pull both individuals into a low frequency of mind. I make no judgment against such a choice, however, because the individual may need that experience to understand the futility of it, just as I did.

Once, a self-described psychic, having met me for the first time, said she had a message for me. I went to her house later, and she gave me the message. She told me that I was dating a girl who was toxic for me and that I would be well advised to leave her. The message was correct, but I loved the girl, and I believed that I could help her, so I did not follow the advice. In the end I was not able to help, and I saw that I had been acting in spiritual arrogance. This psychic gave me good advice, but in reality I needed that experience to understand not only that I could not fix someone, but that the very desire, in my case, stemmed from arrogance. If I had not learned that lesson, then even if I had left her, I would still be attracting the same type of toxic relationship now, which is how life works. Sometimes we need disharmonious experiences until we no longer need them. This pattern of learning is perfectly normal and natural for those tuned to mind.

Meditation can enable us to receive other options. If they feel right, then go with those options. Ultimately we do not want to turn life into an "if, then" routine, right? Tune to unconditioned love and look into the issue, and you may find better answers than anyone, however well-meaning, could ever give you.

Malicious Mind

Once, Sensei stopped during practice and said, "Never try to throw people because it will make your mind sick. It's wrong to try to throw people." It struck me as a strange comment since we are always throwing people in this training. Later that afternoon we had a party, so I took the opportunity to ask Sensei what he meant by his admonition not to throw people. He seemed pleased with my question and filled my sake cup. "In Daito-ryu [the name of the martial art style], we use aiki, which is to say, we use harmony. To try to throw someone is a malicious intent, don't you think? That is not harmony, is it? Instead of trying to throw someone, just move your body here or there in harmony. If the person is attacking you, they will naturally fall down, even though that was not your intention. Just move in harmony."

Since that time, I have found that trying to change people does not serve anyone. If we remain in harmony, we can allow inspiration to do the work. Harmony is inspiring. Of course, that does not mean that we can't make a suggestion here or there when asked, but remove force and expectation from the equation, and, of course, continue to move in harmony.

I have found this to be most challenging with regard to family relationships because of the degree to which they are bound in expectation. For this reason, family relationships provide great learning opportunities. You may think you have the perfect answer to solve someone's "problem," but they reject it outright because, really, they do not want to solve the problem; they just want to complain. Or maybe they do not see the cause of the problem as having anything to do with their own energetic projection; instead, they would like to blame others. In such cases your suggestion will not be accepted, and if you push it, argument or avoidance will follow.

Therefore, whenever making a suggestion, we put it out there lightly, and if it meets with rejection, let it be. At some point, another opportunity may arise to make another suggestion, at which time we may put it out there again, but without expectation. We treat the situation as if casting out our fishing line. We do not expect a fish to bite every time we cast, do we? Of course not. We cast without expectation. In this way we may communicate with people while remaining tuned to consciousness.

Many times people who ask for advice really do not want to receive any advice at all, but instead seek a shoulder to cry on. It's up to you to decide whether you wish to lend your shoulder. Beware, for sympathy only feeds identifications, and pity helps no one. In the event that we give advice, the temptation to make the person see the solution may be strong. Often we are in fact identified with an imagined outcome. We may feel that we are helping them by pushing them to see it. But, in truth, other people are not our responsibility, and we cannot make them do anything. They have their own free will, and it's wise to respect that.

If we push too far and stir up conflict, then it's only proper that we apologize for being pushy. If this happens, instead of digging in further, apologize and forgive immediately once you realize the disharmony that has arisen. If the individual continues down the path of disharmony and their problem gets them into trouble, know that you need not feel bad about being unable to help because feeling bad serves no purpose. We can love and care for people and not feel bad when things do not go well for them. Instead, we remain in a calm state, ready to be of assistance when the opportunity is ripe. At some point, their situation may grow so uncomfortable for them that they will honestly seek help, at which time they may listen.

Authenticity

Although I have been extremely fortunate with my teachers, not every teacher offers a good, healthy demonstration of humanity. I have seen many teachers over the years, and I have come to the realization that the majority act from selfish and egotistical motives.

It seems to me that many teachers who pretend to be wise sages and all-knowing masters actually fear to reveal their humanity. One such teacher even told his own mother, who was not a student of his, that she must call him Grand Master. She called him lots of things, but Grand Master was not one of them. Some teachers seem to have collapsed into caricature. I have seen many times that this condition leads to abuse of all sorts that students then pay forward to those lower on the totem pole, both in and out of the dojo.

In the West, many "Masters" buy and exchange ranks, certificates, and titles. I have received several letters from "Masters" requesting that I grant them rank in the arts I teach in exchange for rank in their arts. They expressed no interest in training; they just wanted the rank so they could add to their collection and bragging rights. This displays a lack of integrity and authenticity.

I suppose such teachers are trying to live up to the Hollywood image of a "Master," and so they try to bolster their position and stoke their image. Liberated individuals do not identify themselves as being masters, and people walking the path of unfoldment with integrity know they still have much more to learn than they have yet to touch upon, so how can people call themselves master and maintain integrity?

Be authentic; admit mistakes and imperfections when they show up. Apologize authentically when an apology is in order. This is part of being human, and this inspires. At the same time observe teachers carefully, and note any lack of integrity so as not to be led astray. Live with integrity, heart as light as a feather, attracting other human beings seeking that same lightness.

Complacency

When I joined my first dojo in Japan, not knowing anything, I asked Sensei, "How close to perfection are you in your technique?" He replied, "I never believe in 100 percent because if I believe in 100 percent then I have nothing more to understand, no more depth to explore. In reality, there is always more to uncover and to understand. So I always try for an ever-expanding 97 percent, leaving room to believe that 3 percent remains that I have yet to discover. Then I am eager to find that last 3 percent. And no matter how much my understanding grows, I have always another 3 percent left to discover, because as my understanding grows, so does the remaining 3 percent."

The realization that we have always more to understand is very helpful in the unfoldment process. I am constantly asking questions in silence, seeking insight about the nature of the mind and suffering. I write the questions and the answers and then look back on that information repeatedly to ask deeper questions still. No matter how much I realize, I find there is still more to learn, more to refine.

Remain Behind

Once, while I had dinner with my teacher after training, he spoke of the tendency for some students to believe that they should be given a higher rank than they actually deserve because they are high ranked in other arts or traditions. He said, "They have a strong desire to demand recognition for their accomplishments even though they do not understand the art I am teaching. I think the better way is the exact opposite of this tendency. Your job is to become so effective that others push you up because they feel awkward when compared to you because you are of equal rank with them even though your ability is obviously beyond theirs. In this way, you may be pushed up without ever desiring it, and therefore there is no ego involved. Your job is not to push your way up, but instead it's to perfect, to refine and purify. If you are not pushed up, that is okay too, because you have no ego about it."

This teacher's words are very wise, but even if we embrace this philosophy we might still have an unconscious identification that creates the desire, unbeknownst to others and even to ourselves, to be at the top. It takes constant observation of the mind to notice this type of identification.

I remember once, about six months after I was given the instructor's license, one of the other students in the dojo took his test for the same license, and I was there as an observer. I felt a strong desire for him to fail the test. I did not want him to pass the test and be equal with me. Suddenly I realized how absurd the feeling was, rooted entirely in mind and carrying no harmony whatsoever. I resolved that identification and found myself cheering for this individual, who, fortunately, did pass the test. I would have felt awful had he failed it, knowing that I hadn't completely supported him.

Many teachers of ancient arts intentionally withhold knowledge from students in order to keep them down. This desire springs entirely from the mind and causes both short-term and long-term disharmony. The immediate effect is that students believe the teacher is naturally superior, that they can never match his or her level. The long-term effect is that key knowledge does not get passed down, and the arts become useless shells of their former glory. Teachers who are tuned to consciousness see the uselessness of such a selfish desire. Rather, they hope to train students who one day will surpass the teacher's abilities. In this way, the arts become stronger and stronger through the generations. So much ancient knowledge has been lost because of the ego-driven desire of the mind. Only students of ancient arts who have rediscovered some of this lost knowledge will have any idea of how destructive "secrets" have been.

On an emotional level, we may have a tendency to compare our lives to those of people who have it worse than us to feel better about our own lives. This strategy is entirely of the mind and indicates a very low-frequency identification indeed. We can also see that at the lowest frequencies of mind, identifications feel threatened when others succeed, and thus the desire is to tear down those successful individuals in any way possible. All of these feelings come from a conditioned mind. They do not even exist when the self fully resolves. Comparisons can never bring any form of clarity or joy, but consciousness can.

Butter over Bread

A sword instructor in Japan used to say that our techniques should happen as smoothly as spreading warm butter over bread. He wanted us to remove any clunky, abrupt, or disharmonious movements so that the techniques could lose their edges, flow with no telegraphing. In this way, our movements become effectively invisible to the attacker. Although attackers can see the body moving, their minds cannot feel changes until it's too late.

With regard to unfoldment, we can take this same approach and apply it to the whole of life while removing any sense of an opponent. In this manner, unfoldment will occur quite naturally at a much faster pace. We can use the "spreading butter over bread" feeling when observing the flow of our breath or our pulse to easily notice when disharmony begins to arise within us, even before we have any recognizable emotion or thought. In this way, we can resolve disharmony before it overwhelms us.

A person on the path of unfoldment seeks to become as aware as possible of the workings of their own body and mind in the moment. Since all thinking and feeling have their mirrors in the body through the breath, pulse, and tension, we should develop such sensitivity and awareness that we know whenever tension grows in the body. Can you feel the pulse in all parts of the body by mere intention? Can you feel the pulse in your fingers and toes without touching them? Can you feel the pulse in your eyes?

Diligence

I once asked my teacher what it takes to master aiki. He paused for a moment and then responded, "Practice every day but do not train yourself inflexibly. Instead train to be flexible and open because, quite naturally, your expression of each technique will change gradually and simplify as you perceive deeper through training. If you just come to class, this is insufficient. Each student who has completed my training has come to class regularly and practiced on their own diligently."

To practice flexibly means to practice without identifying ourselves strongly with the expression of our techniques, which is to say, we do not have the feeling of, "This is how I do it." If we notice this feeling taking root, we might consider softening it to be more like, "This is how I do it at this stage of my understanding. But the future may hold many other practices of which I am not yet aware." Eventually, the "I" will slip out of the story and the technique. Movements will just happen spontaneously, and therefore the expression may vary each and every time.

With regard to practice, I personally did it so much that I trained in my dreams. I practiced on the train, while walking, and when at home. I practiced so much that my wife became annoyed. Eventually I learned to hide my training so that it could happen all the time without anyone noticing. Of course, this level of training occurs only after a great deal of dedication.

Spiritual unfoldment's process does not really reduce to training or ingraining, but we do need to set a regular schedule for consistent meditation, which resolves darkness within to reveal the fundamental truth at the core of our very being. However, in one area ingraining is helpful: when we develop a habit of taking regular intervals for introspection. Without having curiosity as to what we are feeling and tuning to, we cannot correct the tuning. Add in a regular self-check, so that you will not go too long without one. Then, little by little, decrease the intervals between checks until eventually your level of awareness around these matters remains constant. Be aware that at some point along the path even "good" habits need to be released, because a habit is a rut. We are moving toward consistent awareness, which transcends habits.

The Philosophy of One

One day at the dojo a new student who was practicing with Sensei, after repeated failures of a basic technique, mumbled in frustration, "It's impossible; I can't." Sensei seemed to understand this person's feelings exactly, for surely he had also been in the same position in his early training. Kindly, he replied to the student, "Never believe that you can't do something. If you say that you can't, then you are right, you can't. But if you say that you can, then even if you can't do it right now, some day, you will be able to do it. You just need to keep at it."

A story about a young samurai who was caught in a great storm at sea tells how, centuries ago, a young country man went out, off the coast, with his boat for a day of fishing. As he was of low rank, his stipend was insufficient for him to make ends meet for his family. Therefore he supplemented his income of rice with fishing whenever he had the opportunity. He went out into the deep waters, hoping to bring in some large fish for his family.

He left well before sunrise, and after a few hours he was quite far out to sea. He found the spot where he felt he was going to make his catch and lowered his line. The day was warm and comfortable, and before he knew it he dozed off.

He awoke to the crack of thunder and large drops of cold rain bashing his skin. During his sleep, storm clouds silently filled the sky so that he could barely see the shore. He knew that the sea became extremely violent during storms like this, and that being out on the water in such conditions probably meant death. He needed to get to shore before the storm really picked up.

He began rowing as quickly as he could for the dim shore, but the moment he put his oar in the water, the sea began to undulate violently, the waves growing feet at a time. He had waited too late. He would have to hope for a miracle.

He plowed through wave after wave for an hour, but it seemed he traveled no closer to the shore. He began tiring, and the thought that he would not make it took root in his mind. He started counting the waves, and as the number rose he lost more of his confidence — the shore still miles away.

Rowing over each wave felt like a monumental task, and the desire to give up grew in his mind. He began to think that the task was impossible, that he would never reach the shore. He found himself wanting to give in to death, to let the sea swallow him up.

At this point he realized that he was allowing the negativity of his mind to overwhelm him, and that counting the waves and trying to guess the distance to the shore was too discouraging. He decided to forget that distant goal and to instead keep things simple. He would tackle each wave one at a time and stop counting them. All he would do was focus on the wave there and then.

Wave after wave came, and with each one he would say to himself, "One." In short order, his mind rested, and his energy was dedicated to the task of navigating the one wave in front of him, no longer projecting to the future and the monumental task ahead. Again and again: "One." "One." "One ...."

That samurai survived because of the Philosophy of One. And with the wisdom of that experience, he eventually became an inspiring leader, teaching others to live powerfully in the present.

During my training in Japan, I noticed that within three to six months most students gave up. The art is so difficult that we are certain to fail repeatedly hundreds or thousands of times before having a real taste of success. I spent three years working on just one technique before I could do it well enough to pass my test to begin the next higher curriculum. Can you imagine going five nights a week, for two hours each night, doing the same technique over and over and over, only to fail repeatedly for three straight years? Imagine how many times the voice of the quitter tried to convince me to give up. Whenever I heard that voice, I dismissed it and just kept pressing forward after calming myself. How many people can do that? Actually, everyone can do it, but few do, because they empower the quitter identification rather than embracing the Philosophy of One.

Remaining present in this way applies to all avenues of life. My martial arts students often laugh when, after a technique, I say to them, "Just one more." After doing it once more, I repeat, "Just one more." Of course, there is never an end to "Just one more." Through presence, we can accomplish the impossible. Just one more.

In the process of spiritual unfoldment, we will pass through many times in which we may perceive no progress or feel that the road ahead is too difficult to travel. At times we may feel down and out, that we can't go on. Remember, there is no shame in crying, but when the tears are over, get back up and start moving again. Just get back up.

Many times while training in Japan I just didn't feel very motivated to go to the dojo, especially after a hard, stressful day of work. The dojo was about an hour from school by train, and getting on the train to go to the dojo, knowing that I still had another hour on the train to get home, could be discouraging. But instead of projecting my mind to the entirety of the trip, I would just focus on getting myself out the door with my gear. If I got that far, I knew I would not turn back. Almost without exception, nights like that afforded the most profound breakthroughs.

Most people go awry when they give in to the feeling of not wanting to go, and they entertain the thought, "I'll take tonight off and go tomorrow instead." Those feelings and that thinking don't come from consciousness, do they? Get up, grab your gear, and get out the door. If you can make it that far, the momentum will carry you the rest of the way.

This applies to meditation as well. We just make the space for the meditation in our life and follow through every time unless Isness indicates otherwise. If, during the meditation, the mind drifts, don't give up. Simply stay there for the allotted time, regardless. We may not realize it, but even though it may seem that the time is wasted, it isn't. Half of the process is making the space and time for the meditation and doing it. Do not expect that each meditation will be comfortable or easy. This teaches us to have follow-through even in times of great difficulty.

Chapter 16 — Inspiration

The multiverse is founded on self-definition and ignorance, but there is an unseen power throughout all, Isness. Remember, in every breath we take, Isness is there. In every cell of our bodies, there is Isness. In each person we see, in each surface we touch, Isness is present. In the empty spaces, it is there. The key to effective conscious unfoldment is tuning to consciousness in every possible moment of our lives. As we tune ourselves to consciousness, we will find inspiration in the "ordinary" because the common and mundane becomes extraordinary when perceived through the light of Isness. Here are some key points about recognizing Isness in our daily lives.

Be Mindful of Hints

Every incarnate human being experiences at least one moment in its existence when Isness gives it a hint as to the possibility. This may seem a bold statement, but it's true. The question is whether you remember any of these hints. I have spoken of a number of personal visions and communications with Isness, but now I will mention a more common hint of its presence that I think many people may overlook: being in the zone.

We hear professional athletes talk about this phenomenon quite often, but the zone is not limited to professionals or athletes. In "in the zone" moments, grace flows through us. Our minds become totally silent, and our bodies just do the right thing at exactly the right moment. It's an absolutely wonderful feeling when it occurs.

My first "in the zone" experience happened when I was in the sixth grade. I was not a good athlete as a child (aside from running), primarily because my body grew too quickly and was ungainly but also because I had no confidence in myself. Being constantly self critical is a crippling disorder, which I had in spades. Consequently, I was usually one of the last kids picked for any sporting team, so I tended to avoid playing sports to spare myself the embarrassment.

One day during lunch break, I walked along the outdoor basketball court watching a game between some of the best players in my grade. They found themselves one man short of even teams, and since I was the only one watching at the time, they asked me to join. I declined at first, but Rick, the best athlete, an honor-roll student and a really nice person, kindly came over and asked me if I wouldn't reconsider. I had a strange sense that I should join them, so I agreed.

I tried to play defense as much as possible, as I didn't want to be a ball handler. I had never been any good at making shots in a game under pressure. Unexpectedly, however, the ball ended up in my hands and from that very spot, without any thought, my body launched the ball at the hoop — perfect swish. It happened from quite a distance, and everyone was surprised but dismissed it as luck. The game went on, and someone passed the ball to me again.

Jump-shot, swish.

Once is luck, but twice in a row means something, so no sooner than my team got the ball, it was in my hands and swish. Over and over and over again, the ball just could not miss. Needless to say, our team won by a wide margin. Everyone huddled around me when the game was over. They were amazed at how good I was. Rick said, "Man, you are better than Magic Johnson." Boy, that felt great. The bell rang, and we had to head back to class. I thought all the rest of that day and night about that game and began to believe I was a basketball phenom. I guessed that I had found a hidden talent, and I was eager to go out and play again.

We got together at lunch the next day and divvied up teams. I was the top pick for Rick's team. The game started, and the ball went straight to me. I thought I should do the same thing I did the day before, throwing it from wherever I got it, so I tossed the ball at the hoop, and it flew over the backboard. A little later, I got the ball again and – another wide miss. I tried and tried, only to miss every time. It was humiliating. We lost that game, and they did not invite me to play again. I felt really embarrassed and didn't know what to make of the magic I had just a day before.

Years later I understood what happened that day. I had been in "the zone"; there was no thought, just Rightness. My body was abuzz with this feeling, and my mind was silent. It was a hint from Isness. Later, of course, my ego kicked in, and I falsely identified myself with the feeling, trying to own it.

During the game the following day, all I had going for me was the noise of ego and thought, so we lost the game.

Surely many people have had similar experiences in one activity or another and probably suffered similar results when they tried again on another occasion. It can be frustrating especially if we egotistically try to grab onto the feeling and own it. We must stay present and unconcerned with outcomes such as success and failure. Just flow in the present with clarity of spirit, allowing the body to be moved.

Isness gives us hints in other ways, too. We might suddenly feel that we should go somewhere specific, without reason, and then something miraculous happens. We may have an inspiring realization, an answer to something that has puzzled us for a long time. You may have an extremely vivid dream such as flying, for example, which is of Isness. These things hint as to the freedom that comes from unbinding Soul.

Look back over your life, even into early childhood, and feel through your memories. You are likely to find moments of total wonder and inspiration that catch your attention; chances are, that feeling was one of your hints. If you do not remember anything right away, just keep it in the back of your mind and recheck your memories from time to time. I have found from many conversations with a great number of individuals that often they have forgotten these moments because they could not make sense out of them. But after looking back over their lives, again and again, eventually they remember.

Allow Isness to Express

While I was living in Japan, I worked in a private middle school, which is quite an eye-opening experience for a foreigner. You see, in Japanese culture drinking socially and having parties is part and parcel of having friends. Business people, schoolteachers, club members — almost any adults, really — will find any excuse to get together and drink. In sober moments, tight social order and etiquette keep everyone restricted. But while drinking, such bindings, for the most part, go out the window. So people drink to release stress and get to know each other on a more intimate level, without the shackles of the usual social rules.

These parties tend to be a lot of fun and can get pretty wild as party number one (at a hotel conference room or traditional restaurant) turns into party number two (at a Japanese pub), and, finally, the 2 a.m. taxicab-ride-home party number three (at a hostess club). My school had a long tradition of great parties, and teachers considered the year-end party as the best of them, as all the accumulated steam of the year could be released with the froth of beer and the exhaust of sake. Mr. Shino, our school's vice principal for as long as anyone could remember, was an expert at getting these parties rolling by taking the stage and shaking his hips to a Rod Stewart karaoke tune.

But that year we had a new principal and a new vice principal to go with him. Although the new vice principal had the right heart and was more than up to the task, the principal, by his nature, made everyone tense. He all but forbade anyone from having a good time by his very presence. During the tenure of this principal, people attended official school parties out of obligation, and the only dancers were the ticking hands of the clock.

I showed up at the party a little late and took a seat at a table of teachers I did not know well. Our campus combined middle school and high school, and all teachers came to the same year-end party. Somewhere near a hundred teachers were distributed in groupings of six in a large hotel conference room. I took my seat and felt the atmosphere: tepid.

Suddenly I felt a strong inspiration to go outside for a minute. As I left the conference room, I felt inspired to allow Isness to take over and see what would happen. I set Richard aside and felt a lightness envelop my energy field and body. I went back in and sat down with my group.

Within a minute or two of my arrival the party started heating up. We were going to play a trivia game wherein the table that could answer the most questions won. The prize was that someone from the winning table would have to take the stage and sing karaoke. Logic told me that we would not win because I could not speak very good Japanese, and I was never any good at trivia, either — I was dead weight. Isness, on the other hand, made it clear that our table would win and that I would be performing on stage. I surrendered to this idea should things pan out that way.

The game began, and our table quickly took the lead and held it strongly. While the other teachers at my table answered questions unfailingly, I considered which song should be sung. As our table's resident trivia genius answered the final question, all the teachers at my table, as if they had planned it, looked at me and asked if I would like to sing. Of course, all of them were able to answer at least one question and I had yet to put anything into the process, so I suppose it was only fair. Anyway, seeing as this experience was Isness inspired, I agreed and took the stage. With mic in hand, I requested, the Beatles — "Twist and Shout."

Normally I would have been extremely self-conscious, but not this time. My body was twisting and shouting just as wildly as the song was meant to be performed. The house was on its feet as the inspiration spread around the room, and the ice melted. People danced and sang along with me, and even the principal allowed himself to be caught up in the fun. It was an out-and-out miracle as far as I could see.

The song came to an end, but the party was just beginning. The music teacher got on stage following me and dizzied up a great song. The teachers sang and danced, drank and socialized, and forgot their worries. Truly we had an amazing night to launch us into several weeks of winter vacation.

Unfortunately I didn't find out about it until several weeks later, when some of my friends at school asked me where I had gone after my song. Just as the song ended, Richard was back, and he was embarrassed. He left the stage in a state of panic, failing to notice all the teachers gesturing for high-fives as he walked back to his table. He sat down awkwardly and within a few minutes got up and left the party.

An individual who is still too tightly bound up in the self is unable to touch in with Isness easily. If they do successfully set aside the self and allow Isness to express, they may find themselves utterly stunned at the result. The more we start to release the limiting content of the self and tune to consciousness, the more we are able to enjoy the fruits of the process. In my case, on that night, everyone got to enjoy the fruit except me. Such a shame, isn't it?

When we begin deeply tuning to the frequencies of consciousness, the self-conscious, analytical, overbearing mind rests, and life becomes inspiring and infectious. We begin to know things that "can't be known" and do things that "can't be done," and best of all, we are not egotistically connected to this knowing or doing. We, like everyone else, just have a ticket to the greatest show on Earth — Isness in expression.

When you can, set aside the self and allow inspiration to take over. Don't worry, the self will be there waiting for you if you want to suit back up again. Allow the blessings to flow. And when you come back to the self, take a deep breath, relax, and allow yourself to enjoy that, too.

Appreciate Beauty

During my vision quest, thanks to nearly three days of limited visibility caused by constant drizzle, I made a resolution to myself to notice the simple beauty of daily life and to appreciate everything more fully. I noticed when I went back to Tokyo, a city with some of the most incredible sunsets you will see, that people, without exception, walked at a breakneck pace, eyes glued to the concrete, stress written all over their faces. In the midst of heavenly glory, they hurried by without so much as a glance to the horizon. In their rush to live their lives, they were missing life.

On the path of unfoldment, it's vital to slow down the pace and relax into an appreciation for all that is. Be careful about turning beauty into a mental picture, as that pulls us back into mind. What do I mean by a mental picture? When you look at a sunset, for example, turn off the mental words that describe it. Open up all of your senses, and place the horizon in the center of your vision without limiting your awareness to it. Take it all in purely and relax into it. Absorb it deeply and share the feeling of deep appreciation for the totality. In this way, you remain conscious throughout the process instead of going into mind. Looking at a sunset then becomes inspirience instead of experience.

Taking it a step further, loosen your definitions of beauty and start to observe the whole with unconditioned enthusiasm, taking in the details that others might dismiss as commonplace and not worth noticing. In this manner, more and more, we can find beauty and inspirience through the senses almost anywhere. Even in the busiest most crowded places in Tokyo, I found it easy to have sensory inspirience simply by changing my attitude toward my surroundings.

The truth about beauty is that such awareness comes from consciousness, not the mind. When we look at beauty through the mind, the critical function begins to dissect it, to analyze it, and — worse still — to acclimate to it. You could have the most beautiful woman in the world at your side, but sooner or later you will just regard her as normal if you view her only through the mind. The mind will find a way to sap the magic out of everything if you feed it.

Relationship with Nature

Jon Young, naturalist and survival instructor, asserts that nature is a nutrient. Truly, the body draws sustenance just from being in nature and absorbing the atmosphere or presence. Nature tends to be tuned to calm awareness, and by being in nature, so long as we are open to it, we quite naturally begin to tune to calm awareness as well. For this reason, having regular access to a natural environment is exceedingly helpful in the process of unfoldment.

I highly recommend that individuals take survival and nature awareness classes from instructors who have learned to live in harmony with Earth. Many schools out there support the mindset of humanity versus nature. These schools are not teaching in support of the unfoldment process; they base their methods and intentions upon opposition. Instead, seek out instructors who teach the approach of blending and attuning with nature. These methods will help to get us out of opposition, fear, and dominance and into the Garden of Eden.

When I took my first survival class, something amazing occurred after about the fourth day there. I noticed that my dreams changed quite dramatically. Whereas my dreams had normally taken place in the backdrops of buildings with squares, angles, and edges dominating, they changed to being set in nature with flowing, smooth transitions and circular shapes. More than the visuals changing, the feeling in my body also changed, and I felt as if my sleep became more productive. It took a few days to reach this state. Until I settled into the environment, I slept poorly because I was not used to camping in tents. As with anything, such attunement requires a transition phase.

Remember, nature is everywhere, not just the great forests, grasslands, and deserts of the world. Nature exists in the city and in your backyard. Most importantly, the closest physical thing to us, the body, is nature. Learn to be quietly aware of your body, feeling into its processes. Allow it to calm and teach you. "Or do you not know that your body is the temple of the Holy

Spirit who is in you" is a very wise saying of Paul in the New Testament. Learn from your temple, and treat the temple with great respect. The body is not you, nor is it your prison, but your place of realization. Love and respect it as such, and the body will teach you more than you could ever imagine. Even more than that, love and respect nature as such, and all of life will open to you.

Chapter 17 — Caring for the Physical Body

The Amazon vision indicated that the three pillars of humanity will soon collapse, and great chaos will arise on Earth. I no longer hold any belief or opinion on if or when this might happen, as neither belief nor opinion will assist in defusing such a possibility; both are of the mind and not consciousness. Instead, I tune to unconditioned love and allow that to express into the world. In this chapter I discuss ways to care for the body. What I have written here will both assist in unfoldment and help us to survive during times of hardship.

Humans have a lot of disagreements over how to take care of the physical body, and this confusion has led to stumbling blocks in the unfoldment process for many. If we can address these issues early in the unfoldment process, we can save ourselves a lot of grief and let ourselves serve whenever the need arises, as the body will be as ready as possible.

What is the physical body? A lot of people think that their body is themselves, but if we take a look at what makes up the body, we find it is more like an ecosystem filled with a great variety of living entities, all of which are made up of earth. If we count all the bacteria in our body, we contain more bacteria than human cells. The bacteria alone in a healthy body number about 100 trillion, the vast majority of which provide beneficial services. When we add to that total the estimated cells with human DNA, another 50 trillion to 100 trillion cells, we have somewhere between 150 trillion and 200 trillion cells in the body. If our body is made up of more foreign cells than cells with human DNA, then it is quite difficult to call it us, isn't it? Each of these bacteria has requirements to survive, a purpose, and a mind of its own, just as does each human cell. What we call the body is just the sum total of all the varying cells that make it up, which changes constantly, much like the great jungles of the earth. So, just as the mind is made up of countless identifications, the body is also made up of countless individual identities.

The body functions like an energy transference system, just as the rest of nature does. Consider that the body is constructed from all of the elements that we feed it. Are the elements we consume sufficient to meet all the needs of a healthy ecosystem? If our food comes from a farm, does the soil have all of the necessary elements to constitute healthy produce that our body can then digest? If our soils are highly depleted of minerals due to overuse, then those vegetables do not get the elements that they need in sufficient quantities, and, therefore, neither do the cells in our bodies. In turn, if the cells in our bodies lack what they need, then they cannot provide all of the services that they are purposed for, and the health of the body wanes. Thus, if we wish to have a healthy body, then we need to have healthy soils, too. We cannot properly take care of our bodies yet not take care of the earth's ecosystems, which provide the elements and services that our bodies need to be healthy. To be healthy we must realize that just as consciousness is connected to everything, so is the body.

Considering that the body is an ecosystem made up of a huge variety of different organisms, all with their own needs, we need to be aware that the body also has a mind of its own, designed to represent the needs of the organisms that make it up. Although the physical body is not us, it does obey us, mostly. Sometimes it rebels or breaks down. Let's say that you are the general of the body, which is an army. A good general listens to subordinate officers and makes decisions according to the information that he receives from them. He also observes the overall condition of the service personnel when making plans. If we act as wise generals, respecting and leading the body properly, it will accomplish a great deal for us and teach us more than we can imagine.

Exercise

The human body at its current stage of development functions as a hunter-gatherer collective, and it needs to be moving around every day as if it were hunting and gathering. Walking is one of the very best activities for the body. All other bodily systems are toned by walking, and if we are not getting enough exercise, no matter how healthfully we eat, the body is not going to digest and use that fuel nearly as well as it can when well exercised. If the body were exercised well but had a generally poor diet, that is preferable to a body receiving a perfect diet but just lounging around all the time. I say this because exercise tones the digestive system, allowing it to absorb nutrients and separate out toxins much more efficiently than it would otherwise. The body needs to be walking about five miles each day. But instead of walking we usually drive or go nowhere at all. I see people get in the car to visit a neighbor!

Many possible exercises benefit the body, but yoga, tai chi, and other internal martial arts systems, dancing, hiking, and swimming are probably among our best choices. Some of these exercises do very little for the cardiovascular system, however, because the movements happen slowly, so you may want to consider adding fast walking or other cardio-building routines. If at all possible, try to find an exercise that you enjoy doing, because that will keep you motivated. Fitness routines driven by a sense of obligation or duty are less likely to become a regular structure in your life.

I practice swordsmanship, as well as my own energy-balancing methodology called shinkai-ho. These work very well for keeping my body lean and functional. I also chop lots of wood for heating the house and take regular walks in the forest with my dogs and goat to gather wild edibles and medicinals. I enjoy all of these activities tremendously, and therefore no negativity taints the exercise.

If you practice the meditation as I have outlined in Part 2 of the book, as well as Dance of the Self, you may be surprised to find at some point that you can engage in almost any activity and enjoy it thoroughly. When your enjoyment is unconditioned, the specific activity is not a factor in your enjoyment. In many cases as we unfold, inspiration may guide us to very specific activities, which is a real blessing. In any case, if we notice negativity or lack of joy, then that is a perfect signal that we are tuned to mind rather than consciousness.

The basic idea here is to keep the body flowing with some sort of healthy movement. We want a strong, stable, yet flexible body that holds up well in extremes of heat and cold as well as dry or moist weather. We need a toned and balanced immune system, so our bodies may serve whenever Isness indicates. If our bodies are out of balance, we may be unable to serve when the need appears. Because much of unfoldment happens through service, having a disharmonious body can prove quite limiting.

If the body has become frail through accident or disease, then we do all we can to keep it as strong and flexible as possible while working on positive attitudes and without identifying ourselves with frailty. Individuals who have been disabled by accident or disease often find themselves able to serve in ways that those with healthier bodies cannot, so there can be a natural balance if the attitudes are clear.

Trust the Body

Allow your body to choose your food. We have a free-range goat named Hana at our training facility. I find it so interesting to watch what she eats day to day as she wanders around. Her diet changes constantly, with the exception of oak leaves, which she eats year-round. One day she won't touch a certain flower, and the next she craves it. She is extremely healthy because of her natural diet.

I have often heard it said that goats eat anything, but this is not exactly true. A goat that has been removed from its natural diet options will eat almost anything because it's deprived. A goat that regularly has choices is actually very choosy about what it eats. Just as a goat that is deprived eats foods in which it might not otherwise have an interest, so our bodies also go out of balance and then desire strange things.

The physical body has its own needs, and if it's in balance, it will make better nutritional choices than we could make for it. Try this game: get into a good meditation and then turn the reins over to your body. Allow your body to do the food choosing when in the kitchen. Completely forget what you like and just let your eyes go where they want to go, then pick up any food items that the body chooses, but don't consume it yet.

Before you eat any of it, look at each item. Let's say that your body picks up a bag of mixed berry oatmeal. Instead of just eating the oatmeal, ask the body what in the oatmeal it really wants. The body will pick out what it's actually interested in. You might find that your body wanted only the cranberries but nothing else in the oatmeal. Then let it eat some cranberries. With each item, question the body to see what it really seeks, making no assumptions. You will likely find that your body picks out meals that you would never have chosen had you selected your food in your normal manner. Your body knows which nutrients it needs, and it will choose accordingly. However, if you have food addictions, they can throw off the process. Liberation means having no addictions of any kind.

I recommend doing this activity regularly to allow the body access to nutrients and energies that it needs, but do not get compulsive about it. Many times someone else may be preparing food for us, and we should not expect that they will know or abide by your body's desire because that is quite a burden. Eat then what is offered with joy, but as a snack fill in the nutritional gaps by allowing the body to choose.

Structuring Food

On the path of unfoldment we want our food relationship as healthy as possible. All life-forms are like rivers of flowing atoms. We have the tributaries of inhalation and absorption through the skin, but the main atomic river is digestion. Atoms flow out through exhalation, and through the skin by way of sweat, but the primary outlets are from the bowels and the bladder. Consider that atoms we consume today may have cycled through countless other bodies, stretching back over millions of years. What we eat today in the form of a sandwich may have been in a dinosaur millions of years ago! Atoms in your food may have passed through the bodies of Jesus or Gautama or any number of other inspirational individuals who have walked the earth. Just as we might aim to leave a place better than when we entered it, we are well served to consider that atoms leaving our bodies should be in a better energetic state than when they entered.

To eat in a spiritually healthy manner we must address the frequencies to which we are tuned while eating, which has a lot to do with the degree of our presence. Have you noticed how once you start on that bag of chips you find it hard to stop? This is an example of eating unconsciously, a condition in which we are not consciously present and aware of the eating process. Of course, many modern processed foods have been formulated specifically to get us to eat unconsciously by making the food addictive, but ultimately each of us bears responsibility for what we put in our mouths. When we eat unconsciously, we reinforce a very unhealthy pattern. To turn this pattern around, I offer some helpful guidelines to curb the tendency to eat unconsciously.

Consider making a personal rule of not eating or drinking while walking or standing. This cultural rule is the norm in Japan, one I did not appreciate at first, but the longer I lived there, the more I began to realize its value. When we are walking and eating, we are generally in a rush, which of course means not tuned to appreciation. Or perhaps we simply do not realize that spending time with food is important, which may mean that unconsciously we believe that eating is a waste of time. If you notice people who are walking and eating, almost without exception you will find that they are consuming sugary drinks and/or junk food. If you have a tendency to walk and eat, consider taking a look at the structure of your life to see whether you have allowed sufficient time to sit down and eat a healthy meal consciously.

Make access to food difficult. I have noticed that a lot of people sit at their desk and work, having desk drawers filled with snacks. Those snacks invariably end up unconsciously popped into the mouth as we work, don't they? Instead of keeping snacks in the desk drawers, consider putting them in a place a little difficult to get to, such as in a kitchen cabinet, that will require you to get up from the chair. This choice can help make us conscious of the process of eating those snacks. When getting up for a snack, take only a small amount, so you have to get up again to get more. This small change will stop a lot of unconscious eating at work.

A common scenario at home is to sit down and turn on the TV with a bag of chips at the ready, which we munch on unconsciously. Consider pouring the chips into a small bowl to take with you, leaving the bag in the kitchen. In this way, we can eat those chips, but if we want more, we have to get up to return to them. Again, we are likely to eat less in this way, and to give more consideration to what we do eat.

Although the advice given on not walking and eating applies very well to a civilized lifestyle, it does not apply well to hunter-gatherers, who often gather and eat as they walk. Of course, people in such cultures tend to be much more aware of their surroundings and are not tuned to haste or caught in distraction of watching a TV, so walking and eating works well for them. Our goat also walks and eats, but again, she digests extremely well because she attends well to the eating process, even while she walks. In the event of widespread collapse, we may find that we will do the same thing. Grazing is totally appropriate in a hunter-gatherer context.

When I was a young man, an acupuncturist told me that my nervous system was overly amped up. He told me that I need to slow down my movement and to eat more slowly, to chew my food much more. He went so far as to say that I should chew each bite 100 times. That seemed pretty excessive to me, but I tried it anyway. If you've never tried this yourself, I highly recommend it. You will quickly see how habitual the chewing process is and how quickly you forget your count and start to swallow at 20 or 30. The urge is powerful – nearly as much as when we have to urinate badly and approach the toilet to find that suddenly, the urge amplifies dramatically. You have trained your body to swallow at a certain point, and it will continue to do so on autopilot unless you become consciously aware of the chewing process.

I noticed after retraining my body to chew more that not only did my digestion improve, but my body relaxed much more, and my mind stopped racing so much. I used to hate massages before this change because they hurt so much, but after slowing down the eating process, massages became pleasurable because my nerves were not so hyped up. Play with your chewing count, and see what happens.

When you observe yourself becoming overly picky about tastes, consider fasting until the food attitudes change. Consider eating only when unconditionally appreciative of food and when a need emerges. Avoid idle eating and eating while having a negative feeling; first resolve the negativity before eating. Avoid ordering food unless you plan to eat all of it then or later.

As you can see, a lot of eating occurs unconsciously, and when we drink or eat while walking, standing, working, or watching TV, and so on, almost without exception that consumption is unconscious. Consider how many fewer calories we would take in if we stopped eating unconsciously. More importantly, consider how much more we will enjoy the process of eating if we make the space for each meal consciously.

Food Bias

Wealthy countries engender a lot of negative food attitudes. The stress that we create in our bodies and the disharmonious energy that we put into food because of these attitudes often prove worse for our bodies than the denatured food itself. If you find that you must eat something less than ideal, then eat it with love. If you can choose a healthy alternative, then by all means do so, but whatever you do, do it with appreciation and love because some life form ultimately constituted the matter for the food and that food will become part of your own body. Do we really want to add disharmony to the food we are going to eat?

An old friend of mine served in the Peace Corps, stationed in a subsistence tribal area of Africa. Her group went there to teach the locals how to improve their diets. She told me how that tribe's main caloric intake was raw blood drained from live oxen. She and her companions taught the tribe that their diet was unhealthy and that they need to eat more vegetables to avoid diseases which come from malnutrition. Of course, the tribe had to be taught how to farm vegetables, and the land there is not very suitable to farming.

My friend said that the natives were resistant to these changes, and she could not understand why. I asked her what they looked like. She said, generally speaking, they were all very tall, lean, and muscular. I asked how their teeth were, and she said they were straight and white. I asked about the whites of their eyes, and she said they were clear.

I asked her, "What is it that their oxen are eating?" She said, "Grass." I replied, "I think I understand why the natives were so resistant to your ideas. Oxen have four stomachs and are able to squeeze every last drop of nutrition out of a blade of grass. Oxen can digest the protein of plants, something which humans cannot do. Drinking their blood gives immediate nutritional access to all that grassy goodness. Beef blood contains more nutrients than we could ever get from eating vegetables. I am not surprised that those natives resisted what you were teaching. They look at your co-workers, and they see comparatively unhealthy, weak bodies. They see all the work you are telling them to do in order to downgrade their diet, and they wonder, 'What is wrong with these people? Are they crazy?' Considering all that they put up with in this situation, it's amazing that they didn't tell you to leave."

This type of situation occurs throughout the world, and its origins are arrogance, ignorance, and sometimes, corporate greed. Not everything that we in the West do is better. Later, I discovered that African farmers are being pressured to use Genetically Modified Organisms (GMO). Might there be corporate and government-level motives for "helping"? That said, my friend believed she was doing the right thing when she was in Africa, but after our conversation, she no longer felt so confident.

Learn not to take food for granted, because it might not always be so readily available. Wealthy countries around the world may soon find themselves facing dire food shortages. In that case, we will be very thankful for developing appreciative and highly flexible palates with the ability to go without for long periods of time, still remaining in appreciation.

Once, I found a couple of grubs while out in my garden. I took them up to the house, put them in a pan with a little olive oil and fried them. My wife entered the room and without seeing what I was cooking, she said, "Mmm. That smells good!" I asked her what she thought it smelled like. "Fried chicken," she replied. I showed her the fried grubs, and she was aghast. They tasted better than they smelled, I can assure you!

Most of us grimace at the thought of eating insects, but about two thirds of the human population includes insects in its diet. They number among the healthiest foods, so long as they are not toxic. We may find them to be a ready source of nutrition when other sources grow scarce. Consider acclimating to this food source.

Wild Edibles

A good idea in any food climate is to acquaint yourself with the wild edible plants in your area and start incorporating them into your diet, little by little, through salads and soups. Wild edibles are great sources of vitamins, minerals, and phytochemicals that you would otherwise have trouble getting in sufficient quantities even in the best of modern diets. Just remember that anyone can have food allergies, so try things a little at a time to make sure your body handles them well.

I first began eating wild edibles after taking survival courses. The number of wild edibles right outside my door in Tokyo surprised me. I found the young leaves of dandelion to be a fantastic addition to salads. The entire plant is edible and extremely vitamin and mineral-rich. I also enjoyed plantain (the herb, not the fruit tree), which grows almost everywhere I have ever been. It makes a great boiled green that you might prepare like spinach. It actually tastes a lot like spinach but is even more nutrient rich. Almost everyone will find these two great plants in their lawn, but make sure you are not gathering from a lawn that has been sprayed with poisons.

Before gathering and eating anything, be sure to get a good plant identification guide and learn to identify plants thoroughly. Also, be sure to pick plants from non-polluted areas. Herbicides are used in a lot of places, so beware. Roadsides are not a good place to gather from because of herbicides, brake dust, and oil runoff. Even though gathering and eating wild edibles requires a bit of a learning curve, developing this practice is well worth the time and energy. I cannot tell you how fulfilling it is to be able to step into any environment and find something to eat. What will happen is you will learn two or three easy plants and go out in search of them, and, before you know it, you'll have collected a number of other interesting plants that caught your attention. After you bring them home and look them up, you will know four or five plants. Those four or five plants will beckon to you every time you walk past them and thereby introduce you to still more plants that catch your eye. Before you know it, you have relationships with dozens of plants, who welcome you into nature everywhere you go.

Contextual Balance

To have a healthy body, you should adjust your diet to your local environment. Each place calls for a different combination of carbohydrates, fats, proteins, and fiber. The percentages of each nutrient you need will vary according to your environment and your individual body. When living in a very warm place, the body may need a lot more vegetables and fruits than if in an extremely cold environment, where the body would need much more fat and protein.

The important goal here is to eat what is naturally and locally available, as that food is balanced for the particulars of that environment. If you self-identify as a vegan, vegetarian, or fruitarian, imagine taking a few weeks to go camping in the far north, where average temperatures tend to remain extremely cold. You will quickly realize that the body cannot survive naturally on vegetable-based diets in the cold. The body will simply not be able to produce the necessary heat. For years, as a self-identified vegetarian, I found that I could not handle subzero temperatures, for no matter how much clothing I put on or how much I ate, my body would not produce the heat necessary to keep me warm. Unfoldment is not limited to the temperate and equatorial regions of the planet. Therefore, eating animal products is not a limiting factor with regard to unfoldment.

For most of my life, I suffered from digestive disorders, and I tried a variety of diets. For a long time I remained vegetarian, but that did not solve my issues. Although this regimen seemed to keep me healthy in many respects, I began losing weight and feeling lethargic after a few years.

Out of ideology, I remained vegetarian for several more years. I gave up after breaking several bones during training in situations that should never have resulted in breaks. I adopted the standard Japanese diet, and my body weight and energy normalized, as did my bone density, but still the digestive disorders continued.

Recently, I suddenly lost the ability to move my left arm, and signs of similar impending loss were showing up in the right arm as well. I was diagnosed with arthritis in my neck that was impinging on nerves. Upon further testing from a specialist, we discovered that I had nerve damage in my arms as well as extensive myofascial damage in the neck and shoulders. I was in tremendous pain and unable to work. I was told that there was no cure for my situation and that my condition would continue to deteriorate. My only option, I was told, was to manage the pain with medication.

I could not practice the martial arts, write, or work by any other means, and according to the doctor, the condition was only going to grow worse.

What was I going to do?

Not accepting that diagnosis, I meditated on the issue and questioned my body, and to my surprise, the answer I received was that I needed to change my diet to eat only meat and organs for a time. This was a very counter-intuitive approach to my situation, so I researched meat only diets, and I found that people have been eating only meat for years without ill-effect.

My biggest concern was scurvy, which comes from a lack of vitamin C. Scurvy is the breakdown of connective tissue in the body, including the skin. Deadly disease can result if one does not gain access to sufficient quantities of vitamin C.

How would my body get all the vitamins and minerals it needed on only meat? According to people on meat-only diets, eating the skin, connective tissue, and organ meat covers everything except vitamin C, but you don't need the vitamin C if you are eating the collagen found in the skin and connective tissue.

Was this true? I didn't know for sure.

As I faced a dire situation with no other options, I took the leap, cutting out everything except meat, salt, and water for two months. I ate no eggs or dairy products. After one month I could move both arms properly, and after two months my strength had returned. I never got scurvy, although most people who heard about my choice warned that I would.

I began adding plants and other foods back into my diet, omitting only eggs, which would cause shooting pain in the nerves and arm paralysis a few hours after eating them. In retrospect, I suspect I have always had some minor issue with eggs, but never realized it because I have been eating them daily all of my life, having grown up with chickens on the ranch. As I aged the issue exacerbated. My body, in a weakened state, became reactive to many other foods. Cutting out everything but meat allowed my body to recover. I revisited my doctor, who, after testing me, admitted that medical science knows next to nothing about diet and the digestive process.

I'm not suggesting that everyone eat only meat. I suspect that a natural variation occurs between individuals as to what they can eat harmoniously. We may go through times when eating only vegetables is healthy, and other times when only meat is better. Be very careful not to be seduced by food ideology, because your body needs what it needs, and adherence to ideology may result in illness.

Some interesting and unexpected effects emerged during my meat-only months. Body odor completely disappeared, and the passing stools were tiny, perfectly formed, comfortable and odorless. My body became lean, and my little gut entirely disappeared.

After several months, I added vegetables back into the mix, but without concentrated carbohydrates such as rice or potatoes, as my liver would hurt when eating those. Body odor returned, as did stool odor. Those stools were larger and less consistent. About a month later, I was able to add in carbs without liver pain. The gut began to bulge at that time, and I was having issues with foot cramping whenever I ate carbohydrates. I started having vivid dreams about drinking lemon juice and eating dandelion greens. Drinking lemon juice while eating starches prevented cramps, I found. I suspect my body was quite low on vitamin C, so maybe vitamin C helps to digest carbohydrates properly.

I am not advising any particular diet. Take my anecdote for what it is — just one person's experience. I do suggest that we pay attention to our bodies and set aside assumption and ideology. To quote my doctor after I showed her my recovery, "We know very little about digestion, and much of what we think we know may well be incorrect." The nerve specialist, equally surprised by my recovery, agreed.

If you digest legumes well — and if they are locally available — you can get a lot of good protein from nuts and beans. Try to get a large range of natural colors into your foods as well. Below I have listed a few examples of colors that we may want to include in our diets. Numerous vegetables offer each color, so enjoy getting as many as you can, because each provides unique benefits to the body:

> Yellow (squashes, bell peppers, corn, grapefruit)
> Orange (bell peppers, pumpkin, carrots, oranges, sweet potatoes)
> Green (spinach, kale, broccoli, asparagus, green beans)
> Red (radishes, red tomatoes, red peppers, watermelon, guava, beets)
> Blue/Purple/Black (blueberries, blackberries, plums, cabbage, eggplant)
> White (turnips, cauliflower, daikon radish, leeks, garlic)

Finally, give the body access to a large variety of fermented foods. Fermented foods provide the body with a great variety of healthy bacteria for the digestive process. If we look at any ancient or primitive human culture, we quickly see that a great portion of their caloric intake came from fermented foods, because that method enables us to preserve vegetables and beans for long periods of time without refrigeration. Not only was fermentation a practical way of preserving foods longer, it also provided people with a food source rich in B vitamins (which the bacteria produced in the fermentation process), and digestion-enhancing probiotic bacteria. Modern diets are severely impoverished when they exclude fermented foods such as kombucha, sauerkraut, kimchi, natto, miso, pickles, kefir, and live culture yogurts. Bear in mind that some people have allergic reactions to fermented foods. If that describes you, it would be wise to avoid fermented food.

If we are getting regular exercise, eating consciously, limiting sugar and salt, and if we are careful to have a contextually balanced diet for vegetables, carbohydrates, proteins, fats, and fiber that regularly includes all colors and a variety of ferments, while allowing the body a little time to do its own food choosing, then we are heading in the right direction, so long as it's all motivated by love and appreciation.

Hydration

When I was a boy, a friend, Jeff, visited late one summer evening on his motorcycle and invited my brother and me to go camping by a stream, many miles from our house. It was a spur-of-the-moment decision, so we really had not prepared properly. It was already getting late in the evening, so walking was not an option. Our only means of transportation at that time was Jeff's motorcycle, with all three of us piling on.

Because we had no storage space on the motorcycle, we had to keep our supplies to a minimum. We brought sleeping bags, one strapped on each fender and another carried by my brother, who rode in back. We taped a flashlight on the handlebars, and we were off. We rode out to the stream and set up camp, then we headed to the nearest store several miles away to get some snacks and drinks.

We messed around on the motorcycle for hours and hiked in the hills before returning to camp for sleep. Being kids, we didn't think about keeping hydrated. I probably went to sleep mildly dehydrated, but after a few hours of sleep in the dry air combined with the mosquitoes pulling every last bit of blood from my face that they could, I awoke in severe dehydration.

I have been through a lot of physical pain in my active life, but nothing compares to the overwhelming pain that comes with severe dehydration. I awoke unable to move, think, or speak. I knew I needed water, and that was all I knew. I tried to move, but my body would not respond. I tried to scream, but all that came out was a moan.

I don't know how it happened, but Jeff must have heard my weak moans. He came over and asked me what was wrong, I tried to say water, but it came out more like, "Waaar."

I repeated it a few times, and he asked, "Do you need water?" Not waiting for my answer, he lifted my head to a cup of water. I somehow managed to drink it down, and before long I was back to myself again. It's a scary thought, but I was probably not too far off from unconsciousness, which would probably have resulted in death. To me it's a miracle that Jeff woke up because of my weak moans. But thankfully he did.

All of us have experienced minor dehydration, which we would feel first as thirst, but relatively few of us have experienced severe dehydration, thankfully. I don't recommend it. Severe dehydration can kill quickly and painfully, but minor dehydration also exacts a toll on the body and the mind.

Transpiration probably took most of the water out of me. Many of us are familiar with perspiration, which happens when the body releases water through the pores onto the skin, which slowly evaporates and cools the surface of the body. Transpiration is the same except the water evaporates immediately and, therefore, we do not realize that we are sweating. When the air is extremely dry, transpiration happens, and it's a silent killer. When in arid climates we must pay close attention to our sense of thirst because the body is constantly losing water through transpiration, and we can find ourselves in severe dehydration in a snap.

Extremely humid environments are also dangerous because we can easily suffer heat stroke as the sweat remains on our skin, failing to evaporate in air that is already saturated. In such a case, the body does not cool through perspiration, yet it still produces sweat. We need to keep up with our hydration while also being careful not to overheat.

Even in the case of minor dehydration, the body loses strength, flexibility, and reaction time. The brain no longer functions as effectively, leaving us in a mental fog. Many people confuse the feeling of dehydration with being hungry, and they eat. Doing so exacerbates dehydration as the body uses water to digest. This is just one of many reasons drinking any sort of sweetened liquid with calories is ill-advised. When thirsty, avoid any caloric intake.

Let us consider for a moment the progressive symptoms of dehydration. When the body is properly hydrated, it operates at optimal physical and mental performance and regulates heat normally. At the onset of thirst, the body has lost about 1 percent of its water, which causes slight performance decline and altered heat regulation during exercise. At about 2 percent water loss, thirst is further increased while heat regulation and performance decline further. The decrease in performance runs between 20-30 percent when water loss is at 4 percent. At 5 percent water loss, headaches, fatigue, irritability, and feeling "spaced-out" are common. At 6 percent water loss the body's ability to regulate heat is greatly compromised, and one experiences obvious weakness. When the body has lost 7 percent of its water, collapse is likely if exercise is not discontinued. By the time the body has lost 10 percent of its water, it is likely comatose. Beyond 10 percent loss of water, death is likely. (Grandjean & Ruud, "Nutrition for Cyclists." *Clinics in Sports Medicine.* Vol 13.1 [Jan 1994]: 235-246.)

Overhydrating can be dangerous, too. Surprisingly, long distance runners have died from drinking too much water, which hyper-increases blood volume, diluting salt (electrolyte) concentrations in the blood. When saline levels become lower in the blood than in cells, water starts to move into the cells through osmosis, oversaturating them. This imbalance can lead to breathing disorders, headaches, and even death if the brain cells swell too much. The increase of blood volume in the circulatory system stresses the heart and kidneys, leading to damage of kidney cells.

Some symptoms of overhydration (water intoxication) are as follows: fatigue, headaches, confusion, nausea, vomiting, irritability, restlessness, cramps or muscles spasms, seizures, unconsciousness, coma, and, sometimes, death.

As with all things, we seek to achieve a balance between the elements of the body. Those individuals who consume less salt and eat more vegetables, which contain water, do not need to drink as much to maintain a balanced water/saline ratio in their blood. Individuals who consume a lot of salt need to consume more water to balance saline levels in their bodies. The climate, with regard to heat and humidity, and physical activity also factor into the salt-to-water ratios.

How, then, do we figure out how much to drink? The basic rule is to have constant access to water, which we sip little by little as we feel thirst. If we observe that the mouth is not dry and we have no thirst, then we hold off drinking. A lot of people have learned to ignore their sense of thirst, which causes hydration issues. Overdrinking can easily occur during times of high physical activity, so consume no more than seven ounces, or about seven normal swallows, of water in a 15-minute period to avoid overhydration. The body tells us through thirst when to drink and when not to, if we only listen, but when drinking, do not guzzle. We can look upon this as another opportunity to observe.

Biorhythm

Another common challenge we face in modern culture is maintaining a healthy biorhythm, the rhythm of bodily processes. When people do not keep to a consistent schedule for both eating and sleeping, this causes the body not to digest or sleep well.

When I first moved to Japan, I suffered horribly from lack of a stable biorhythm. I had three different part-time jobs, so each day my schedule differed tremendously. On Monday morning, when I had to be at work early, I got up at 6 a.m., but on Tuesday I didn't have work until 1 p.m., so I slept in. The schedule differed every day! After a few months of doing this, I simply could not sleep, or I would wake up at odd hours if I did. Even if I did sleep, my body never felt well rested. Eventually the situation got so bad that I was in a constant mental fog, and I fell into depression. I had very little stress tolerance, so I got upset easily during this time, and my body was hyper-reactive to stimulus as the nervous system was stressed to the maximum. My body felt hard and brittle at this time.

Fortunately, for me, I lost all my part-time jobs in the very same month when those businesses closed their doors permanently. Only a month before the regular school year began, I applied for a junior high school job, which I got. This regular job gave me a fixed schedule that had me out the door by 6:50 a.m. every day. My sleeping pattern improved tremendously from the regular wake-up time, as did my digestion thanks to eating at regular intervals.

The biggest challenge for people with regard to biorhythm is finding a reason to get up and move out every day at the same time. Even those of us with regular jobs tend to sleep in on the weekends to make up for the exhausting week. This is not a good idea. Get up at the same time, even on weekends, but take it easy during the day to recover. In this way, the body's rhythm will not be disturbed.

Many health problems result from having insufficient sleep and a mixed-up biorhythm. For a person on the path of unfoldment, being mentally fogged, exhausted, or overly nervous will make the meditation process quite challenging, so addressing biorhythm issues early on is well advised.

One of the best ways to correct biorhythm issues is to wake up at the same time every day, regardless of the day's planned activities, and not take naps during the correction process. This can present a real challenge for individuals who are already sleep deprived, but if you allow yourself to sleep during the day, then the rhythm never can correct. Stay up until that time when you would ideally go to sleep, and then go to bed, and no matter how poorly you sleep that night, get up at a decided-upon time and stay up. The biorhythm will correct itself in short order if new habits are maintained faithfully.

If you find that you awaken in the middle of the night and have trouble getting back to sleep, it may be what you are consuming before sleep that causes the restlessness. Consumption of alcoholic drinks, certain medications, caffeine, or high concentrations of sugars in the evening can disrupt the sleep cycle in the night and bump us out of sleep.

If we do not sleep deeply and sufficiently, then we will feel dull in the morning, and this will affect our levels of awareness throughout our day. Be aware that the body is very sensitive to light and the seasons, as well as the zone where we live on the planet. All of these factors regulate sleep. During the summer months, we naturally require less sleep due to greater light stimulation than in the winter months when daylight is shorter and the body needs more sleep.

The standard of getting seven to eight hours of sleep a night is probably insufficient for meditators, especially in the early stages. Allow your body to get good, long, deep sleep if at all possible, and allow the body to acclimate to the natural light cycle. Even those who claim they are "night people" will end up going to sleep much earlier when natural light is the only source available. The high-intensity light from bulbs and computers has created the "night person." So, turn off all sources of unnatural light early if you want the biorhythm to correct. After doing so for a time you should find that you awake at or just before sunrise, refreshed and ready for a good, productive day.

Bodywork

During the active process of unfoldment, the body will at times bind up with disharmony as stresses of life reflect deeper issues within. During such moments, it's extremely beneficial to have access to a good, energetically aware, body worker who can get the body flowing again. In Japan, before any meditation session with Sensei we would practice shinkai-ho therapy to open up the body's flow. After doing this our minds would clear, and then tuning to higher frequencies and remaining tuned to them became exceedingly easy.

Of course, we were still not very grounded in the tuning process, so we used shinkai-ho to leapfrog us into consciousness. Ultimately we do not want to become reliant on bodywork for the tuning process, but bodywork is important to care for the body and keep it flowing so that it does not rebel or fail us by making our path of unfoldment unnecessarily difficult.

I continue to practice shinkai-ho regularly; it amounts to a totally formless and inspired yoga, I suppose. The body moves entirely on its own during this time, with no forms or planned movements. Reaching the point when movement begins to occur spontaneously is vital to the process of unfoldment, because then the spirit is doing the work, and the mind and the self are no longer being fed.

Still, it takes a great deal of time before this process will become active in an initiate's body. Usually, I can pass this on to students directly through repeated touch that awakens the body, but most individuals will not have access to such direct experience with me, so we will need to find other means through which we can open up the body.

I found that energetic massage therapy can be very beneficial for individuals who are physically bound. I can imagine that numerous therapy types would work well for such situations, so long as the practitioner is energetically sensitive. For practitioners of bodywork, you will find the meditations that I teach will bring your energetic work to extremely powerful levels if you practice them regularly.

Every day, spend a little time after waking lightly stretching to get the body flowing. We can do this through a light intent on opening the body in all directions. Do not focus on any one point, but instead relax into the frequencies of consciousness.

The teachings of non-concentration, non-will, and non-method are probably quite distinct from most approaches. Just try it out, and I believe you will find that you are able to open up the body without injury or willfulness. Use the intention of unfoldment and the principles of meditation to enlighten your movement. In this way, you will make rapid progress.

Chapter 18 — Caring for the Mind

Through most of the process of unfoldment, a great percentage of time may be spent unconsciously tuned to the frequencies of mind as we release and resolve identifications, little by little. The frequency classes of mind start at the bottom with very low-frequency emotions such as hate or depression and low frequencies of thought such as "I am a loser" or "Nobody likes me." These low frequencies have no direct benefits to the body; they are almost entirely disharmonious. By contrast, in the higher frequencies of emotion, such as personal love or self-confidence, and in the higher frequencies of thought such as "I am happy" or "I am loved" we are still tuned to the mind, but with less disharmony. We would at least like to be in the higher frequencies of mind as much as possible, so that making the leap to consciousness does not present such a challenge. For this reason, we must address certain seeds of darkness that frequently complicate the process of tuning to consciousness.

Expectation

Expectation is defined by the Merriam-Webster Online Dictionary as "a belief that something will happen or is likely to happen." However, this definition lacks the other half of the picture, the emotional rebellion that occurs when expectations are not met. To expect is to sow the seed of disharmony.

Imagine: on Monday morning, time to leave for work, you get in your car and turn the ignition. The starter clicks a few times, but the engine doesn't turn over. You turn the key multiple times, first praying that it will start, but soon those prayers turn to curses under your breath. You have a dead ignition, and now you are going to be late for work. Of course, you expect that your car will start, so you have an emotional reaction. We understand that the function of a car ignition is to start the car, and, of course, we gain value from that function, but at some point that ignition may fail. Having the ability to understand a function and to be able to anticipate that function allows a person to be able to make plans, but when we allow our emotional stability to depend on those plans, that is the problem. The emotional tie to expectation causes the reaction. Ultimately we want to be free of the tie, as well as of the emotional reaction, so that expectation no longer binds us.

> The Master can keep giving because there is no end to her wealth.
> She acts without expectation, succeeds without taking credit,
> and doesn't think that she is better than anyone else.

— Tao Te Ching

Lao-Tzu here describes the life of an individual attuned to the Tao rather than egoic desire. Many of the structures and relationships of our lives are heavily impregnated with expectation. We want to slowly and surely defuse the power of expectation from these structures and relationships. To do this, we relax into an aware flow without going into willfulness.

Observe the emotional reactions that occur every time expectation is not met. For some individuals, reaction to expectation is obvious, for others barely noticeable, but do not get caught up in comparing reactions. Any disharmony, no matter how small, is still disharmony, so we observe and resolve it.

Notice how we use emotional force to push people to do things that we expect of them. They may do as we wish, but the services rendered are steeped in obligation and disharmony. Currently our entire economy operates by expectation, which places tremendous stress on the entire planet. Humankind is so habituated to this kind of interaction that we do not know there is another possibility.

Because expectation is of the mind, we have no way out of it so long as we are tuned to the mind. If we relax into consciousness, then, little by little, we can function more without expectation. The transition should not be willful or forceful, so we will ease our way toward less expectation, less anxiety, which means less disharmony, all the while acquainting ourselves with unconditionality.

Life without expectation does not equate to a life of nonproductivity. The more we are tuned to consciousness, the more inspiration we will find. Inspiration becomes our primary motivation, rather than expectation. When this begins to happen, our lives become much more positive.

Start to map out how and when expectation pulls you out of the present, turning you into a machine of obligation, anxiety, and stress. Correcting other people may be the tendency, but this is not really helpful, so make it a priority to observe and resolve your own habitual disharmony instead.

Integrity

> "He who is faithful in what is least is faithful also in much;
> and he who is unjust in what is least is unjust also in much."

— Gospel of Luke, *The New Testament*

Your word is your oath, and nothing more need be added to it. Otherwise it loses power, and you bind Soul. If you agree to do something, then in order to maintain integrity and not bind Soul, you must fulfill your word. Of course, if you gave your word in the past, and now your conscience speaks against it, then apologize for not fulfilling your word, for to act against conscience is ill-advised at any time.

Such a simple teaching but so difficult to master, it seems. The vast majority of people speak from the tip of the tongue, so what they say is not what they do. They make promises lightly and do not follow through. For a person walking the path of unfoldment, this habit is highly detrimental. A great deal of unfoldment, once one is past the initial phases, occurs through service; if one is not trustworthy, then what service is there? We can meditate all we want, but if we have no trustworthiness or follow-through, then there can be no true service. At some point, we will hit a wall that will halt our progress because our motivation is selfish and our word is weak. Then we might wonder why we aren't respected, why we are aimless.

Whenever committing to something, observe the mind. You may find that it isn't harmony doing the talking. Better yet, observe the mind whenever talking, and do not allow for too much idle talk. Through idle talk, we bind Soul tremendously.

A good exercise, once you feel ready, is to carry around a pocket notebook and a pencil. Keep a record of every time you say you are going to do something. Write down exactly what you have committed yourself to, and date it. At the end of every week, look over those notes and check the commitments that you have completely fulfilled. Doing this exercise improves our awareness of idle commitments and reminds us to keep our word.

Painting

As a child, despite my generally quiet nature, I loved nothing more than to play tricks on people for fun. One Christmas I was gifted a two-foot, ribbed, plastic tube that mimicked the sounds of an Aboriginal bullroarer — a string with a wooden instrument at the end that makes a special sound which travels for miles when swung around.

I found that I could produce myriad strange sounds by blowing through this tube. One Sunday afternoon, while playing with it, I found that I could make quite believable animal sounds — especially the singing, whining, and howling sounds of coyotes, which were numerous in our area. While I was practicing coyote vocalizations outside, I noticed one of my neighborhood friends riding her horse up a trail in the hills behind my house. I decided to see if I could convince her that there was a coyote in the bushes on the hillside.

I quickly climbed the hill where she was heading and positioned myself out of sight, behind a large tumbleweed. As she drew nearer, I began my calls. I started out somewhat erratically, sounding as if a pack of coyotes had just made a kill. I suppose she didn't really understand what my calls meant anyway, so I could do any coyote sound I wanted and she would not know the difference.

When she first heard the sound she was obviously quite interested in checking it out. She turned her horse to bear down on the sound and approached slowly. As she got closer I was worried that she would be able to see me, and the joke would be spoiled, so I started making growling and yipping sounds intending to put a little fear into her. Luckily she responded exactly as I had hoped; she stopped her horse immediately. Her stopping told me that she was worried that there might be a danger, and being the fun-loving boy that I was, I reveled in her fear. I intensified the growls and yips even more, well beyond what any wild coyote would conceivably do. To my surprise, she whipped the horse around and galloped away, downhill, into the neighborhood.

I was pretty satisfied with the convincing sounds that my new instrument could make, but a little disappointed that the fun was over so quickly. I decided that I would have to find a new victim. I was having too much fun to stop with just one scared girl. So I decided to come down the hill and see what she would do after she calmed down, all the while keeping my eyes open for new prospects.

To my surprise, she didn't do at all what I expected. I thought that she was going to tie up her horse and go into her house to tell the story to her father, which would get me into trouble if I were caught. He wouldn't be too happy about me scaring his daughter while she was riding her horse, a potentially dangerous situation. I certainly didn't want any angry parents on my hands, so I abandoned the location where I was hiding and stashed my toy until I was sure the coast was clear. Fortunately, instead of going to her home, she went to mine. I had to assume that it meant her father was not home, so she decided to go next door, to my house, to tell her story.

This got me thinking. Knowing my brother and sister, they would be way too curious to let an adventure like searching for some coyotes pass them up, and if I were right, I could expect them to be coming up my way in very short order. I decided that I had better get back to my previous hiding place and wait for the posse.

And what a posse it was. Clearly, my brother and sister called some of the other kids in the neighborhood, as there was a little horde of people: Natalie, the horse rider; my brother and sister; and two other kids from next door, as well. This was getting good.

They were coming up the opposite side of the hill that Natalie had been on earlier, which was good for me, as I could put more underbrush between the posse and myself.

I started making coyote sounds when they were just halfway up the hill, which turned their dead-run into a freeze session. After a few expletives they started out again, but this time at a slower pace. The trail they were using was quite narrow thanks to the thick sagebrush and tumbleweeds, so that they had to come up single file, which limited everyone's view except for the leader's.

The kids in back were excited and obviously hungry for information. They kept up a constant barrage of questions to the leader, who did a stop-look-turn-answer all the way up the trail. Their progress was slow, and from what my ears could gather, the leader, my brother, loved all the attention he was getting. He had them believing that he could see a coyote and its pups well before they were even 50 yards from me.

Being on a hillside made their voices echo pretty clearly, and I could catch a lot of what they were saying. Of course, my brother couldn't actually see anything except for the bushes between us, but he certainly was convincing. By this time, my adrenaline was pumping pretty hard. I knew if they discovered that I was playing a prank on them, they would beat me to snot. My brother wasn't one to be made a fool of, and the people who would typically have protected me from a beating were unfortunately also looking pretty foolish at this point. I couldn't count on their protection this time around. I had only two options: to try to sneak away unseen, which was going to require a miracle, considering how close they were to me at that point; or to put on such an impressive sound show that fear would prevent them from coming closer and discovering it was me and not a coyote. I chose option number two. Not only was it safer than sneaking away, I thought it by far more interesting. I figured that if I got caught, at least I could have a good laugh before my beating, and if I survived, it would make a great story.

I started snarling with more intensity as they came closer. I also made some whimpering sounds as if there were puppies present. I figured that my brother would know enough about coyotes to realize that they do not normally make noise in this type of situation unless they were backed into a corner, injured, or protecting pups. Of the three, a mother with pups is always the most dangerous.

Once my brother heard the whimpering, he started pointing to the bush I was behind and saying he could see the mother and pups. Soon the others came up next to him and started leaning forward to peer toward the bush. I was wearing blue jeans and a white T-shirt with white sneakers. I knew at this range that they could probably see me, and that if I didn't turn them on their heels immediately I would be caught.

I deepened the growling sound to an ominous level. It didn't stop them from coming up any further. By this point, they were within about 10 yards of me, and I tried not to look in their direction for fear that they would see the whites of my eyes — always a dead giveaway.

At this point, my brother was counting the pups and saying that he could see the legs and tail of the mother, which had a gray coat. I was beside myself as my fear took a sudden detour into humor. I had to use all my willpower to repress the giggles that were bubbling under the surface, threatening to burst into howling laughter.

They got within five yards or so, judging by sound, before the reality of my precarious situation hammered humor back into fear. I broke into a panic-fueled primal growl and began shaking the bush. It was so intense that it would have caused anyone to fear for his or her life. I wasn't acting anymore — I was panicked.

My brother froze. Silence. This was the deciding moment. I knew his fear was overriding his curiosity. I poured on the violence. He made his choice, a blind-panicked, run-for-life retreat.

I peered over the bushes to see if they were far enough away for me to make my own escape. I knew it wouldn't be long before my father came up the hill to check out the situation.

The posse was heading toward my house, and I wanted to beat them there. I ran straight down the hill, where no trails existed, crashing recklessly through the dense underbrush. I was determined to beat them to the house, even though I knew I was risking injury, as there were many holes and large rocks that I couldn't see under the brush. I wasn't worried about the racket I was creating, as they were making so much noise that they wouldn't hear anything above their own terrified screams.

I reached the bottom of the hill, ran straight for our backyard fence, and quickly scaled it. Fortunately for me, my mother had been doing laundry earlier, so the back utility room door was unlocked, which was not usually the case. I ran through the utility room, into my bedroom, locked the door and shut the drapes.

My clothes reeked so badly of sagebrush that I tore them off and stuffed them in my closet. I doused myself with some cologne, another Christmas gift, and put on new clothes. This whole process took less than a few minutes, from the top of the hill to new outfit.

There was still no sign of the posse, but I knew they would be showing up soon, so in order to look completely oblivious to what was going on I made like I was busy doing my chores. I ran down to the barn, which I usually did at that age — running everywhere, I mean, and fed the cats, while singing out, "Here kitty, kitty, kitty," which brought in hordes of cats for food every time. I could hear my brother coming up behind me, and I suddenly felt a wash of self-consciousness. I was certain that he must have suspected something. Surely, someone must have seen me. Or maybe I had some unchecked cockleburs in my hair. That would be a dead giveaway.

To my surprise, he came into the cat room and started blabbering on incoherently about some crazed coyote and pups on the hill, and how I missed it all. My self-consciousness turned to a strange sort of objectivity bordering on the scientific. I pretended as if I were completely in the dark about this whole coyote business and started asking him questions about it to see if he really believed his own story.

To my amazement, he seemed to believe wholeheartedly that he had seen the mother and pups. He told me she was wounded and that he was sure she would have attacked if they had taken one step closer. I was having trouble accepting that he really believed his own story. My curiosity kicked in, driving me into potentially dangerous territory. To test his conviction, I would have to tell him the truth — that I had been on the hill, making the entire ruckus. It was the only way I would know if he really believed his story or not.

So I told him everything, in detail, even going so far as to reproduce the sounds. He told me that I didn't sound anything like what he heard on the hill and that I was full of crap. He swore emphatically that he saw everything with his own eyes and that there was no way that it could have been me.

Baffled by his hard stance, I showed him my concealed, sagebrush-smelling blue jeans and T-shirt and pointed out the location where I played the coyote on the hillside. He still didn't believe me. And to my greater surprise, he wasn't the least bit angry with me. If anything, he seemed somewhat bewildered.

Before I knew it, my sister walked into the house and started blathering on about the coyote to my parents. Bewilderment turned again to conviction as my brother chimed in with full force, wanting to outdo my sister with tales of his bravery and leadership and how he saw everything while the others had merely gotten a glimpse of the coyotes.

So I pushed even further and told my story to my parents. Nobody believed me. This was one of my first experiences with how the mind can play tricks on us. Sometimes, we want to believe something so badly that our minds actually fill all the holes and paint in the elements that we need to reinforce our beliefs. I have always held that experience close to my heart, and I have been as careful as possible not to jump to conclusions or "paint" experiences.

Unless a person is aware of this painting tendency of the mind through an actual experience such as I had, painting is likely to be a common way of interpreting reality. The most common way that we paint is with regard to other people's motivations and intentions. If we are being truly honest with ourselves, we must admit that we do not know what is going on in another person's mind. To assume otherwise is extraordinarily arrogant. And for one walking the path of conscious unfoldment, this kind of reflexive tendency to think we know the story can be extremely disadvantageous. We must strive to remain as calm and centered as possible when we observe people or experience things and not get caught up in emotional fervor, which gives rise to the painter within.

Devil's Advocate

A thousand years ago people believed that the world was flat, a notion we now discredit, but were you to go back a thousand years ago and speak to anyone on the planet at that time, most would think you were nuts if you asserted that the earth was actually spheroid. Looking at science a hundred years ago and comparing those ideas to contemporary science, we find that much of what past thinkers believed to be true does not hold much water now. How much of what we assume to be true now will hold water a hundred years from now?

Just as the popular beliefs and "facts" of a thousand or a hundred years ago no longer hold much water, the beliefs and ideas that we personally hold onto may also prove incomplete. Instead of trying to justify and protect our ideas, we might reverse the process, and try to prove them wrong. In this way, not only will we no longer be feeding the ego, but we are also likely to find any weaknesses in our perspective, which will eventually cause us to look much deeper than we might have otherwise.

During the years I trained with my teacher in Japan, we would intentionally try to counter each other's techniques. This testing process allowed us to go beyond technique to something more profound and irrefutable. Had we continued practicing purely in a cooperative fashion, then we likely would not have attained this deeper level, which is consciousness.

The basic idea of this approach is that no matter what you believe or what you practice, try to prove it wrong or find a weakness in the method. But don't test just once. Keep at it over and over, from differing angles and perspectives. Otherwise you can easily overlook something valuable by way of assumption. Be the devil's advocate for yourself, because if you have not found the holes, then as you go further down the path of unfoldment, the devil surely will.

This approach will turn off a lot of people. Certainly others are likely to become frustrated when you punch holes in their theories, ideas, and methods, so do not be rude or egoic about being the devil's advocate, as that will only kick up identifications. Instead of directing this approach at other people's ideas, direct it at your own beliefs.

This simple change of intent will goad you deeper and deeper until you find the root of ignorance and resolve it to Isness. Any time you find yourself protecting a certain position or building up a belief system, do what you can to disprove it. When you have stripped away all, and nothing remains but pure being, which really is no-thing, then you will have found harmony.

When we consider the incredible amount of strife in the world over belief systems, methods, and cultures, we can see that if all people were to embrace this one simple approach, those divisions would disappear as each nation resolved to harmony. Of course, we cannot expect that other people will do this. Instead, we always begin within ourselves and allow that to project into the world through the radiance of consciousness.

Starting with ourselves may seem like the slowest way, but actually it's the fastest. The ego will always tell us that we need to promote this idea or that idea to change other people's minds. But the war of ideas and the desire to change minds is itself of the mind, and, therefore, we remain stuck in the matrix of mind that is disharmony. Instead, take the seemingly slow route by tuning to consciousness and questioning your own mind. Be your own devil's advocate, and disprove your mind time and again until you lose faith in the mind. In this way, consciousness will be revealed through you, which will light a spark for all who are ready to take the same step.

Memory Identification

While I lived in Japan, I worked as a middle-school teacher. I had a homeroom class and a group of students with whom I grew very involved as I taught them throughout their middle-school lives. They felt to me in some ways as if they were my own children. We were very close.

Toward the end of my career at that school, numerous factors brought me to stress levels that were too much for the body to handle. Probably the most important factor was the vision that I'd had in the Amazon and the trauma that I held onto after being shown the probable futures of collapse toward which humanity was unconsciously moving. Add to them the great earthquake and tsunami that hit the country in March of 2011, knocking out electricity and causing a nuclear plant in Fukushima to go into meltdown. The entire country was thrown off kilter. We were rationing electricity and wondering whether life in Japan would ever be the same. The economic stresses of the world had been hitting the country hard as well, and some ensuing harsh policy changes at our school had divided the teachers, creating animosities. I didn't have the clarity to move gracefully through those circumstances.

One morning after midterms, I went to my desk and sat down to grade tests. I began with my homeroom class, picking up the stack of tests, unfolding them, and turning to student number one. Strange, I thought, who is Ai Wada? This was not one of my students. I flipped to the next student and again could not recognize the name. I rechecked the class, and indeed it was 3A, my homeroom class. Someone must be playing a joke on me, I thought. Then I got out my grading book, which had been locked in my desk, to verify the names. I flipped to 3A, student number one — Ai Wada. I knew that my grading book was unmolested because it contained my own handwriting, and, therefore, the data must be correct.

Ai Wada *was* my student, and she had been my student for years. I had helped to raise her through her junior high experience, and suddenly I could not recognize her name. I had forgotten her. How terrible. What's more, I had forgotten all of my students, whom I loved very much. "What is wrong with me?" I thought. "Do I not love my students enough to remember their names?" Then it occurred to me that I had forgotten almost everything. I knew my name, but I could not recall the names of other teachers, apart from a few old friends at the school.

Tears began to pour uncontrollably down my cheeks, and my body began shaking. I felt terrified panic. Another teacher came over to talk to me. I turned my head away so as not to reveal my shame. He didn't realize that I was having an emotional breakdown right in front of him, and he walked off, seemingly offended to be ignored. I walked out of the school, telling no one. I remembered how to get home, and there I went. My wife called the school and let them know that I was taking sick leave for the remainder of the week. I spent the next few days in a depression, not remembering enough to be able to do anything useful. I called my father by phone and told him what had happened. He said that he'd had the same experience many years earlier, a temporary memory loss due to too much stress. He assured me that the memories would come back soon, and that I should just take it easy and rest for a few more days.

The next day, I had an unexpected insight. I realized that, although I couldn't remember anything, I was still me. My existence was not dependent upon memory. And as soon as I realized that, the depression lifted. Of course, without memory, I lacked a certain functionality, but I was still me, which meant that I could still be happy, regardless of the loss of memory. I began to enjoy my days off, and in short order memory returned.

Memory, which is in the ninth spectrum of disharmony thanks to our identification with it, is a necessary tool to function in daily life. However, it can also be a curse when we identify with our memory, because, for a start, memory is not stable. Once we understand that memory consists of a biased recording of events, constantly being rewritten in our minds every time we tap it, and that the data there corrupts with time, then we can see how unstable it really is. Memory is not actuality. Memory is not even the past. Memory is similar to imagination in that it's quite mutable. For this reason, we cannot use memory as a way of being present. Memory is never present, and its accuracy degrades over time. Of course, we should appreciate the functionality that memory allows, but we need not attach our sense of self to "our past."

One interesting exercise is to play with the idea that you have no memory at all, apart from essentials. Forget things like your favorite food, what you like to do, or where you like to go, and then just change up what you eat, what you do, or where you go for a day. Try something new, or do something old but in a new way, but don't be foolish about it.

Many of the most healthy attitude changes occurred in my middle-school students when we went on field trips. They just needed to get out of their usual rut in order to reach a new perspective. Do not seek to be comfortable during this type of exercise. Just soften your pattern to the point at which you are willing to try something new with an open mind.

Identification with memory can be quite the prison, limiting your outlook greatly. Take a holiday from memory, let go of old stories, and enjoy discovering new insights and understandings. Often we cannot embrace new viewpoints or step out of old patterns while maintaining our usual life situation, with its ruts and habits.

Positionality

The questions "Who am I?" and "What am I?" have vexed philosophers and laymen alike since humans developed the ability to speak the words. These questions stem from Soul, so anyone on the path of spiritual unfoldment will eventually ask them. Of course, the way these questions typically come through the mind are so limited and biased that the framing actually prevents insight.

On occasion, throughout my childhood, I went outside on clear starry nights to lie down on the lawn and gaze up into the vastness of the universe. Because I lived in a small rural town, few lights interfered with the cosmic beauty of space. Sometimes the skies were so clear and the stars so distinct that it felt like I could just reach up and pluck one from its dark nest in the heavens.

I would relax so much into the gazing that it began to feel as if I no longer had a body, as if I were the cosmos. But if I did not have a body, then what was I, I wondered. Curiosity began to move me into a search for self. If I was not my body, then was I thought? But then, I had moments with no thought at all, and during thoughtlessness, I still was, so I could not be thought. Was I emotion? No, because during the time of thoughtlessness I also experienced no emotion. Was I memory? When gazing at these stars I was so relaxed that memory was not even present, so I was not memory. "What am I?" I wondered. All I could say at that time was that a very clear sense of "me-ness" existed without any further defining attributes.

Little did I know at the time that those experiences were profound moments of insight into actuality. Of course, I would come out of me-ness and pop right back into Richard, who was a body, thought, emotion, and memory. Still, unknown to me at that time, a seed was planted that began to grow.

As an adult I had unexpected insight into the unconscious identification process while watching the movie *Avatar* at the cinema in 3-D. I remember being drawn into the movie so deeply that, at some point, I was no longer Richard, but one of the tall, lean, blue, Na'vi natives in the forest. I snapped out of it and realized what had happened. I had unconsciously identified myself as an alien from a distant planet.

It sounds ridiculous, doesn't it? If we watch our children, they identify with characters on TV all the time, becoming so entirely engrossed in the process of identification that they make games of it. Adults, for the most part, might not get so deeply into this imaginative process as children do because much of their identification is already tightly defined, but we do identify ourselves unconsciously with thoughts, emotions, opinions, places, and things almost constantly. And when someone challenges those connections, well, we may not like that so much. Such challenges cause the frequent violence that occurs during sporting events. Whether adult or child, the automatic identification process is so smooth and habitual that it happens nearly constantly, without our noticing it, through association.

A nice game to counter-balance this unconscious process is the game of nonpositionality. In this game, we lovingly allow space for everyone's opinions. We have no stake in opinions and positions during this game, and instead are interested just in allowing for communication. Spend the entire day without defending any thought, emotion, opinion, position, and so forth.

Consider all things to be equally possible, as if we lived in a fantasy world. Allow people to express their ideas fully and question those ideas to draw them out even further. Do not confront their ideas, even if they seem really illogical. When questioning an idea, do it with love, and be careful not to shut the idea down.

Do not be spineless or wishy-washy. You may still suggest an idea, but take no emotional stake in "your ideas" or "facts." Do not make yourself "right" and the other person "wrong." If the person likes your idea and accepts it, then fine. If they ask for clarification, then clarify if you like, but if they argue against it, do not defend anything. Instead, flow with them to see where they are heading. They are free to accept your idea or reject it, just as you are free to accept or reject their idea; moreover, you are free to change or reject the idea that you thought you supported originally.

After this exercise, you may find that your perspective has changed. It's not that anyone changed you, or even that you changed your perspective willfully, but more like your perspective just opened up and began to flow. Do not concern yourself with whether the other individual changed or learned anything. That is not the goal. The goal is to soften the content of the self and "our" positions.

Structural Change

One of the biggest and most frightening challenges that one faces in the process of unfoldment is structural. I refer here to the structures of your life. Your relationships, job, social standing, your home, comfort zones, habits, addictions, interests, entertainment sources, opinions, likes, dislikes, diet, language (including body language), movement of the body, and so on, begin to change to match the shifts occurring in your perception as Soul unbinds, your mind silences, and you begin to see the world more clearly.

It's not that some outside source tells you who you need to hang out with or what you need to eat, but, instead, the flow of your very being inspires you to move in new directions. In many cases, your family, friends, coworkers, and so forth may not be spiritually unfolding at the same rate that you are or who may have no interest in unfoldment at all. They might try to hold you to their expectations of who you are to them. As you change you may encounter resistance from those who feel frustrated that you are not the same person they thought you to be. Some may even outright try to prevent you from "changing" because they want you to be the person that they have in mind. Many may simply not find you interesting anymore and move out of your presence. If we worry about other people's opinions of us, then that is just another level of binding that will prevent us from realizing oneness. Liberation is not for the weak or cowardly. It takes great courage to face all of the fear and illusion that we hold onto. Embrace courage, and let it flow through observation.

Remember to do the Dance of the Self often so that when these changes occur you do not become too imbalanced by them. Allow developments to happen at a smooth, even rate, and enjoy the process; it's not a race. The people who no longer suit your energy field will eventually distance themselves, and new people more in accord with your energy will gradually be magnetized to you. The process will take time, and you may go through a long period wherein you feel that you have no one with whom you can speak of spiritual matters, but that will pass eventually. Joining a meditation group for companionship through these changes may be a good idea for some.

Idol Worship

The greatest idol worship is not the worship of objects but the worship of the self. Worship is not limited to times when we have clasped our hands in prayer or joined in fellowship; we worship with our attention primarily. How much of our attention dwells on the self? That is how much we worship the self. The only time we are not idolizing the self to some degree either directly or indirectly is when our attention is on silent, unconditioned love and, ultimately, Isness.

Personality worship is just an extension of idol worship, reverence directed to the superficial, the non-essential, to things, including ideas. *Person* shares the same root as *persona*, which in Latin originally referred to the masks used in theater. The persona is a mask that the individual has created over many lifetimes to protect the self and/or to gain a social advantage. The person is just a mask, no matter how much we believe it to be us. Do not confuse the personality with the actual individual. Neither Soul nor the Spirit is the personality.

Regardless of someone's intentions about consciously unfolding, we are all susceptible to this confusion about personality, and that often creates misjudgments about individuals. I have noticed that on first introductions people tend to be attracted to extroverted, sparkling personalities, and that less glittery individuals get overlooked or underrated. But when we watch relationships over the long-term, often those sparkling personalities fall short. Frequently they suffer from critical issues like lack of follow-through, untrustworthiness, narcissism, and so on, using personality to insulate themselves from consequences. Those who are far down the path of unfoldment very rarely have flashy personalities.

> "The Master views the parts with compassion,
> because he understands the whole.
>
> His constant practice is humility.
> He doesn't glitter like a jewel
>
> but lets himself be shaped by the Tao,
> as rugged and common as stone."
>
> — *Tao Te Ching*

We will find that as our energy withdraws itself from maintaining the person and focuses more on Isness, we lose interest in flashy people. In all likelihood, we might seem somewhat dull to ordinary people but captivating to those who are consciously unfolding. So the question, then, is, whom do we want to attract? Once we have insight into the personality, then we understand the motives of the self and others, and we are no longer misled by glitter.

Belief Systems

Sometimes people join my meditation group and become upset because these teachings appear to conflict with a pre-existing perspective or belief system. The conflict comes when the individual holds a belief system to cover for a sense of insecurity and/or a sense of hopelessness. When we look into any belief system, we find that it attracts because the self gains some sort of hope through envisioning its place within a constellation of ideas. It gives the self a feeling of location, of having a concrete foundation to hold on to.

But the self is itself a mental construct, not ultimately true. The self is the first belief system. Precisely because the self is inherently insecure, it needs to construct layers of story to try to patch security holes. Just as there is always a weakness to any patch, though, weakness is inherent in any belief system. The end of belief systems does not come from no longer believing in them, but instead from the deep realization that the self itself is a belief system. Some would call what I am saying, "killing the self" or "the death of the self," but how can something that never actually existed be killed? How can an illusion die? We are not killing the self; we are just seeing through it, which is to say, we are opening to the infinite.

I know that many self-described atheists and agnostics claim that they do not have belief systems, but actually they do because they believe in the self, even if unwittingly. They also tend to believe in physicality, in the senses, in the mind, and/or in science. Even science can be a belief system because it's based on the mind. Mathematics, for example, may be seen as the attempt to measure what is inherently immeasurable. Mathematics creates artificial constructs to temporarily encapsulate the infinite. We can best see this in the calculation for the area of a circle, which uses pi. The number 3.14 represents pi, but in fact this number has no end. Pi's first 30 digits are 314159265358979323846264338327, but the number actually stretches on into infinity. The benefit of using 3.14 to represent pi is that it gives us a functional enough circle to work with. Mathematics benefits us in that it allows for a practical construct for the mind to function within the universe to a degree, but if we attach ourselves to it, it becomes a barrier that does not allow for the realization of the infinite. If we were able to soften the emotional ties to mathematics and view it only as a tool of the mind for functional purposes, then that would not be a binding belief system. In this way, we might still make use of mathematics as a tool, if we wish, without binding to it, which allows us to be more open to the infinite and the undefined.

Because all beliefs represent the content of the self, I encourage students, little by little, to untie from belief systems. We may not be able to fully untie instantly because, for a lot of us, belief systems compensate for traumas and deep-seated insecurities. Thus, to give up all belief systems immediately would feel extremely threatening to the self and most likely create defensiveness, avoidance, or even aggression. Therefore, we release little by little as we gain trust in the infinite and undefined. Once we realize the degree of flowing stability and strength that comes from being free of belief systems and ultimately the self, then we find it very easy to take that final step into the infinite. Until then we take it very slowly and carefully.

Paradoxically, when all has been released and the infinite shines through, we find hope and belief, but hope and belief of this type are not of the self. They innately come from the infinite and, therefore, they are unconditioned, which is to say without mental construct or emotional tie. To have unconditioned hope and belief, we remove all conditions of the mind through tuning to the frequencies of consciousness. Then we find, counter intuitively, that we achieve clarity and hope by default without any ascertainable cause. These qualities have power so long as they remain unconditioned. Why is this so? When we feel connected to all that is, fear and anxiety quiet, and a powerful inner strength emerges that is capable of flowing with what life has to offer, so hope is no longer focused on ideal circumstances, but instead on our capacity to be present and work positively with any circumstance.

True freedom begins with freedom from belief systems through unbinding. Such unbinding and embracing of the infinite lie at the core of what I teach. Truly, Isness cannot be taught, because it's formless and free of all definition. Therefore, the only belief that matters is the one that blocks us from resolving to Isness. "Empty your cup," as the old Chinese saying goes — but let us do it gently and carefully, starting with what we are ready to release. To release more than we are ready to causes willfulness, and that does not aid in this process.

The Danger of Teachings

Several students have confided in me that they used to buy every spiritual book that they could get their hands on. They played spiritual audiotapes when driving, recite mantras and affirmations. For all of it, they found themselves with more mental noise than they had before reading any spiritual books. When they tried to meditate, their minds would repeat wise sayings and insights to them. The teachings had become millstones around their necks. One student became so frustrated that he took all of his books outdoors and burned them. He decided not to read any more spiritual books because he was so fed up with the noise.

The mind will feed on any information that you give it, and it can turn any great teaching into disharmony. A Bible verse that might offer insight on this dilemma is "Do not give what is holy to the dogs; nor cast your pearls before swine, lest they trample them under their feet, and turn and tear you in pieces" (Matthew 7:6). If we consider that the dogs and swine in this statement represent the mind, then this teaching helps us to understand the dangers of the mind and what the mind will do to spiritual teachings.

A true danger comes with any teaching: the individual receives the teaching through the mind. Whatever the teaching is, if it's received through the mind, that teaching will become just another set of trivia in the mind to think about and debate. This thinking and debating all derive from the mind, and they feed identifications, which ultimately bind Soul even further.

Therefore, true teachings can be either binding or enlightening, depending upon which route they take, the mind or consciousness. Jiddu Krishnamurti, in his book *Total Freedom*, has audiences with various scholars who end up debating with him in frustration. This is the inevitable consequence of teachings being received through the mind. Had those individuals listened through consciousness they would have seen clearly, with insight, what Krishnamurti was saying, with no need for debate. But because they were working through the mind, each little point elicited resistance and debate, creating more disharmony than before they had spoken with Krishnamurti.

Instead of debating about the transcendence of self, which is the route of mind, the way of consciousness would be to directly experience life without a sense of self. When one directly experiences no-self (consciousness), one no longer needs to theorize about what it feels like, and thus there is no longer a need to debate.

If we receive Krishnamurti's teachings through the mind, we suffer from thinking or create a belief system, both of which are of the mind and disharmony. But if we go deeply into the higher frequencies of harmony and receive the very same statements from Krishnamurti, we will find that we understand much of it clearly — it appears obvious because we are directly experiencing that to which his words point. The words will not get us there, but they can help motivate the individual's interest to experience consciousness.

Tune to consciousness, and many spiritual teachings become simple and obvious, assuming they were passed on through consciousness. Unfortunately, many teachings, the majority, probably, have come to us through the minds of the teachers and dogmas of traditions. Such traditions are not transformative. They sound wonderful, and the mind tends to crave them because the mind can feed on them, but they do not resolve the self. The only way to realize the difference between accurate teachings and inaccurate teachings is through consciousness.

If we are tuned to consciousness, then we no longer feel the need to burn our books. Instead, we can enjoy reading them and feeling the degree of accuracy of each book. Through reading while tuned to consciousness we can gain a lot of great insights from almost any book, really, possibly beyond what the author was intending to teach because we are no longer bound by expectation.

Wanting Needs

The vision quest has proved an extremely valuable experience for me in so many ways. One of the biggest takeaways I got from that time alone in the forest was the realization of really how little I actually needed to be happy. I also became more aware of how owning lots of things can be a burden as the things in our possession actually own us. I reflected on my life and realized all that I truly required was shelter, food, water, love, and an inspired purpose. I saw then that most of my "wants" were in truth attempts to fill an empty space inside.

I began to notice how, when we buy something new, like say a car, for the first few months it feels fresh and exciting, but after a time, the mind begins to adjust to the item, and it no longer feels special. Pretty soon we are hungry for a different new car. We might or might not buy that other car, but the urge for that new car experience is there, and we start comparing it to our old new car, causing the one we already own to lose value in our minds. This desire is an illusion that traps many of us in the never-ending hamster wheel of debt and misery. Once I became aware of this tendency of the mind, whenever that tendency arose, I could see through it. I began to be quite happy with my meager belongings. I pruned down my possessions to fit into 10 or fewer cardboard moving boxes, so that I could just load them into my car and move with ease as Isness pulled me here or there to study.

Since that downsizing I've met a number of wealthy individuals who, despite their holdings, have little or no ease of mind. They have asked me how I can be happy owning so little and having so few desires. "The answer is simple," I say. "Our desires actually represent the content of the self. If we have a lot of wants, it reflects disharmony within. Once we understand the tendency of the mind is to try to patch over insecurity and lack of clarity with desires, then we find it easy to choose consciousness instead of mind and needs instead of wants. And the more that people do this with dignity, not identifying themselves as 'poor,' the easier it becomes for other people to make the same decision."

Sense of Purpose

Many on the spiritual path struggle with finding a sense of purpose. Depression runs so rampant in first-world countries in part because, although people are busy and work a lot, in general they do not have a sense of purpose beyond the self. For someone walking the path of unfoldment, a lack of purpose beyond the self is all the more difficult to deal with. Many get stuck at step one because they do not know what that one special purpose is, so they just wait to find out.

In a few rare cases, individuals may have a clear indication of purpose very early in life. Unfortunately the accomplishments of these individuals usually receive a lot of publicity, whereas we hear little about how the process normally works for most other people. Just as not everyone's true love shows up in high school, neither does our one true purpose show up easily (assuming everyone has one true purpose). In fact, for most people many smaller purposes may emerge before they find a big one. Or maybe the individual is well suited to many varieties of service beyond the self. We should have no assumptions here.

Soul often speaks through passion. If we are inspired or passionate about something, so long as our conscience is in accord, then pursuing that passion will open doors for the unfoldment process. Whether others consider the passion important does not matter. This pursuit could be something as simple as a hobby, or as large as starting a business. Once we give our attention and energy to our passion, it will lead us to the experiences that expedite the unfoldment process.

If this compelling sense of interest eludes you, look into the health of the body as physiological issues may be blocking passion. If curiosity and engagement still do not rise, then consider doing a vision quest to reveal what you do find compelling. If that does not help, then simply apply yourself to something beyond the self in accordance with your conscience. This will get the flow going, and through this flow of purpose, you may realize that you have found what you were looking for, or you may move from one thing to another. In any case, you have a purpose, a sense of service, and that buoys the spirit. Remember, have no expectations, but remain open to the possibilities.

Forgiveness and Reconciliation

One of the most difficult and sensitive areas of the unfoldment process deals with forgiveness and reconciliation. Forgiveness is a misunderstood process. And due to this misunderstanding there is a lot of resulting disharmony and victimization in the world.

First and foremost, forgiveness comes not from mind, but from consciousness. The mind does not have the capacity to forgive because the mind is conditioned. Any forgiveness that the mind conjures up is conditional, not forgiveness at all. The second misunderstanding concerns the belief that forgiveness and reconciliation are the same. Forgiveness is a realization that you come to on your own through resolving negativity, by tuning to consciousness, but we cannot expect it of someone bound in the mind. Reconciliation, meanwhile, requires the agreement and follow-through of all parties involved. The crux of the matter is that we do not control what other people do. They are not our job. We can do only our part, which is to tune to consciousness so that negativity can resolve.

Because of the confusion between forgiveness and reconciliation, victimizers will often take advantage of the commandment to forgive, pressuring people into forgiving and then interacting with that individual again. Take an alcoholic, abusive spouse as an example. He drinks and beats his wife. The next day, when he is sober, she says she will leave him. He apologizes and cries, saying he will never do it again. The next week the same thing happens again, so his wife decides to draw the line and says she is leaving. He then says, "You're supposed to forgive me. Jesus says you must forgive, right?" The abuser guilts his wife into giving him still more chances.

If we step back and look at what is really happening, we can see that by staying with him she enables him to continue the same negative cycle. She is willing to forgive in hopes that he will change, but he is not doing his part to reconcile, which in this case means to make the change he promised. In light of the lack of reconciliation, often the best thing she could do for herself, this individual, and her children, is to end the relationship. He is not going to change so long as he is comfortable. People do not change when things are comfortable. Only when there is some pressure, either internal or external, that creates some discomfort does a person wake up and change their ways. Of course, for the sake of Soul, forgive, which means to release any emotional negativity toward the individual. But for the sake of all involved boundaries may need to be clear and firm.

Usually when we think of forgiveness we might imagine one person forgiving another, but that covers only a part of the picture. A great portion of forgiveness needs to be directed toward ourselves. Through my unfoldment process, memories of things I said or did to myself or others that I felt bad or embarrassed about will pop up. I locate the negative feeling in the body and dance it out. In the same way, if the memory of someone else arises and I harbor negative feeling toward them for their actions or even just for "bad chemistry," I dance it out, which keeps things from getting intellectual.

Dance of the Self is an extremely useful tool that we can apply to a great variety of situations on the path of unfoldment, but it's a tool that we use only until we are so consciously connected to Isness that we no longer have any need to dance out negativity because there simply is none. Isness never forgives because there is nothing to forgive, which is to say Isness always forgives instantly. When we have reached that point of grace, nothing gets stuck emotionally, yet we are still able to make clear rules and boundaries for the sake of all involved.

When I was suicidal, a voice spoke through my chest, giving me direction in life. One of the first things it said was, "Find friends who are working for something positive, who have a purpose in life that you respect." One of the best and easiest choices that we can make in life concerns our companions. If we are surrounded by people who are tuned to low frequencies, our own frequency will tend to drop unless we are already far along in the unfoldment process. Thus, if we wish to tune to a higher frequency, we can choose to be around individuals who are tuned to consciousness, right? In order to do this we must begin to take command of our space. You must be the general of your space, or others will be.

Allowing Prayer

"But seek first the kingdom of God and His righteousness,

and all these things shall be added to you."

— The Gospel of Matthew, *The New Testament*

Great wisdom can be found in the above statement when we realize that Allness has no specific gender. We must be mindful that in Hebrew, all nouns and pronouns have grammatical gender. According to the grammatical rules of Hebrew, God had to have gender. Grammatical gender has greatly distorted the original message. Written properly, we must omit all gender related words. Corrected for obvious language distortion, "His" and "Kingdom" would be removed. Once corrected, the passage would read something like this: "But seek first the presence of God and its righteousness, and all these things shall be added to you."

I consider prayer, as commonly expressed, to be a very dangerous thing, indeed. What I have noticed is that even when people get what they want, it rarely benefits their lives, which is to say they are not happier in the long run from getting what they want. If you could choose to grant everyone's prayers just as they request, would you? Would that be healthy? How long would it take before we destroyed the planet with our prayers? Human beings are still bound in the self, and, therefore, our desires are quite dangerous.

I personally never ask anything for myself through prayer because to ask for something for myself is indicative of mind-based prayer. Oftentimes, though, prayer does come through spontaneously, and when it does it's always through the higher frequencies of consciousness, which means that the mind is not directing the prayer. Instead prayer is happening of its own accord through the body. Such a prayer is truly powerful and more likely to have an outcome that aligns with the highest good for all.

The danger comes when we are in mind and praying, which is what commonly occurs with people now. Such a prayer, whether we realize it or not, even if we pray for other people, is inherently selfish, as the mind is entirely of the self. What I would suggest is that tuning to the frequencies of consciousness is prayer — the highest and truest form of prayer. Even if we requested nothing, the frequency alone benefits all that is. Therefore, how could there be a better prayer? When a specific prayer needs to be stated, then it will come through us spontaneously and effortlessly if we are open to it.

Consider de-ritualizing, de-willing, de-personalizing prayer; instead, allow prayer to happen in its rightful place, which is embodied consciousness. Sometimes personal prayers happen through the frequencies of consciousness, so they are not of the self; instead, they come from Isness to express through the body into the world. In this case, the prayer is not from the self but from Isness.

Consider the statement of Jesus: "Most assuredly, I say to you, the Son can do nothing of Himself, but what He sees the Father do; for whatever He does, the Son also does in like manner." Corrected to remove grammatical gender, it would read something like this, "Most assuredly, I say to you, the awakened one can do nothing selfishly, but what the individual sees Isness do; for whatever Isness does, the awakened one also does in like manner."

Once grammatical gender is set aside, this statement is full of insight; what a beautiful hint of consciousness. Untrue prayer issues from the self, whereas true prayer flows from Isness through the body to the world.

Chapter 19 — Beyond Mystical Experience

For some reason, certain people are excellent dreamers, whereas others rarely have dreams, or if they do, they rarely remember them. The same can be said of mystical experiences. I don't often remember my dreams, but I have had many mystical experiences. Why do some people have these experiences, while others do not? I don't know. Judging by the many people to whom I have spoken about mystical experiences, the desire to have them is powerful in many. I suspect mystical experiences are more common than we tend to think they are. Modern humans tend, for many reasons, to overlook or forget the mystical experiences they have had. First, these experiences seem so beyond our normal sense of "reality" that they might frighten us, so we later deny the experience as just a brain glitch, and then, as time passes, the experience slips from memory.

This tendency to forget such experiences was revealed to me while teaching conversational English in Japan. I taught a game called Truth or Lie. During the game, each student tells two unbelievable stories that happened to them, one true and one a lie. The fun is in telling both stories as if they were true. After each story is complete, the listeners can ask questions to help them figure out which story is a lie. Once all questions are answered, the listeners each guess which story is true and which is a lie. Once everyone has verbalized their guesses, the storyteller reveals which story is true and which is a fabrication. The class then opens for discussion about the stories. To give every student ample time to tell their stories and have a good discussion, I dedicated multiple lesson hours to this game.

As I used Truth or Lie with classes for several years, I observed a certain pattern in students. Usually a relatively small number of students could easily recall an unbelievable story. After they revealed their story, I would ask them had they ever before shared the true story. The vast majority of students said they had never told anyone because they feared appearing strange. The "true" stories ranged from ghost experiences to premonitions to visions. Most students admitted that telling the story in class felt liberating once they realized that everyone was enjoying the game. Listeners commonly voiced incredulity, exclaiming, "Really? That can't have happened," even when they themselves might have experienced something equally astonishing.

Upon introducing the game, some students invariably said that they had never experienced anything unbelievable, so they could not tell two stories. I recommended that those students take time to reflect on their lives over the week to see what memories might arise, and I scheduled their stories for a later lesson to give them time. Very often, the content of another person's story would jog a long forgotten memory in a student who claimed to have never had an unbelievable experience. In the event that a student could not recall any such experience by the last lesson, I allowed them to share an experience of someone else that they knew. Doing that allowed everyone to share something.

As the lessons passed, I found that the vast majority of students, roughly 75 percent, could eventually share a personally experienced unbelievable story. I suspect this might be true of society as a whole. In some cases, the mystical experience deviates so greatly from our normal experience that it fades out of memory much like dreams often do a few minutes after we wake in the morning. Or perhaps the experience so shocked or frightened us that we did not want to remember it, and thus suppressed the memory. And of course we may simply forget an unbelievable experience just like we forget a lot of things as we age.

Every moment of life offers an opportunity to question reality and ultimately our perception of self. Mystical experiences make it easier to question because their immense power can break us out of a perceptual rut, so that we begin questioning our assumptions, biases, and beliefs.

Visions, for example, are sometimes described as being more real than real because they tend to be much more vivid and meaningful, standing clearly apart from regular experience, which tends to be dull by comparison. Other visions are so powerfully absorbing that when they happen they feel impossible to differentiate from the real. The person might not understand in such cases that they have experienced a vision until perception returns from the visionary state to normal experience.

Sometimes the vision itself includes a moment of understanding that it is a vision, much like what happened to me as a child when the horse tried to kick me in the head. After I put the horse away, my attention was drawn up to a cloud, which initiated a vision. I immediately knew it was a vision meant to direct my life, but how I knew, I cannot say. I just knew. Furthermore, an experienced individual might come to recognize that a vision was in process due to a greatly magnified feeling of meaningfulness during the vision.

One of the great benefits to having visions occurs at the moment of return to normal perception: the individual might feel unfamiliar within their own body, as if it is somehow foreign. Dissociation from the physical body and the environment can last from a few seconds to days, weeks, or more before one fully re-associates with the body.

This feeling of disconnect with the body is similar to what one feels when the content of the self is resolved. At that time one has a sense of being that is not identified with anything in particular. The clear spaciousness does not stop at the body. The time of dissociation with the body provides a window onto the awakening process, even if it lasts only a few seconds.

Dissociation itself can create another form of suffering, however, which is that one thereafter feels trapped in the body, or that the bodily experience is somehow wrong. This is another form of identification that causes great suffering. Allow for dissociation without the identification of condemnation. Accept the body as an experience to be with, and do not identify with or against it. It simply is as it is.

Mystical experience can come in a variety of flavors. Aside from waking visions, other common ways in which the mystical experience expresses are through visionary dreams, which occur during sleep. An example of a mystical dream is my repeating dream of Jesus that I detailed in Chapter 1. I classify that dream as visionary because it was saturated with meaning and served as a guide for my entire life.

Another common mystical experience is what I call "the download". In downloading experiences, one does not experience any sensory information related to the mystical experience. Instead, one has a feeling that he is receiving some vital information, the content of which he can't yet access. Much like other mystical experiences, a profound feeling of importance or meaning accompanies the download. The precise information that comes through the download often does not reveal itself until days, weeks, months, or even years later, at which time you will likely recall the download experience, when the information originally came to you.

Still another form of mystical experience arrives in a flash of insight or knowingness. People frequently describe this type of experience as a psychic phenomenon. Here is an example of the flash. When I was working my way through college in Southern California, I had a tech support job at a call center. Call centers can be extremely fast-paced and stressful places to work, so sometimes during my lunch breaks I would drive to a nearby nature preserve called Elvin Forest.

Elvin Forest had several good hiking trails, so I would park my car and eat my lunch as I walked, absorbing the good vibes of nature. I was ever mindful of the time because I didn't want to be late returning to work, of course.

One day after a rejuvenating thirty-minute hike, I returned to the parking area, only to realize that I had locked myself out of my car. I searched my pockets for my keys, but they were nowhere to be found. I looked inside the car, and there they were, still in the ignition. I had no time to call AAA for a professional jimmy to unlock the door. My only option was breaking the car window, which I really did not wish to do. Breaking a window to retrieve keys is a poor return on investment!

Even if I broke my window to get the keys, I saw, I would need green lights all the way back to the office just to be on time. Just then, another vehicle pulled into the parking area, and a middle-aged lady got out with a walking stick, ready for her hike. Suddenly my body surged with energy as I saw her fumbling with her keys. I knew without doubt that her truck key would open my car. It made no sense that a Ford truck key would work on a Nissan Sentra, but the feeling was strongly telling me otherwise.

Without another thought, I greeted the woman and told her my predicament. I asked her if I might try her truck key on my car. She assured me that there was no way it would unlock my car door. We compared the keys — totally different. I told her I just had a feeling that her key would open my car, and I had to at least give it a try. She gave me her keys and followed me over to my car out of curiosity. I gave her a wink, put the key into the slot, and turned it.

The lock-nob popped up! It worked! The woman was visibly astonished as I returned her keys. I hopped into my car and drove off, leaving a wall of dust in my wake. By then, I had just two tasks ahead of me: one, I needed to get back to work on time, and two, I needed to figure out how I knew that the truck key would work. By what mechanism had I received that information? Was there a spirit whispering in my ear? Did the car tell me? Was it the key that told me? And, if for example, the key itself had told me, how was I able to hear the voice of the key when the woman could not?

By some small miracle I was not late for work, but my mind rode the key enigma like a wild stallion for the rest of the day.

As soon as I got home, I told my roommate the story. Tim was an extremely intelligent person — a certifiable genius by standard measures. But due to his attitude, his intelligence was a mixed blessing. For him, nothing could possibly be true that was outside of what modern science could prove or what the senses could verify. He was a devout atheist, and I knew even before telling him this story that he would not believe me. I told him anyway.

Tim was an unabashedly arrogant person, one who did "not suffer fools" as he so often reminded me. Obviously amused, he patiently listened to my entire story before bursting into laughter. He reached into his pocket, pulled out his Dodge truck keys, and said, "You mean to tell me that your car opened to a key like this?"

"No, the car opened to a Ford's key, but your key will work too," my mouth said with certainty.

Tim, laughing even harder, tossed me the key and said, "I gotta see this!"

We walked out to the garage, and I put his key in the keyhole with full confidence that the door would unlock. The nob popped up in a snap.

Tim was dumbfounded and yelled, "What the fuck!?!"

We walked back into the house. I sat and pondered the key mystery for a time and then suddenly energy surged through my body again as my hand reached into my pocket and pulled out my keys again. I looked at the house key and said, "This house key will unlock it too!" We went out to check, and, sure enough, it unlocked the car door. Then, in a flash, I had the answer. I knew why all these keys were working. I realized that my Nissan had been broken into before I bought it, and the locking mechanism was destroyed and never repaired — almost any key would have unlocked it!

The lingering problem was that I knew why all of these keys could unlock the door, but I still could not understand how I knew. If Tim were in my exact circumstances at Elvin Forest, it would have never occurred to him to try another person's keys, because his logic would not accept the possibility of another key fitting his door lock. He would have been forced to break his window or call for assistance, and he would have been late for work. How could I know, when Tim would not have known?

As with all experience, having mystical experiences can be helpful or harmful depending on the attitude we take toward them. For those on the awakening path, visions, premonitions, and other mystical experiences can cause the mind to leap into overdrive in the attempt to understand the nature of those experiences. Through the attempt to understand the essence of mystical experiences, limiting identifications or belief-systems are birthed. Awakening individuals reaching any fixed conclusion about anything is anathema.

Not realizing the dangers of identification, I spent a great many years in my search before I came to the understanding of what was happening in my mind during my attempt to grasp mystical experiences. In retrospect, I needed to know out of ego. I wanted to create some sort of supernatural story out of these experiences — something grandiose to make me feel special. For example, with the car-lock experience, I wanted to know if it was spirit that taught me, or God, or the key. I wanted to believe in something — or more precisely, I wanted the situation to fit a belief system, or at least to find a belief system that could account for this phenomenon — and I did. But years passed before I realized that the phenomenon happened regardless of any belief system, that any belief system was too small to encapsulate the mystical experience, let alone life. I then saw that I did not need to have a belief system for such "knowings" to occur, so long as I was not opposed to such things when they came to me. What's more, it is actually easier for these knowings to occur without any belief system clouding my mind.

I found it surprisingly liberating to have no need for a belief system! There is no need to force every experience into the framework of a belief system if you simply do not have such a system. You can be more aware and more present simply by resting in the present moment, open to all that is, without trying to control it or grasp it with the mind. Truly, a marvelous way of being!

Once you have a sufficiently powerful mystical experience, you realize that your brain is capable of creating experiences far more vivid than "reality," and then you might begin to wonder, "If my brain can create vivid experiences that are not objectively 'true,' how do I know that my normal reality is real?" You might try getting someone else to verify your experience by asking them if they are seeing the very same thing that you see, but regardless of their answer, you can't be sure they are not just a part of the hallucination. Realizing this, you might wonder if all experience is illusory. What if everything that you ever valued or thought to be true were just a dream? How can you prove your existence? What you will find is no matter how you try, there is no way to verify your existence. The attempt to verify one's existence is extremely valuable, though, and I highly recommend everyone take the time to really look into the matter, for in such explorations one awakens from the dream of self.

The reader might never have a vision, but that is fine, because the inquiry process is what matters. Visions help to stimulate these questions, just as vivid dreams do. If you believed a dream to be real while you were in it, then you were duped. Could it be that you are also duped by your sense of self?

If you take such questions seriously, they can lead to a terrifying place that I call "the abyss," wherein all that you ever believed to be true falls away leaving nothing but eternal, black emptiness. If you fear letting go, the experience is horror beyond description, and you will do all that you can to claw your way back to identification with your life experience.

Transcending the abyss does not happen through identification, but by fully relaxing into and loving the abyss even if you could never come back. By loving nothingness, you might find that the void transforms into blissful clarity that then shines through your life when perception returns to the physical experience.

What are you willing to give up for spiritual clarity? It won't kill you not to have a belief system. People often confuse my teachings as being a belief-system. But what I am teaching comes of direct experience and is expressed merely to help others set aside their biases, assumptions, and beliefs so that they can experience life more directly for themselves. All models of reality break down at some point, and so we only use those models so long as they serve the awakening process. Any model that I put forth is a tool to be discarded once its usefulness has been exhausted. So rather than aiming to be right, we simply aim to be.

Part 4 — Soul and Spirit

Have you ever wondered what is the difference between soul and spirit? Is there a difference at all? Judging by the many religious and spiritual writings that use these words, there is little or no difference between them, as they are commonly used interchangeably. Looking these words up in the Merriam-Webster Online Dictionary does little to clarify, as the meanings are nearly identical.

> *Soul*: the immaterial essence, animating principle, or actuating cause of an individual life ... the spiritual principle embodied in human beings, all rational and spiritual beings, or the universe.

> *Spirit*: an animating or vital principle held to give life to physical organisms ... a supernatural being or essence.

So, what is the difference between spirit and soul? For the sake of this book, I define them distinctly, to highlight their differing functions within the multiverse. These terms may be used differently by other teachers, but I need to differentiate these two things to clarify function and allow for a flow of understanding. Please forgive if this seems tedious.

Before I go on, please understand that none of what I write here constitutes a belief system; that is, I am not identified with the information conveyed here. I am merely sharing what I have received through the visions during my unfoldment process. I have no way of verifying the "truth" of it, but what I have seen has proven helpful to me in my awakening path. I include it here in the event that you too might find it helpful.

To personally identify with any model of "reality" would be to place a roadblock in my own unfoldment path, something I would prefer not to do. From my perspective, that which is true of life happens regardless of belief, and since we don't get any spiritual bonus points for believing, it is wise to soften beliefs so that they serve the awakening process and discard each that does not serve as soon as possible. I'm not saying that beliefs are devoid of value, for beliefs, in their rightful place, do serve a function — to motivate action in the world. After all, if you did not believe that a door would allow you to enter into another space, you would never use a door.

Finally, to convey the content of this chapter in words, I must necessarily sequence and refer to this content in a way that the mind can digest it, which means I must take what is inherently beyond time and place, and run it through the lenses of time and space.

As I stated earlier, everything in the multiverse has/is Soul, including elementary particles and atoms, but only life-forms have individuated spirits. Soul is the image-free energy within each individual in the multiverse and beyond. Each and every atom in the multiverse has Soul. All cells and organelles within cells have Soul. Plants and animals, planets and stars have Soul. Humans also have Soul.

Soul is immortal and timeless. Soul cannot be bought or sold, nor can it be killed or destroyed. Soul can be likened to water in that it is formless as a gas but mutable as a liquid. Like the way frozen water maintains the form of its container, Soul also takes on the dimensions of its container.

Soul provides the possibility of unfoldment. When Soul energy is used responsibly, in alignment with its pure nature, great love, integrity, and service are possible. Soul is not the self, although the self is constructed of Soul energy.

The spirit is the body-image-template of the individual life-form within the multiverse. The spirit, like the self, is entirely made up of Soul energy. We could say that spirit and Soul are different phases of the same energy.

We can think of the self as a temporary construct that serves functionality within the immediate incarnation. Because the self is meant to serve functionality in the world, it contains much more detailed information than does the spirit. The self is found entirely in physical memory. The spirit contains overarching themes such as incarnational memory, incarnational/unfoldment trajectory, virtues, vices, talents, passions, et cetera. By contrast, the self contains much more specific information that is subject to rapid change relative to the information held in the spirit. The information of the self includes your personal name, likes, dislikes, proclivities, specific knowledge, tastes, preferences expressed in the five senses, and so on.

In this section, we will learn of the relationship between the self, the spirit, and Soul and how that plays out in the wheel of life. From this foundation, we rediscover the true transformative power of unconditioned love, a power without which humankind would be eternally bound in the matrix of the mind, suffering from the trauma that inevitably results from our sense of separation.

Chapter 20 — The Wheel of Life

During the physical death of the body, the individual perspective continues into a nonphysical phase commonly referred to as the afterlife. In truth only one life exists, and that life is not limited to the body. The individual perspective goes into a bodily experience and expresses, and when that perspective departs the bodily experience, it rises or falls into what can be likened to blissful or hellish experiences. Neither of these experiences are eternal, nor are they ultimately true, but they feel true and eternal during the experience.

The Ascent

At the end of a bodily experience (death), the individual's perspective rises from self, through spirit, and finally to undifferentiated Soul, like ice, to water, to gas. As perspective ascends metaphysically, identifications, limited to the self strip away.

Once all negativity has been shed, the spirit goes through a phase similar to dreaming, wherein the spirit vividly projects extraordinary experiences with other spirits that the individual may perceive as having known for eternity in environs that would defy the physical mind's capacity to conceptualize. These spirit dreams contain no negative emotion and are therefore much more vivid and meaningful than experiences of physicality, which contain negativity and disturbance. These projections are occurring at the very instant of death, and because the time discriminating aspect of mind is shutting down, what feels like years or eternity may be a mere fraction of a second in physical time as the body dies or nears death.

Once all spiritual projections cease, Soul is in formless, blissful oneness — Pure Soul. Like water drops entering the ocean, the individual no longer is.

The purity of Soul shining through a fully functioning, identification-free body in service is what humans are ultimately gravitating toward during incarnation. I suspect that this condition is the Heaven on Earth that Jesus spoke of 2,000 years ago, when he said, "behold, the kingdom of God is in the midst of you" and "the kingdom of God is within you." We are tuning to the frequencies of consciousness to unveil this inherent purity while in the body, not just in the "afterlife." When functional purity becomes our reality, then we experience unity.

As the time nears for the next incarnation, perspective descends into spirit, which takes the form of its next incarnation, to become familiar with the perspective of the new life-form. The nascent being may perceive that it is being instructed by others of that species, learning what it is to be in that form. It's a timeless, loving place in an ideal body that does not age, practicing, playing, and preparing. When the spirit has completed its preparations, it is conceived through the right genetic combination, time, and place for its incarnation so that the individual can have the experiences it needs to prepare it for eventual unfoldment.

The stages of the afterlife are the same for humans as for all other life-forms, but certain differences occur in details thanks to belief systems that color the experiences as the human perspective gradually dissolves into Pure Soul in the process of death. We can get a glimpse of the subjective nature of these experiences through comparing afterlife stories as represented by different cultures and religions. When Buddhists die, for example, they may have to cross a river, whereas a Christian may perceive climbing a staircase and going through a doorway or gate. Many cultures seem to travel through a tunnel into the light, while many other people experience being met by family members, ancestors, or spirits who guide them into a brilliant light.

Individuals who have had near-death experiences report a brief ascent into a heavenly experience, only to be sent back to do more work in their current incarnation. Their stories often differ in the details, but the fundamentals are the same. These individuals had unfinished business and needed to go back into the body to complete that business. This type of business is always for betterment on a spiritual level. The personality that gives the message is not as important as the message itself. A Buddhist may perceive that the message comes from Buddha, whereas a Christian may perceive speaking with Jesus. One might just hear a voice in the light and perceive it as God. Still others are greeted by family members who give them the message. The point is not to get caught up in the personality or the images. Look deeper, for when the spirit is shed and all that is left is unconditioned Soul, these details will mean nothing.

As one's perspective nears the threshold of "Heaven," one will be in the atmosphere of knowingness yet still have conditions that alter the perspective, which is to say that one feels deeply what is being experienced as absolute truth, even though it has illusory aspects. The difficulty here is that while sufficient connection to the conditions of self and spirit remain, the truth perceived is conditioned to some degree. For this reason, a Buddhist, a Christian, a shaman, and an atheist could reach the edge of "Heaven" and come back with significantly differing stories that to them are absolutely true.

Whatever and whomever we see during the ascent is a projection for the sake of communication and is not entirely real. However, these projections carry a message that helps to get the individual back on track in life according to the individual's stage of unfoldment. Forget the messenger and pay attention to the message, because back on Earth there will be conflicting accounts of other individuals' differing experiences of "Heaven." The only stage of such ascent that is not at least partially a projection is the stage of Pure Soul wherein the spirit is fully shed.

Once the Self is fully dissolved, and perspective is in the pure spirit phase of the ascent, the presence of Isness is almost palpable. At this phase, we will perceive Isness through the filter of the spirit and positive memories. Thus, a Christian may perceive Isness as a white light, for example, or an old man with a long, white beard. A Hindu may perceive Isness to be a totally formless presence, or as a favorite god such as Vishnu. The possible projections are as varied as there are individuals. In any case, it's a profoundly peaceful inspirience.

Perspective then transcends spirit, and all that remains is formless, timeless, unconditioned bliss wherein projection ceases. In this deepest and truest state of the ascent all are having the same inspirience, which is to say that the individual perspective is no more, although the inspirience of unity probably will not be remembered once perspective reincarnates again, because mind is not active during the inspirience of Pure Soul.

Once the Pure Soul stage is complete, perception descends like a funnel cloud to reform spirit and prepare for the upcoming incarnation. During this phase, the individual may perceive being instructed by a wise teacher or mentor. The individual sees the degree of darkness and division that they are working toward resolving in their next incarnation. At this time the spirit takes note of higher learning, core relationships, and important events to be encountered. During the upcoming incarnation, these forces will attract experiences and people that serve to draw the individual, often in unexpected ways, toward unfoldment.

The pre-incarnation phase for each spirit is unique, but regardless of the details, the feeling of the afterlife is timeless, like an eternal moment of bliss. When the time is right an intense pressure builds to pull perspective back into physicality.

Like water evaporating as heat rises, only to condense back into drops to rain down onto the earth, and refreeze — so does the spiritual perspective rise and fall.

The Descent

Just as there is a blissful ascent, there is also a painful descent. The descending experience happens for individuals who are so unconsciously blocked and or identified with the sense of separation that they have effectively shut down, drowned out, or distorted conscience to a point where it no longer speaks to them in a beneficial manner, if at all. Only potentially unfolding individuals experience the descent; the perspective of flora and fauna does not descend beyond the physical.

Although ordinary people may have done many things they are not proud of, and maybe continue to do, each of them still has a conscience that at least attempts to speak to them. These individuals may lie and cheat, or they reactively think and harbor negativity, but they do not consciously identify themselves as being evil, nor are they constantly wallowing in their misery. They do not revel in their negativity or malice, but instead regret it to some degree, even if they are not able to entirely stop the destructive attitudes and behavior. These types of individuals are not the people who experience the descent.

Primarily, the fall is experienced by individuals who are so self-identified with the sense of separation (darkness) that they enflame, defend, or revel in it. Let's use a murderer as an example, one who loves the feeling of power he gets from the fear in his victims, and who is a perfect example of a being self-identified with malice. Such a perspective is too heavy to ascend and quite naturally falls into an uncontrollably separated, what we might think of as hellish, experience. Although what one experiences during the fall is entirely illusory, it does not feel that way during the experience. These individuals believe themselves to be surrounded by potential victims to slaughter, and they kill seemingly endlessly until they grow utterly sick of the hollowness that always arrives once the thrill of the kill fades. They begin to wonder whether there is any meaning in their lives, and whether killing will always leave them feeling hollow in the end. Once this observation sets in, they eventually reach a point at which they grow sick of killing and would rather die than to kill again. They begin to yearn for some deeper meaning in life.

At this moment they begin to ascend out of the hellish experience, and the once deactivated conscience becomes active again. At this point, they may acutely experience the underlying suffering that motivated their murderous compulsions and thereby open to learning.

The individual may perceive himself to be in the presence of a respected teacher or mentor, whom he trusts deeply and instinctively. He reflects on his life with the support of this teacher or mentor. The individual ponders his former incarnation and finds the points at which he made choices against his conscience, and he gets the opportunity to make new choices. When all of his decisions are in alignment with conscience, his spirit prepares for his next incarnation. He is born once more into a physical body with an active conscience, which he now values. During such incarnations the individual still has to account for all actions taken against conscience. With his conscience reawakened, he can continue through the cycle of perception until he discovers the truth within himself and resolves all nonserving divisions.

White-collar crime, in general, offers a very easy way to turn off conscience because this form of criminality is so rarely detected or prosecuted, as compared to street crime. Because individuals can commit such crimes with ease, they commit them often and easily, thus expediting the deactivation of conscience. Another quick avenue of conscience deactivation through acting against conscience can open when we justify an immoral action as legal. Many of humankind's laws are not actually moral or ethical, and conscience will often speak against actions that those laws support. Do not be seduced by the statement, "Why not? It's perfectly legal."

Destructive addictions can also lead to a descent — whether a sex addiction, food addiction, drug addiction, or even a video game addiction. The type of addiction is not the main factor in determining whether the individual will fall. The determining factor is whether the addiction is central to the individual's life so that it results in near-total dysfunctionality — and whether the individual defends or even promotes the addiction. If such individuals do not manage to resolve this problem before the body dies, they will suffer the fall. No matter the type of behavior, if our conscience is turned off, it leads to a descent.

These severe addictions point to deeper emotional issues, ones for which addiction is a mere symptom, and so during one's incarnation, the productive thing to do is to take courage and face whatever is causing such addictive drives. If one takes the time to observe one's mind and the feelings in the body, the cause can be found, and resolution can occur. The difficulty lies in the underlying identification(s) which may have convinced the individual that looking into the issue will be too painful, and that the individual is not strong enough to do so and maintain sanity. What the identification never reveals is that the addiction already establishes a lack of sanity. Observing the issue from the frequencies of consciousness is the most effective way to re-establish sanity.

When addicted persons' physical bodies die, they will have a hellish experience wherein they gorge themselves with their addiction, experiencing its destruction over and over countless times until they become so entirely sick of it that they utterly refuse to touch it again — and don't.

The descent, properly understood, is not a punishment, but is instead a greatly magnified expression of what the individual has been feeling deep down during their physical experience. The process helps us to get out of a rut that has blocked all possibility for a healthy interaction with life. When conscience is turned off, spiritual unfoldment is no longer possible, and a time-out is necessary to face the issue head-on without interruption.

When the right circumstances appear for perspective to return to physical experience, the individual is born into a family that has the right genetics for their physical body, talents, intelligence, and personality traits. These individuals are born at a time when they are able to work out relationship issues they share with others — people with whom they still have unresolved energy. Truly, every condition needed to work through in that lifetime may be met by being born into that particular family, in that particular place, at that particular time. In this way, all that the individual spirit wishes to accomplish is within possibility.

Is there any way for us to get some insight into our potential afterlife experiences?

To perceive the possibilities, we must open up to the perspective of Isness. From the holistic perspective of Isness all experience and inspirience is happening right now, in the instant, which is to say that life and afterlife are a simultaneous occurrence even if the individuated perspective has no awareness of that fact. The conditioned nature and smallness of the individuated perspective veils the experience of the eternal and creates the sense of time and separation. Being cognizant that all experiential potentiality is now, we can see the possibilities of countless life cycles, at least on a feeling level, for each instant contains the seed of uncountable cycles. Take whatever you are feeling on an emotional level in this instant (much of which may be beyond your capacity to articulate with words) and simply imagine the intensity of that emotion magnified a million-fold, and you will have some idea of the experiential possibilities. There is an entire life-cycle revolving around what we feel right in this instant. Magnifying, observing, and resolving our feelings in the moment allows us to greatly expedite the awakening process. Do not underestimate the immense value of the Warrior's Meditation and Dance of the Self in the awakening process.

Rebirth

When a self-identified individual reincarnates, identifications reemerge in phases as the individual matures because they can exist only if the individual has the ability to respond to certain stimuli. As a baby becomes a child, a teen, a youth, a worker, a parent, middle-aged, and so on, identifications reemerge each according to the phase of human development that they are able to feed upon. Whenever identifications emerge, we have an opportunity to resolve them to Isness, given the awareness, right attitude, and understanding.

In order for an individual to unfold to express Pure Soul through the physical body, all identifications must be resolved to Isness so the energy that was bound up in them can be put to use in true service. Ignorance creates, sustains, nurtures, and protects identifications through a sense of otherness, and through self-protection. For this reason, we do not want to simply push identifications away, which would be just another action based on otherness. Unconditioned love rooted in Soul is the alchemy that allows for identification resolution.

Many of us will discover that we feel an urge to condemn identifications, even if we know better. Whether we admit it or not, we believe that such condemnation is an effective strategy to protect ourselves. The irony is that condemnation is a strategy born of the identification process. Once we realize fully that condemnation is born of identification, and also that condemnation does not bring about positive change in the world, we stop investing Soul into that strategy. Identification resolution occurs to the degree that we consciously embrace Soul, while also perceiving the identification.

Taking this notion further, we also learn to hold people who would call themselves our enemies, people who would do us harm had they the opportunity, in the space of unconditioned awareness. Once we unveil and fully put unconditioned awareness to work in our lives, malice cannot enter our experience. If we still fall prey to malice, that is because there is still a certain amount of condition to our intention, some disharmony or dysfunction within.

How is reincarnation a just way for life to express? Looking into it, we see that through reincarnation we create the world that we will again be born into. Considering the degree of corruption throughout society, the rate that we are overpopulating, depleting resources, polluting, and destroying ecosystems through action and inaction, what kind of experiences are we creating? It's a frightening thought, isn't it? Nonetheless, an unfolding individual makes the best of whatever life brings, without blame, for to do otherwise is to feed victimization — an energy that often leads to a hellish descent.

Because we create the world that we will be born into, simply complaining about our life and the world serves no purpose; instead, we must do something to improve that world, to reduce suffering, which ultimately means that we must resolve the darkness within and act through purity of unconditioned love to actually exert some beneficial impact.

That stated, it's not necessary to believe in reincarnation. What's important is to tune to unconditioned love, rooted in Soul, and allow it to express into the world. In this manner, quite naturally, the world will improve through our expressions and actions of unconditioned love. Many of our beliefs are really excuses not to love; thus, we soften all beliefs and remove all excuses not to love. No matter the situation, turn to unconditioned love, rooted in Pure Soul, and there can be no regrets.

You say that belief leads to suffering, but it seems to me that you believe in reincarnation. That is a big inconsistency.

As the entire "afterlife" experience varies so much from individual to individual, my only unwavering belief concerns what happens when the content of self is cleared. At that moment, Pure Soul is inspirienced. The revelation of Pure Soul is self-evident to anyone who resolves the content of self, so it does not require belief to be true.

Chapter 21 — The Gateway to Understanding

The content of this chapter will affect the awakening soul at multiple levels. I recommend that readers open themselves to receive this information as deeply as possible. The seed of awareness that it plants in the subconscious mind will eventually unravel the matrix of the mind to reveal the most fundamental you, Isness.

Each of us will receive the essence of this chapter at a level that pertains to our personal path of awakening right now; we have no need to compare one level of understanding to another, for we must move from where we are, not where we wish we were. As we move through the awakening process, revisiting this chapter from time to time can reveal something fundamental that will pertain to larger and larger swaths of your life experience. Fully exploring the content of this chapter through daily life can accelerate your awakening.

Spiritual unfoldment is a process of letting go to reveal that which is most fundamental, Isness. What we are letting go of is that which unconsciously limits or biases perception — identifications. Identifications make up the self. One might wonder why, if letting go of the self is the path to Pure Soul and the end of our suffering, do we hold onto the self so tightly?

Human beings are self-conscious, so we have varying levels of fear that stack up pyramid-like within us from what we think of as the most basic, relating to physical survival, to the most complex and ego-based fears at the top. Compared to those of animals with less self awareness, our fears are quite complicated and layered. People tend to think that the most essential form of fear is physical death, but we have more fundamental ones — unbridled suffering, absolute meaninglessness, and eternal aloneness are just a few flavors of fear that we all wish to avoid.

All experience is potentially useful for the unfolding individual, though, even our most fundamental fears. This chapter addresses these deepest fears and explores how they can aid the unfoldment process.

In my description of the Isness inspirience (Chapter 5), I recount meeting a great void: "I went through spirit worlds and what felt like Heaven. Finally I encountered a great void, and just beyond it there was a presence, intelligence, and power so perfect and loving that there are no human words that describe it satisfactorily. It was utterly whole — holy." In that description I glossed over a lot that now needs to be discussed, namely, the great void.

> "The tao that can be told is not the eternal Tao.
> The name that can be named is not the eternal Name.
>
> The unnamable is the eternally real.
> Naming is the origin of all particular things.
>
> Free from desire, you realize the mystery.
> Caught in desire, you see only the manifestations.
>
> Yet mystery and manifestations arise from the same source.
> This source is called darkness.
>
> Darkness within darkness.
> The gateway to all understanding."
>
> — *Tao Te Ching*

"Darkness within darkness" is the void that I describe in Chapter 5. Lao Tzu states that the void is "the gateway to all understanding." He is correct. But there is more to it than that. The void or the abyss, as I variously call it, is also the source of your suffering.

The awakening soul never knows for certain when they might encounter the void, but the ways that it can be encountered are fairly predictable. People typically encounter the void as a result of unexpectedly losing their sense of self, and thus they are most likely to experience it upon reaching deep states of meditation, creating powerful psychedelic trips, or having psychological breakdowns.

Here is an example described by a friend, Rob, who encountered the void during the very first meditation he ever experienced. The meditation was simple. The instructor guided students to half close their eyes and gaze down at the floor at a 45 degree angle, then count down from one hundred, with each breath representing one numeric descent. As they exhaled, they released all thought and physical tension.

As the count descended, Rob's perception of the room began to change in strange ways. The floor and walls began undulating, the colors of the room changed, and then suddenly a field of blackness consumed him, and he found himself in utter void space, with no body and no sense of self. Time disappeared, and he was struck by unbridled terror, for he was absolutely alone, in utter, black, meaninglessness, fearing that he would never return. While in the darkness, he could not even recall what it was that he might return to. He knew that he had lost all that he ever cared for, but the content of the self that he had lost, he could not recall. In blind panic, he began trying to force his mind to create something to cling to, anything to hold onto, so that he would not slip away forever in the dark abyss.

Rob eventually clawed his way out of the void and back to himself, but he swore he would never meditate again and didn't. For Rob, the experience of the void was horror beyond words. If you imagine your worst fear magnified infinitely, you'll still come up short, for in the void there seems to be no limit to fear. In comparison to the void, "hell" is easy.

As I said, during the lead up to the Isness inspirience, I too encountered the void, but when I encountered it that day, I was able to release the fear and relax into it, which transformed it into the Isness inspirience.

If an individual who is fearful of losing the self experiences the void via psychological breakdown, psychedelic trip, or deep meditation, he might very well feel so overwhelmed by the everlasting emptiness, utter meaninglessness, and fear without bounds that he is unable to get past the fear and inspirience Isness.

The void experience is absolute, solitary, eternal, empty, darkness with no form or sense of whom and what you are. The perception is that everything that you have ever known, loved or valued is suddenly stripped away leaving, only the horrific realization that you will be stuck in unformed meaninglessness forever.

Words do the experience of the void no justice, for there can be no greater suffering than is found in the abyss. And an individual who encounters the abyss might gladly choose physical death to escape the abyss if death were possible. But in the abyss there is no perception of the body, so death is not an option.

For individuals with fear of total release, the instant that they encounter the void, blind panic overcomes perception as they try with all their might to anchor onto time and form, hoping to reconstruct a sense of self. Even a second by the clock can seem like eternity in the abyss. If we can relax into the void, the experience shifts to that of Pure Soul. But if the individual is unable to let go of fear and relax, eventually, perception shifts and returns to physicality.

The process of identification born of fear motivates the clouded mind to continue identifying, and it engenders countless universes, as I describe in Chapter 10. Most of us do not directly experience the void as did my friend Rob, but we do experience it indirectly through our lives. The void or abyss reflects an unconscious fear that our lives are utterly meaningless. The uncontrollable thoughts and feelings that swamp your mind are unconscious attempts to avoid that underlying fear, so that you can continue to get up and go about your day as society says you should.

When we are depressed, we are experiencing a tether of the abyss. During depression it is hard not to think that our life is pointless. We might begin entertaining thoughts of suicide during this time because death seems to appear reasonable when life has no meaning.

Here are a few typical thoughts which reflect that the abyss is rising up within us: "I'm worthless," "I'm not good enough," "The universe is so vast that my life is just like dust in the wind," "In this vast universe, my suffering means nothing," or "Human beings are like a cancer on the earth. The planet would be better off without us." Repeatedly identifying with such thoughts and feelings will take us to very, very dark places over time.

It is entirely possible to have these feelings without the thoughts that accompany the feelings. In such a case, the individual feels dull and flat, like beer with no suds but without any idea why they feel that way. Given enough time, nihilistic thoughts will arise.

Most every adult on the planet has had these or similar thoughts and feelings from time to time. These experiences can be very instructive if we are determined to learn from them.

But the void offers an inverse experience, also most commonly accessed during states of deep meditation, psychological breakdown, or psychedelic trips. Instead of absolute meaningless, eternal, empty, darkness, the inspirience is absolute, eternal meaningfulness, with no form or sense of whom and what you are. It is a blissful, Pure Soul inspirience.

Counter intuitively, at an unconscious level, unawakened individuals tend to fear unbound meaning just as much as meaninglessness, and that fear blocks the inspirience of Isness. Why would we fear unconditioned bliss, you might wonder? Maybe because one has to give up everything that the ego clings to to have the inspirience. Inspiriencing Pure Soul, while living, is the metaphorical equivalent to reentering The Garden of Eden, a metaphor used in Chapter 11. The guard at the gate of Eden is not cherubim and a flaming sword, but, is, instead, the void. Only Pure Soul, which is no thing, can pass through that gate.

Experiences of the abyss and Pure Soul are not mutually exclusive. If you spend enough time visiting the abyss, you could eventually let go of fear, and suddenly the experience will transform into unconditioned meaningfulness, Pure Soul. From such a transformation we can realize unconditioned love.

Only highly awakened individuals who come close to the void will recognize that they harbor a fear of absolute meaning. As they approach unconditioned meaning, a sudden visceral fear arises – fear of letting go and assuming the immense responsibility that comes with realizing absolute meaning. The fear is overwhelming, and the individual might be unable to articulate the fear until after they have awakened still further.

At a certain point of awakening, our nervous system constantly compares our lives with Pure Soul, and the more we fall short, the more anxiety and depression we feel. To get a sense of what I mean, take a look at how much of your life is spent living trivially by your own standards. Consider how your life would be different if you felt that all that you did or did not do was vitally meaningful. In short order, you would start making better use of each moment, spending less time distracted, or you would step off the path until you were ready to make those changes.

To live unconditioned meaning, one must release the self and fully engage in life in the moment, holding onto nothing. Until we do that, what we hold onto will hold us back. But we can only let go when we are ready to do so. This process is like a flower blooming. It happens only when all is ready for blooming. You cannot force awakening, but you can feed and water the plant.

Once we have sufficient insight, we realize that unconditioned meaning and absolute meaninglessness are actually just two faces of the very same thing. The profound differences between these two fundamental experiences derive from the attitude through which perception filters the experience. If the attitude is fear, then that fear comes to the fore and paints the experience, creating the abyss, from which one must either claw one's way back to self identification or relax into in order to pass through it. The individual who masters unconditioned gratitude and love perceives no abyss, only Pure Soul.

Very few human beings on the planet right now have realized they have been unconsciously avoiding the abyss. The mere realization that one is avoiding the abyss indicates a highly aware individual. And as the number of individuals on the planet who are thus awakening increases, those not open to spiritual awakening will cling to identification even more desperately. Those who identify traditionally will cling ever more strongly to the past, while the more liberal leaning might identify with whatever is new. In extreme cases, individuals begin to play with identification, morphing from one persona to another much like role-playing, or they might identify themselves as things that most people would consider to be absurd, like a dragon. All of these responses are born of deep fear, which stimulates constant thought and emotion, and the desire to identify.

During a common day, we go about our lives bouncing between relatively meaningful and meaningless experiences, failing to perceive what is going on at a deeper level — the ever present potential represented by void and Pure Soul. Our daily experiences range from the pleasant to unpleasant, meaningful to meaningless, but we automatically associate our sense of self with all of it unwittingly.

Unconscious avoidance of the abyss keeps us in a near constant state of low-level tension as mind runs on and on in the attempt to distract us from underlying feelings that we aren't good enough or that our lives are meaningless. We also avoid the realization of absolute meaning because deep down we instinctively know that such awareness would require us to take full responsibility for our attitude and require a lot of hard changes in our lives. Our entire body is programmed to sense meaning and give feedback as to when we are living meaningfully or meaninglessly; so as long as we are in the body, we can't entirely avoid the message.

Early in the awakening process one might be tempted to give up identification with the negative or unpleasant, while remaining attached to and identified with the positive or pleasant. This tendency will last until we realize that we can only go so far while anchored down by any identification, even a "positive" one.

One experience with the void demonstrates beyond all doubt that most of our suffering there comes from the sense of losing what we knew and loved. So if we identify with the "positive," then we suffer that loss when we enter the void. This principle reflects in our lives as well. Our greatest suffering comes from losing that which we love, which was positive. You love and identify with your baby, who unexpectedly dies, and you spiral into suffering. You have assumed that your baby is yours, and that it should have a long life, so you suffer. Can you fully love your baby and let her go when it is time? Why do we assume that death is wrong? Why do we assume that a longer life is better? Let go of these assumptions, so that you can begin to love less selfishly.

Looking at the "negative," we can see that much of what was unpleasant in our lives constitutes the path of our awakening. The perceived polarities of positive and negative actually just form opposite ends of a circle that curves from pleasant to unpleasant and back again repeatedly. So long as we identify, we move from one to the other quite naturally. Upon realizing that even identification with the positive leads to suffering, we let go all identification and begin to fully engage in life, no matter what it brings, while fully releasing it once the moment has passed. Life then overflows with meaning beyond words.

Put simply, our two greatest fears are that our lives mean nothing and that our lives mean everything. When you are ready, you will step through "the gateway to all understanding." But until then feel free to identify with anything that you wish for as long as you wish. At some point, you may seek to leave the prison of identification. At that time, you will be ever more careful to identify with neither the pleasant nor the unpleasant, for to identify with anything is to imprison awareness within the confines of self, which reflects in the seemingly endless avoidance cycle of ego death and rebirth — the wheel of life/suffering.

Chapter 22 — Removing the Veil

The path into the light seems dark,
the path forward seems to go back,

the direct path seems long,
true power seems weak,

true purity seems tarnished,
true steadfastness seems changeable,

true clarity seems obscure,
the greatest art seems unsophisticated,

the greatest love seems indifferent,
the greatest wisdom seems childish.

— Tao Te Ching

Visit www.richardlhaight.com/links to download a pdf document listing the frequencies.

8 - Emotion, Feelings, Will

9 - Thought, Imagination, Memory

10 - Curiosity, Relaxation, Innocence

11 - Observation, Sharing, Compassion

12. Silence, Acceptance, Appreciation

Observing our reactions to abyss experiences, we can see that the identification process is in large part an unconscious strategy to keep us from falling into the abyss. Yet only by letting go of identifications and the fear that stimulates them are we able to transcend the abyss and experience Pure Soul in daily life. In reality, we are always connected to the abyss/Pure Soul at a deep unconscious level, and that connection provides the blockages we face in life. Just as a change of attitude toward the abyss can transform it into a Pure Soul inspirience, so too does a change of attitude toward the blockages in our lives transform them from obstacles into stepping stones on the awakening path.

So long as we fear the abyss, at an unconscious level we will desperately continue to feed identifications because they appear to keep us from falling into the abyss. Thus, although identifications are vampiric in nature, we have a co-dependent relationship with them that sustains and empowers them. The irony is that the fear generated by identifications creates the abyss experience. But until we recognize that fact, we will continue paying the price of the identification protection racket. In a way, the abyss is not ultimately real. We only experience it when we fear letting go. Thus, exploring identifications, fear, and attitude is vital to the awakening process.

Everything within the multiverse has and is Soul, even atoms, because all is ultimately an expression of Isness. Just as when ignorance defines itself it produces a mental bubble, a universe, so also does the individual, when self-defining, produce a mental bubble that is fueled by Soul. As that bubble is filled with the fundamental energy of perception and life, it takes on a life and identity of its own, which I call an identification. All identifications are inherently unstable because there is no stable answer to the question "What am I?" The furthest one can go toward that answer and not create a disharmonious mind-bubble or identification is to say, "I am."

Identifications, both positive, such as, "I am kind" or negative, such as, "I am a loser," are disharmonious because they are untrue; consequently, they are always leaking energy and need to feed in order to survive. They parasitize their creator, the individual, by agitating and causing stress.

The individual feeds identifications by reacting to the agitation, unconsciously binding a little more Soul energy into these dark bubbles. With each reaction awareness of Soul grows more veiled. I call this a bound soul. As Soul binds, the individual is pulled deeper into the matrix of the mind, a very disharmonious and insecure place where thoughts and emotions constantly harass. Therefore, bound souls know no peace until they unfold to express Pure Soul in daily life.

Identifications all exist within certain energetic frequencies, and when we live our lives tuned to those frequencies, quite naturally we feed and create identifications. As a result, we suffer from the matrix of the mind. But still higher frequencies are available that do not feed or create identifications, but instead resolve them back to Pure Soul, which is harmony. When we remain in these higher frequencies, the energy of Soul gradually unbinds, which ultimately leads to true liberation.

When one tunes to the lower-frequency classes — emotion, thought, memory, or imagination — Soul energy is bound. When incorrectly using the senses, which means to focus on one sense to the exclusion of others or to focus all senses on one thing to the exclusion of the totality, the sensing stimulates memory, imagination, thought, and emotion, which also bind Soul energy. But once we realize that we have a choice as to what we tune to, we may begin tuning into higher frequencies and, thus, gradually find freedom.

Whenever we use consciousness incorrectly, this binds up some Soul energy into a dark form. Just as the multiverse is the projection of self-definition, so does projection within the consciousness of an atom or an animal or a human cause Soul-binding. For the human, the birth of a thought-identification(9) begins when an individual identifies the self with a mental statement such as "I am ugly" or agrees with someone's assertion "You are ugly." At that moment a sliver of Soul energy gets bound up as the ugly identity, which will then assert "I am ugly" whenever it needs to feed. The individual's mental/emotional reaction is the food.

It's probably easy to see how the statement "I am ugly" would create disharmony for the individual, but what about the opposite statement: "I am pretty"? Isn't that good for the individual? No, it's not, because it's using the mind, which is based on opposites, contrasts, and comparisons. If I am pretty, does that not by definition mean that other people are uglier? I am holding myself up and unconsciously putting others down. What happens when someone is prettier than I am? If my sense of self is tied to my appearance, then I have been put down. This comparison process, a process born of a sense of otherness, is the imbalance. Whenever we play this game, we sliver off a little Soul and lose a little more clarity.

These identifications are very unstable, as they are based on disharmony, so they need to feed regularly. They buzz around in the mind constantly, seeking to agitate and catch our attention to inspire thinking. The thought "I am ugly" now leads us into thinking about being ugly, for example, by way of remembering a time when we were told we were ugly and how that made us feel, or maybe by going into a problem-solving mode to consider how we might be less ugly through applying makeup or getting our hair done, et cetera.

Many teachings say that we should make positive statements to ourselves such as, "I am confident," but those statements create and sustain identifications just as surely as do negative statements. Consider any activity that you are truly confident at, and pay attention to the mind when doing it. If there is true confidence, we can work in total silence, with pure absorption, at that activity.

Speculation, concepts, theories, and belief systems all come about as a result of ignorance and a sense of otherness. Present-moment curiosity and questioning, by contrast, do not bind Soul, because they are open. What binds energy is thinking, speculation, and the conclusions that we create to answer our own questions. These modes come from our pre-existing paradigm, our perspective on the world, which means, essentially, that thinking, speculation, and conclusions all come from memory. Another common form of binding happens when we blindly accept the conclusions of others without having any insight. To blindly believe anything without insight, whether it is objectively true or false, is to bind Soul energy.

Businesses, cultures, societies are all built around thoughts, concepts, theories, and beliefs. And all are of the mind, which means they feed identifications. Thus, identifications do not affect just the individual; they spread their seed and affect communities. When enough people accept a concept, theory, or belief, then external structures, cultures, and traditions accrue around the accepted idea. Once a concept or belief reaches the stage of popularity, tradition, or "fact," it becomes very difficult for the individual to speak out or act against the communal habit or common sense of what is true due to the backlash of the majority. How can the individual be honest about something when reputation, income, business, lifestyle, social position, sense of self, and so forth, rest on a commonly accepted falsehood? Can we stare in the face of the accepted falsehood and tell the truth when it may cost us our position, our marriage, our status, our friends? Building communities around falsehoods that cause endless frustration and disharmony to maintain – this identification engine has been a common denominator in the history of civilization.

The more powerful identifications, especially ones related to trauma, will try to convince us that we need them to survive; that they help us or protect us. Justification and pride are perfect examples, as they tend to work together in convincing us that, no matter our wrongs, we must defend our words and actions and never admit our mistakes. Of course, this causes tremendous disharmony, but pride and justification tell us otherwise, or blame (another identification) will accuse someone else.

Shame is another identification, one that tries to get us to admit our wrongs by beating us down emotionally. "You should be ashamed of yourself" and "I am ashamed of myself" are perfect examples of shame's negative influence. Of course, admitting a mistake is extremely important, but we should admit the mistake based on alignment with our sense of what is right, not unkind self-talk.

A perfect example of shame is a story a single mother once told me. When her only son was about eight years old, he and his friends stole a hood ornament off a Mercedes-Benz. A mother of one of his friends found the ornament and realized her son had stolen it. She called the school to report the crime. All the parents involved were summoned to the school to meet with the principal and were shocked that their kids had stolen.

When the mother who told me this story returned home with her son, she took him to his bedroom and asked him, "Why did you do something like that? It's wrong to steal." If she had stopped there she would not have fed or created shame, but she continued: "You know you are my only son, and you don't have a father. If you do something good, people will think, 'Wow, he was raised in a good way, even without a father. His mom must be great. But if you do bad things like this, people will think negatively of kids raised by single mothers.'"

Even though this story occurred many decades ago, the mother regrets evoking shame because she feels that, after that talk, her son began repressing himself. Many times parents use emotion such as crying to try to amplify the feeling of shame. This only feeds identifications further. Of course, the child may stop wrong behavior because of shame, but it conditions the parent and the child in unhealthy ways and exacts a toll on Soul.

Identifications like this can entrap entire societies. We can see this phenomenon at the national level, where no matter the destructive actions of one nation against another nation, many in the perpetrating society become angry if the leader apologizes for the destructive action, feeling that to apologize is to admit weakness. But just as we do not respect a person who justifies and is too prideful to admit mistakes, neither does the world respect a country that refuses to apologize. The true damage is not in the arena of public opinion, though, but at the level of Soul. If we justify or defend our mistakes, we are destined to repeat them, and each time we do, a sliver of Soul is trussed up.

The best way to stop feeding these types of identifications is to admit mistakes up front, even if no one confronted us on those mistakes. An ex-convict friend of mine, Steve, long ago exemplified this principle to me. He had told a self-inflating lie in our conversation, which I failed to notice, but to my surprise, he said, "I don't know what came over me, but what I said isn't true." He then explained the actuality. I was stunned because I had never witnessed this type of honesty before in my life. The respect I had for him at that moment was beyond measure.

Steve's honesty so surprised me that my curiosity redirected the conversation into how he came by this method of honesty. He told me that during his stay in prison, his roommate, Lauren, was an older man and a very sincere, repentant Christian. When they were out on the yard, Steve had gotten into a verbal confrontation with another inmate. Steve was clearly in the wrong, but he would never admit it. When he and Lauren got back to their cell, Lauren said, "I have noticed for a long time that you have difficulty admitting when you are wrong. It's hard to admit you are wrong, but you need to do it once. It will be really hard, but after that it gets easy. Then it doesn't really matter if you are wrong, because you don't get mad anymore. Instead, you will be able to laugh about it, and you will be a much better person. You just say, 'Ah, I see. You are right.' Lauren continued, 'You don't even have to say that you are wrong; just agree with the other person if they are right.'" My friend started to apply this honesty deeply in his life. I so loved the feeling of this that it planted a seed in me to be honest like that whenever my mouth rode a lie.

It's not weakness to admit a mistake, but strength, if the admission was done out of rightness, not shame. Still, we may encounter people who will try to take advantage of our admission, in an attempt to shame us. Be aware that it's not them abusing us, but their identifications speaking through them, trying to feed. Of course, the person will not realize this, and it will only make things worse at that moment to teach them. If we become upset because of the criticism, then we are just feeding more identifications. It's healthy to sincerely apologize without expecting it to be accepted. If the apology is not accepted, we allow for that while correcting ourselves. We do not make the other person our project.

When we understand how energy is bound in identifications and how to unbind that energy, we begin opening up to answers through insight rather than through thinking, which is of the mind. In this way, we are able to understand things directly. This occurs naturally in the latter stages of unfoldment as the mind begins to quiet more and more. And this insight further expedites our unfoldment if we make use of it.

Emotion functions in part to reflect thought as it comes through the body, but emotion is not limited to direct expressions of such thought. While we create thought-identifications from identifying the self with such statements as "I am smart," emotion-identifications(8) come to be in a more subtle way through simple association. We may never have had the structured thought "I am angry," for example, but still can have energy bound up in anger. Although emotion does function in part as a physical representation of thought, there is more to emotion than just being a reflection of thought. The mind is like a deep ocean with many layers. The obvious layers of thought and emotion we may imagine like the waves at the surface. But below the surface run many layers and currents that are less obvious. These layers are what I call meaning associations; that is, we have impregnated experiences and words with certain associations.

A perfect example of these hidden associations is an experience that two of my mentoring students had by the campfire one night. I had built a good fire before they arrived, then I had them get into a good meditation and marked their energy field edge. Both students were quite expanded. Finally I led them to the campfire. As soon as they approached the fire, their energy fields shrank down, and they retrenched back into mind. I pointed this out to them and asked them if they knew why they had collapsed back into mind. They both thought about it for a moment, and then one responded, "I don't know; I like campfires, so I would have thought that my energy field would have expanded as I neared this fire."

I said, "Well, energy fields do not lie. You believe you like campfires, and that appears to be true if we look only at the surface of your mind, but deeper down there is a negative meaning associated with fire that you are not aware of right now." They meditated on these words and searched their bodies when they neared the fire. They found that, indeed, there was a subtle feeling in the body that arose whenever they got to a certain distance from the fire, and at that very moment their energy fields began to shrink dramatically. As it turned out, both of them had suffered traumatic burns as young children. They had all but forgotten the injuries, but the association had taken root. In the deeper recesses of the mind, that association was still alive and influencing their experience. That was an example of emotion-identification born of an unresolved painful experience. Both of these students resolved that identification, and their energy fields no longer collapsed when they neared the fire.

Interestingly, before they had resolved the fire association, we did a little experiment with words. Even saying the word "fire" would cause them to collapse back into mind. Later we experimented with other words and their effect on the tuning process. We found that many of the words that they believed they had purely positive associations with actually caused collapse. Many of the "positive" words that we hold dear, like love, honor, courage, respect, and so on, are heavily tainted with disharmony in the deeper recesses of mind. In fact, for the vast majority of individuals, their entire vocabulary is heavily tainted, which means that language itself becomes a huge hurdle, blocking us from tuning to consciousness.

Note: we need not have a direct negative experience to conceive a feeling association. Just hearing and believing a story can create feeling associations. For example, if a child had been warned of the dangers of fire in an emotionally charged manner, the child might well develop a feeling association that is equivalent to being burned. Many of our feeling associations were not born of direct experience, but were instead inherited from our friends and family through word of mouth, body-language, energetic atmosphere, and even through bodily memory hidden in our cells.

A second form of unconscious association can occur at the genetic level. Researchers at Emory University discovered that heightened sensitivity to specific smells could be learned by adult rats and then passed through to their offspring genetically. The process involved issuing a mild electric shock in conjunction with a certain odor. Once the mother rat had developed a fear of the specific odor, her subsequent offspring carried the fear of that odor even if conceived in vitro and having no social interaction with the mother. The inherited association continues even into the second generation or pups.

The Emory University discovery is supported by the research of neurosurgeon and trauma specialist Bessel von Der Kolk and others which concluded that descendants of humans who survived horrendous trauma-inducing events such as the Holocaust and slavery, display heightened cortisol levels and poor health outcomes as if they had experienced these shocks directly.

https://www.ncbi.nlm.nih.gov/pmc/articles/PMC4677138

https://www.nature.com/articles/s41598-018-29107-0

Could it be that feeling associations affect our bodies at the level of genetics? If so, then releasing counterproductive feeling associations offers a way of healing our genetic makeup and that of our offspring as well. Science does not fully understand how the process of inheritance works, but I am certain that life improves when we start paying attention to and resolving feeling associations that have outlasted their initial purpose.

With regard to an emotional identification with anger, the association often has roots in events where we felt that anger made us powerful. Once the association forms between anger and power, then every time anger arises, we unconsciously flame it because we like feeling powerful. Anger then becomes a primary emotional strategy and a part of our personality. It feels like a reward.

The base level feelings are vulnerability, fear, aloneness, and a bracing against change. The most basic emotions are agitation and frustration, so we want to be very aware of these energies within the body. For most identifications, the most successful way to harvest food is to make an individual so uncomfortable that the individual starts trying to escape the present moment by projecting into the future or the past through imagination and thinking, which is psychological time. As the individual reacts to agitation, Soul energy is siphoned off by the identification, which when full goes into a state of torpor and ceases to agitate for a time.

Emotional tendencies come from associating emotion with the self. A person may have unconsciously associated himself or herself with being a kind person. In such a case, that individual has actually created an emotion-identification called kindness, which produces a weak energy projection around the body attracting those who would wish to take advantage of that weakness. Kindness then uses our bodies like puppets to express itself and cause disharmony. How is that bad? Kindness makes it difficult for the individual to say, "No" when "No" is the most appropriate answer. This then causes a tremendous amount of stress on the individual, which feeds the identification. When resolved to Soul the person will naturally express love, gentleness, and service, but will maintain the ability to draw a line when one needs to be drawn because the energy is clear.

All of the traumas of our lives are emotion-identifications. The bigger the trauma, the more powerful the identification. These identifications create such strong emotional urges when they rise up that resisting them may be nearly impossible. An extreme example of this sort of trauma identification is when a young child has been sexually molested. Often when the child matures they re-enact the trauma, wanting to be sexually dominated or the opposite. Many individuals who were sexually abused as children may not even remember it because the trauma was so overwhelming that their psyches blocked it out of accessible memory. Even if they can't recall the abuse, they still carry the trauma that acts out through sexuality.

Weaker identifications may express in common relationship arguments amplifying distrust, judgmental attitudes, and aggression. Here is a common example I hear regularly: "I know that making that negative comment to my partner is not going to help, but I say it anyway, and we end up in an argument. The funny thing is, I am aware enough to know that I shouldn't say it, but often enough I end up saying it anyway. And when I say it, it even kind of feels good — like I scored a point or won. Of course, my partner gets really upset, and we end up in a terrible argument." This situation perfectly exemplifies what I mean when I say the individual was unconscious. They were not actually in control of themselves; they were in the passenger's seat. Their control was usurped by emotion-identifications well before they actually said that hurtful thing. We need to develop the ability to notice signs of an identification coming out of torpor at a very early stage, before the identification fully awakens. Otherwise, we often wait too late to regain balance, and our odds of successfully piloting harmoniously through the situation are greatly diminished.

It may have been just one identification or several that urged the individual to say something hurtful, but regardless of how many created the urge, certainly many identifications fed off of both individuals during the argument. Identifications care nothing for marital happiness; they are concerned only with feeding and will do whatever it takes to get us to act or react in negative ways.

Even though an identification moved us to speak those hurtful words, we cannot say, "The Devil made me do it," can we? True, an identification took over and controlled the body like a puppet, but the individual bears sole responsibility for it because we do have the ability to intervene in that process. We are responsible for all that expresses through the body, either consciously or unconsciously. Imagine this scenario: a police officer is using a bullhorn in hopes of bringing a crowd under control. Someone comes up to the officer and asks to use the bullhorn, and the officer agrees. That person uses the bullhorn to enflame the crowd, and violence results. Doesn't the officer bear responsibility for lending the bullhorn to someone else to use? Absolutely. Similarly, we bear responsibility for all that we allow to express through our bodies, for we have empowered all of it, even if unwittingly.

We should not equate taking responsibility with shame or blame, which are identifications. It simply means making corrections when disharmony arises. People who become good at anything have learned to correct themselves on some level. We can see children making corrections when they play video games. They observe mistakes and then practice correcting their game-play — with joy. We are simply refining our inner space in much the same way we would correct our game play. Blame and shame are unnecessary and do not serve our highest good.

Deeply traumatic identifications can cause a person to jump into a fight, flight, freeze state, heart-rate elevated, blood pressure up, and bladder constricted, just as if in actual physical danger. A person in this state is highly unstable, so even the most innocuous, well-meaning comment could easily be misconstrued as a personal attack. The body always mirrors the type of energy that is within the mind. If we observe the body, we can cultivate awareness of what was formerly unconscious. A common sign that strong identifications are taking over is a feeling of detached emptiness that enables a person to be unfeelingly cruel and harsh. Ideally we will notice a subtle feeling of agitation, tension, or even dullness in the body. This feeling is most often located in the chest; we might notice our breathing is altered. As you become more aware, you will be able to feel how different frequencies of disharmony tend to show up in different parts of the body. By observing this, we can become tremendously aware of other individual's disharmony as those frequencies also reflect in our own bodies in subtle ways.

I have seen longtime friendships ended over deep-seated traumas arising unexpectedly. One individual felt belittled and never spoke to her best friend again. Sadly, her friend and all witnesses had absolutely no idea what had happened to cause the relationship to end. It was an unsalvageable mess.

We can also steal attention by letting emotions run unchecked, and it causes tremendous disharmony. Have you ever felt how draining it is to be in the vicinity of certain individuals? Probably everyone knows individuals who are constantly seeking either "positive" attention by showing off or seeking compliments or "negative" attention by way of sympathy. Really, it does not matter whether the attention is positive or negative, so a person may do all they can just to get us angry. All they are seeking is the reactive attention that we give them. Some individuals have gotten so stuck in the rut of attention-vampirism that they annoy everyone around them without even trying. Once we have realized our ability to observe without judgment, we can see that it is not the individual acting like a vampire, but identifications that they have empowered through their daily lives.

A less obvious way to empower identifications occurs through success and performance. Many athletes and entertainers, for example, egotistically feed off of the attention they receive. The attention, no matter the form, is not beneficial to the receiver, as it is not love.

Let's look at an example of an adult who compulsively participates in energy vampirism: the gossip. This person spends every available moment getting people's attention in order to gossip about other people. The gossip gains an initial emotional high from the attention given them through the gossip process, right? But because energy received is absorbed by identifications, the high that the person feels is the frenzy of the feast. Then, of course, other identifications feed on the chaos created from the aftereffects of gossip: lack of trust, frustration, victimization, and so on. Truly, a whole host is fed, but the humans involved only lose clarity. People participating in negativity actually gain nothing of true value from it. They merely provide for an identification banquet, further degrade themselves, and pull other people down with them. That is, of course, until they have insight into this process, and then, little by little, they cease investing in insanity.

Sensing, emotion, thought, and imagination work synergistically through memory to compose the matrix of the mind; separately and together they keep one from being present. Whenever we go into condemnation or comparisons with regard to the self or others; whenever we fail to forgive ourselves or others; whenever we get nostalgic for the past or look forward to the future, we are stepping out of the present. Each time we allow the mind to leap forward or backward in time for emotional reasons, it binds Soul into darkness. The darkness takes on an identity of its own and now needs us to feed it. Each time we slip into distraction, willfulness, or brace against the moment, we feed something. Any time we aren't fully present and tuned to unconditioned love, something is siphoning off our energy.

Nothing can steal our energy unless we wrongly give of it through an inappropriate response. So, it's useless to go into blame, which is yet another identification. The way to properly manage one's energy is to remain present, calm, and tuned to the frequencies of consciousness, while taking total authority over and responsibility for one's energy. The solution begins right now, within each of us, as we tune to an unconditionally loving, clear, and peaceful perception as often as possible. When we collapse out of consciousness and into the mind, we take notice and open back up again. The more we develop this awareness, the freer we all are.

Chapter 23 — Unconditioned Love

The spirit of Buddha is that of great loving-kindness and compassion.

— The Teachings of Buddha

We can see that unconditioned love has been recognized as the spiritual alchemical agent for many thousands of years, because the teachings of Christianity, Buddhism, and most other major religions indicate it as the great vehicle of transformation. Given love's prominent position among religions, why hasn't the world already been transformed by this alchemy?

Is the violent and forceful state of the world a failure of love? If unconditioned love truly is the alchemical agent of transformation, which is being taught to the estimated 500 million Buddhists and 2 billion Christians, roughly a third of the 7 billion humans on the planet, then why is the earth so fraught with disharmony, war, and division? Could it be that unconditioned love is not what is being taught?

Looking into it, we recall that Soul cannot be taught because it's the default and merely needs to be revealed in order to be active in one's life. Even if the teacher is resolved to Soul and therefore unconditioned love, if the listener is tuned to mind, any teachings quite naturally get filtered through the mind. This in turn brings the teachings into a frequency of disharmony regardless of the words used in the teaching. Thanks to the filters of the mind, the love that people learn through religion is an ideation(9), which is to say, in the frequency of ideas or concepts, and, therefore, it is thought(9), which also represents in the body as emotion(8). No transformative power resides in thought or emotion. So, even though the teacher uses the words unconditioned love, unconditioned love(13+) is not embodied by the listener.

An evil-minded person can hide behind the words "unconditioned love." Any person, regardless of moral or ethical standing, can use words like love to mislead people, which proves that the words themselves do not have transformative power. "Spiritual" words do not have transformational power. If they had transformative power, then any evil-minded individual would fear to use them because it would undermine their identification with evil. Words are of thought and are therefore not transformative. We need to go beyond words in order to find harmony.

Apart from the idea(9) of love, another expression of love requires a moment of discussion: personal love(8). Personal love is what we feel for our family, our friends, our pets, and so forth. The intensity of personal love will naturally vary, depending upon the specific relationship. A nurturing mother's feeling of love for her baby may far exceed the intensity of the love she feels for a friend. Regardless of the object of the love, it's still personal, not unconditioned love. Someone may believe that they love their child unconditionally, but the love is exclusive to the child, which means it's not truly unconditioned.

People often confuse emotional vulnerability and affection with unconditioned love, but both are frequencies of the mind, quite distinct from the frequencies of unconditioned love. Emotional vulnerability is something to share only with the most trusted individuals in our personal lives. To share this energy openly with just anyone might open us up to a lot of abuse. Affection is an energy that will reward any state of mind, even a destructive state. If expressed at the wrong time, affection will exacerbate destructive behavior. And since no life-form can be happy when emotionally turbulent, to give affection at the wrong time causes psychological harm.

Because emotional vulnerability opens one to abuse and because affection rewards even destructive behavior, both of these energies need to be expressed very judiciously, so as not to cause harm. Unconditioned love, though, has no vulnerabilities; it defuses disharmonious intention and behavior, and, therefore, it's always appropriate.

The frequencies of emotion encompass a large variety of both positive and negative energies. Within personal love we have varying frequencies for our pets, our children, our friends, our parents. Some of these relationships resonate at much higher frequencies than others. This is normal and natural.

Just as there is a gradation in the frequencies of personal love, a frequency gradation also covers types of anger. Frustration, anger, rage, hatred, and a whole host of other emotions: between each of these lie levels of hostility for which we have no words. On the emotional spectrum, a large frequency range encompasses a tremendous breadth of emotional possibilities, many of which are so subtly different that no words exist to describe them.

In Chapter 11, *The Frequencies of Mind and Consciousness*, I refer to the frequency of emotion(8). The frequency of emotion spans a great range. If we divide the frequencies of emotion in half, the lower segment of the emotional spectrum manifests as almost entirely disharmonious, meaning that tuning to these frequencies harms the body and has no direct benefit. Such emotions include feelings of victimization, uselessness, purposelessness, jealousy, envy, anger, blame, negative expectation, doubt, and so on.

Although no direct benefit accrues to the lowest frequencies of negative emotion, wisdom recognizes that the awakening process often begins when suffering has reached such an extreme level that the individual starts to question their basic perspective on life. Thus, even the lowest frequency of mind can lead to awakening.

In the upper half of the emotional scale, frequencies have clear beneficial aspects to go with their inherent disharmonious aspects. Examples of these double-edged emotions are positive expectation, hopefulness, optimism, faith, enthusiasm, passion, love, and so on.

"Positive" emotions are tethered to "negative" emotions, so whatever goes up must come down. We have hope(8), but then the hope is dashed by an unwanted outcome. We then feel hopeless. Looking at hope even further, we must admit it is born of negativity. We are unhappy or dissatisfied with the present, so we hope for a better future. Hope, as it comes from the mind, is always for the future, which means it's an escape from the present, a judgment against the present situation of our life.

We could even go so far as to say that whatever we call positive is largely judged so from the conditioned vantage point of the observer. When we are feeling good and comfortable, we rarely question our perspective. Most people only begin to awaken after an experience of extreme suffering. Those who are actively awakening tend to deem the awakening process as being "good." From such a perspective too much comfort could be considered detrimental. The wise individual makes use of every possible moment, whether pleasant or unpleasant, so the specific conditions of any situation do not always matter. Only those who are awakening tend to be aware of the fact that each moment is useful and important.

Everything can be of service to awakening, and we need emotion until we no longer need it. We need thought until we no longer need it. Emotion and thought are not wrong, nor are they right; they simply are. For this reason, we cannot force ourselves or someone else into unfoldment.

Once we have matured and are ready to begin consciously unfolding, we can make productive use of our intention through meditation and daily living toward global awareness and unconditioned love. But even when we are ready to begin the unfoldment process, it takes time because we generally have a lot of bound energy to resolve; also because the body needs to adjust to the changes over time. Just as there is no benefit to being impatient with the body's adjustments, there is no benefit to impatience with the process of unfoldment.

This brings us to the conscious frequency of unconditioned love. No one can teach what unconditioned love is because it's not of the mind. Unconditioned love can only be inspirienced. We cannot create it, because it's innately present yet typically inactive. We can, however, tune to it and activate it, which will bring us into the frequency of unconditioned love(13+), the great alchemical agent that purifies and unveils.

Consider this African proverb: "When there is no enemy within, the enemies outside cannot hurt you." An individual rooted in unconditioned love sufficiently has an energetic atmosphere around them that wards off malicious intent. The effect is such that the would-be attacker's body refuses to launch the attack, feeling fear or confusion as their own dark intent is mirrored back at them. This is the natural effect of unconditioned love. This field remains so long as the individual is centered in unconditioned love. If this individual were to go into an emotional state such as personal affection, he or she would become vulnerable. For this reason, if we intend to actualize unconditioned love in our lives, we must clearly realize the difference between consciousness and mind; otherwise we will habitually be tuning to mind and, therefore, suffering.

Chapter 24 — The Bones of Christ

There is no fear in love; but perfect love casts out fear,
because fear involves torment.
But he who fears has not been made perfect in love.

— 1 John, *The New Testament*

For many thousands of years, much of humankind has followed the code of Hammurabi and the law of Moses, which are based on "an eye for an eye, a tooth for a tooth." The operative idea is that justice is made through equal and opposite vengeance. This mentality often leads to the escalation of violence. We can see by the state of the world that violence, revenge, and punishment are not transformative energies.

Several thousand years ago a distinctly new option was introduced to the world through the teachings of both Siddhartha Gautama and Jesus of Nazareth. Through Jesus' story we call it the way of the cross. Siddhartha described it as the way of suffering. This path is expressed in Jesus' admonition as recorded in Matthew 5:39, "But I tell you not to resist an evil person. But whoever slaps you on your right cheek, turn the other to him also."

Nearly a century ago Mohandas Gandhi, in a testimonial to the idea of such nonviolence, insightfully asserted, "An eye for an eye will leave everyone blind." Through nonviolence Gandhi led India to independence from Great Britain, which had enslaved that country under a then-legal but immoral construct wherein white people dominated people of color.

Although Gandhi's use of nonviolent resistance led to the liberation of India from British rule, the world has not fully embraced this courageous, love-based approach, and we remain stuck in vengeance and punishment. Fundamentally, people seem to believe that violence is more effective than love, and, as a result, all of the civil structures of humankind are based on force and violence in the final analysis. How does turn the other cheek work? It's a nonviolent way of resisting oppression and violence while maintaining the dignity of superior moral position. When you are attacked, you calmly accept the attack while maintaining the moral high ground. By this means the oppressor's very attack is proof that they do not have a moral foothold, which lowers their standing in the public eye. Moreover, a person with any shred of conscience will not be able to maintain hostility as he begins to feel the dignity and humanity of the oppressed.

Nonviolence has proved to be an incredibly powerful way of dealing with the aggression and corruption of the world. Through this strategy, Martin Luther King Jr. and others in the Civil Rights Movement of the 1960s made huge progress against the U.S. government and the dominant white society in desegregating the United States and improving the social status of women and subject peoples around the world.

Nonviolent resistance has proved to be extremely powerful, but it's not a bulletproof strategy. Because it's a strategy whose success depends upon specific conditions, it can be countered. The conditions required for nonviolent resistance to be successful are a just cause, a clear message, dignity, and integrity. The counter to nonviolent resistance is to create the appearance that one or more of these conditions is lacking. If, for example, the oppressor can stimulate the protesters to become violent, to lose dignity or integrity, or, at least, create the image that the protesters are violent, undignified, or immoral by infiltrating their ranks, then the protest will not elicit the respect of the larger community, and it will fail. Infiltration is now a common strategy to tarnish the image of protesters around the world.

Nonviolence is a high ideal that was transmitted to the world through individuals such as Jesus and Siddhartha for the purpose of bringing us up to a higher law, unconditioned love. The time to manifest this higher law is now. Imagine a protest so lovingly nonviolent and dignified that authorities and infiltrators alike are rendered unable to attack, their malicious intent preventing them from being able to swing their batons, spray their mace, or vandalize property. Imagine the seed of consciousness planted in the hearts of the aggressors as they realize that violence, force, and fear have no power over unconditioned love.

The more people tune to unconditioned love, the easier it becomes for subsequent people to do so, and the more profound the effects. I see that the practice of tuning to unconditioned love will spread among the populaces of the world, ending anger, violence, and aggression of all sorts. Imagine a nation practicing unconditioned love so thoroughly that terrorism is rendered entirely ineffective as fear turns to love. Would there be any need of a military? Would we need police? When people understand that unconditioned love neutralizes all other strategies, what would the world look like? We are on the cusp of the greatest revelation in human history, which is actually a revolution. This revolution of the heart will affect all of the structures of humanity for the benefit of all life.

As a young boy I awoke to find Jesus Christ lying on the floor, his eyes filled with sorrow, his body lacking bones. "Find my bones, for they are the core of my teaching. Find the essence of my teaching and give it back to the world," he requested. I have spent more than 30 years looking for those bones. I have crisscrossed the globe multiple times in the search. I have read and contemplated. I have meditated and prayed, and through all of it, I was like a blind man fumbling around in a briar maze, unable to locate the exit. Again and again I crashed face-first into the walls, my flesh torn away. But against all logic, something goaded me on. "There has to be a way out," I thought. After years of bumps and bruises, scratches and tears, I have finally realized there is no way out. But there is a way in.

For more than three decades I have trained and dedicated myself to martial, healing, and spiritual paths, having achieved the highest rankings and titles. But at the very core, unrealized even by many individuals teaching these arts, lies the same fundamental principle, the marrow if you will. Each person that I have met, whether "civilized" or "primitive," male or female, old or young, has at their very core this very same marrow, which is Soul.

What are the essential teachings of Jesus, the bones of Christ? Without hesitation, I declare unconditioned love to be the bones of Christ. Without hesitation, I declare unconditioned love to be the bones of Buddha. Without hesitation, I declare unconditioned love to be the essence of any true teaching. This ethos is the essential teaching of all awakened Souls, the true masters, but also, it forms the ultimate path for all individuals regardless of ancestry, culture, deeds, or name. Only through unconditioned love does anyone realize true mastery.

The vision in the Amazon said, "There is conscious light from the center of the galaxy, bathing the earth with ever-increasing intensity." I now see that we will meet that light with the conscious light of our being, bathing the entire multiverse in unconditioned love and thereby resolving all sense of separation. In this way, we may have no need for the collapse of humankind and the probable futures of Hell on Earth. Instead, we will transition into a sustainable, spiritually fulfilling, just human presence on this planet.

All that is, is within you, and you are within it; there is no other. There is absolutely no judgment or negativity of any sort. There is perfect forgiveness, for there is unconditioned love. Although humans have the ability to perceive the illusion of negativity, there is no binding, fear, or ignorance, only total harmony and oneness.

"So be perfect, as your heavenly Father is perfect." This way of being is not only a possibility for all; it's inevitable. There is a presence, intelligence, and power so perfect, so loving that no human words can adequately describe it, and it's you. Now is the time to awaken from the dream of otherness to the realization of unconditioned love. There is no other. Now is the time to prove it to yourself and the world. Are you ready?

Many Blessings,

Richard L. Haight

www.richardlhaight.com

If you feel drawn to write a review that would be wonderful. You can post a review at www.amazon.com. I read every review, and I would love to hear from you.

For notifications of future book, video, and course publications, click HERE to register.

Daily Guided Meditations with Richard L Haight

If you would like support in your meditation practice, we can practice together. Get a free 30-day access to my daily guided meditation service by clicking here.

Glossary

Abyss: the void; a state of no content, context, or the sense of time or self.

Content of the self: the accumulated meaning associations, feelings/emotions, memories, and thoughts which have become the definition and sense of who and what one is and which are the ultimate source of suffering; identifications.

Emotion: a strong feeling (such as love, anger, joy, hate, or fear); feelings.

Expectation: a belief that something will happen or is likely to happen.

Feeling: the undifferentiated background of one's awareness considered apart from any identifiable sensation, perception, or thought.

Feeling Association: an unconscious association with experiences and words which has impregnated into the sense of self at a very fundamental level; meaning associations.

Feelings: emotional states or reactions.

Identification: a largely unconscious process whereby an individual models thoughts, feelings, and actions after those attributed to an object that has been incorporated as a mental image.

Ignorance: described in this work as willfully focusing to exclusion in order to come to a conclusion.

Imagination: the ability to imagine things that are not real: the ability to form a picture in your mind of something that you have not seen or experienced.

Innocence: freedom from guilt or sin through being unacquainted with evil.

Insight: a direct understanding of the true nature of something.

Inspirience: any unconditioned experience; its roots are inspire and experience.

Isness: the most fundamental foundation of all that is. Formless yet throughout all form. Soul and Isness are interchangeable terms indicating the same thing.

Meaning Association: an unconscious association with experiences and words which has impregnated into the sense of self at a very fundamental level; feeling association.

Memory: the power or process of remembering what has been learned.

Persona: a mask that the individual has created over many lifetimes to protect the self and/or to gain a social advantage. Interchangeable with personality in this work.

Senses: the five natural powers (touch, taste, smell, sight, and hearing) through which most people receive information about the world around you.

Soul: the most fundamental foundation of all that is. Formless yet throughout all form. Soul and Isness are interchangeable terms indicating the same thing.

Spirit: the nonphysical self-image template of the individual life-form within the multiverse.

Thought: an idea, plan, opinion, picture, et cetera, that is formed in your mind: something that you think of.

The void: the abyss; a state of no content, context, or the sense of time or self.

Appendix

Mental Spectrum Classes:
8 - Emotion, Feelings, Will
9 - Thought, Imagination, Memory

Frequency Classes that Bridge Mind and Consciousness:
10 - Curiosity, Relaxation, Innocence

Harmonious Frequency Classes:
11 - Observation, Sharing, Compassion
12 - Silence, Acceptance, Appreciation
13+ - Unconditioned Love

Warrior's Meditation:
Eyes: Initially Open
Position: Initially seated
Duration: At least 15 minutes initially

Open the senses spherically, beginning with sight and continuing in steps through sound, smell, taste, and finally the feeling of the body. Relax as much as possible and gradually incorporate movement and other daily life challenges into this meditation.

If you would like the audiobook edition of *The Unbound Soul*, you can get it HERE for free with a one month's trial of Audible.com.

Alternatively, if you would like the audiobook but without subscribing to Audible.com, you can get it at tremendous discount if you have already purchased the Kindle edition.

Notes

Index

B

being in the zone 1

belief systems 1, 2, 3, 4, 5, 6, 7, 8

Bible 1, 2, 3, 4, 5, 6, 7

biomagnetism 1, 2

biorhythm 1, 2, 3, 4, 5, 6

blasphemy 1

bodywork 1, 2, 3

Buddha 1, 2, 3, 4, 5, 6, 7, 8, 9

Buddhism 1, 2, 3

Buddhist 1, 2, 3, 4, 5

C

California 1, 2, 3, 4, 5, 6

ceremony 1, 2, 3, 4, 5, 6, 7, 8, 9, 10

chanting 1, 2, 3, 4, 5, 6, 7, 8

Charlotte 1

Christ 1, 2, 3, 4, 5, 6, 7, 8, 9, 10, 11, 12, 13, 14, 15, 16, 17, 18, 19, 20, 21, 22, 23, 24, 25, 26

Christ-consciousness 1, 2

Christian 1, 2, 3, 4, 5, 6, 7, 8, 9, 10, 11, 12, 13, 14

Christianity 1, 2, 3

Christmas 1, 2, 3

Civil Rights Movement 1

clairaudience 1, 2, 3

D

divine 1, 2, 3, 4, 5, 6

DNA 1

download 1, 2, 3

dreams 1, 2, 3, 4, 5, 6, 7, 8, 9, 10, 11, 12, 13, 14, 15

E

Ecuador 1, 2

education 1, 2, 3, 4

Elder Scrolls 1

Elvin Forest 1, 2, 3

Emory University 1, 2

emotional release 1

enemies 1, 2

energy fields 1, 2, 3, 4, 5, 6, 7, 8

evil spirits 1

exercise 1, 2, 3, 4, 5, 6, 7, 8, 9, 10, 11, 12

F

fasting 1, 2, 3

Final Fantasy 1

food 1, 2, 3, 4, 5, 6, 7, 8, 9, 10, 11, 12, 13, 14, 15, 16, 17, 18, 19, 20, 21, 22, 23, 24, 25, 26, 27, 28, 29, 30, 31, 32, 33, 34, 35

forgiveness 1, 2, 3, 4, 5, 6

Fukushima 1

J

K

Q

R

S

T

About the Author

Richard Haight began his path of awakening at age eight when he made a solemn promise in a vision to dedicate his life to enlightenment and to share what he found with the world. He took his first steps toward that promise at age 12 when he began formal martial arts training.

At the age of 24, Richard moved to Japan to advance his training with masters of the sword, staff, and aiki-jujutsu. During his 15 years living in Japan, Richard was awarded masters licenses in four Samurai arts as well as a traditional healing art called Sotai-ho.

Throughout his life, Richard has had a series of profound visions that have ultimately guided him to the realization of the Oneness that the ancient spiritual teachers often spoke of. This understanding ultimately transformed the arts that he teaches and has resulted in the writing of *The Unbound Soul*.

Through his books, and his meditation and martial arts seminars, Richard Haight is helping to ignite a worldwide spiritual awakening that is free of all constraints and open to anyone of any level. Richard Haight now lives and teaches in southern Oregon, U.S.A.

Here, I provide proof of my background, as some readers have openly questioned the authenticity of my story. It is my hope that the photos provided will put such distractions to rest. Ultimately, it is up to you, the reader, to prove these teachings true or false through your own life.

Receiving the License of Full Mastery from Master Osaki, Shizen
Kanagawa, Japan, July 2012.

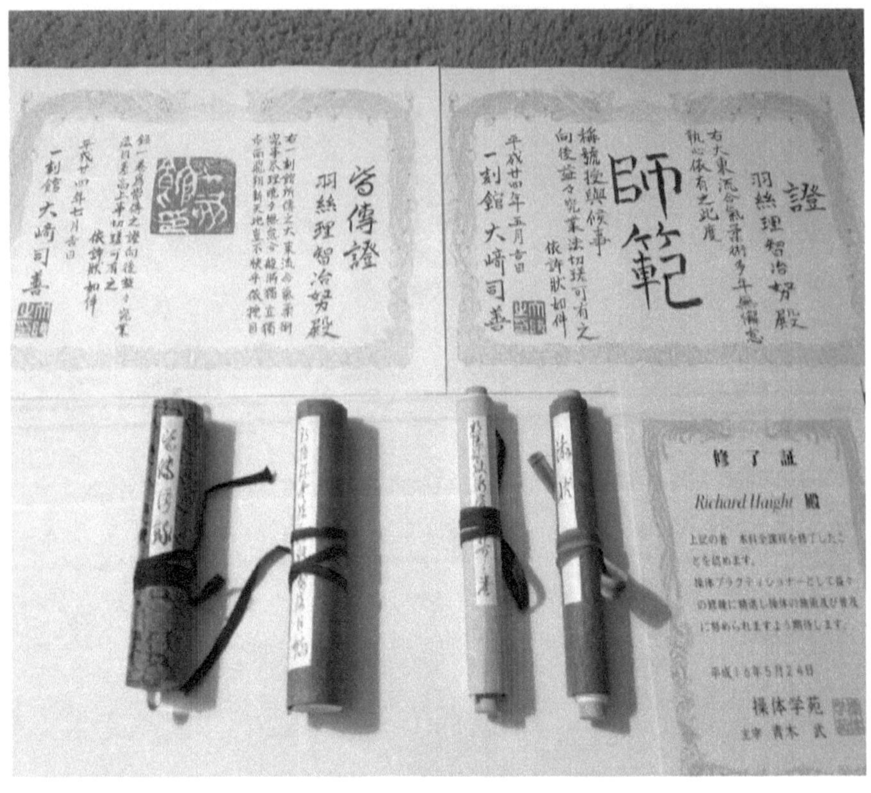

Licenses of Full Mastery (equivalent to 10th degree blackbelt) in Daito-ryu Aikijujutsu, Yagyu Shinkage-ryu Hyoho, Shinkage-ryu Jojutsu, Seigo-ryu Battojutsu, as well as Sotai-ho, which is a traditional Japanese therapy modality

Front row, Haight with Osaki Shizen, Sensei.
Kanagawa, Japan, October 2017

Contact

Here are some ways to connect with Richard Haight's teachings:

Website:
www.richardlhaight.com

One-Month Free Meditation Class Trial:
www.richardlhaight.com/services

Publishing Notifications:
www.richardlhaight.com/notifications

YouTube:
Tools of Spiritual Awakening with Richard L Haight

Facebook:
www.facebook.com/richardlhaightauthor

Email:
contact@richardlhaight.com

Book Club Questions

1. What do you think motivated the Haight to write The Unbound Soul?

2. Why do you think Haight chose to include his personal story?

3. What aspects of Haight's personal story could you most relate to?

4. What aspects of Haight's personal story could you not relate to?

5. In your opinion, what was the most powerful story that Haight shared?

6. Do you think The Unbound Soul would have worked well as a book without the personal story?

7. Do you feel that Haight was being completely sincere and honest in his writing?

8. What is original or unique about The Unbound Soul?

9. What feelings did The Unbound Soul evoke for you?

10. What is your favorite quote from The Unbound Soul and why?

11. Haight shares many stories of his interactions with his mentors. Have you ever had a mentor? How was the experience?

12. Which spiritual vision in the book was most impactful for you?

13. Which teaching in The Unbound Soul most applies to your life?

14. Which teaching in The Unbound Soul didn't make much sense to you?

15. Have you had an unexpected euphoric experience? What brought it on?

16. The author describes a pulling sensation that guides him to various spiritual experiences. Have you ever experienced "the pull"?

17. Have you ever experienced visionary states of consciousness?

18. Can you recall ever experiencing what Haight refers to as frequencies of

consciousness?

19. Haight discusses being depressed with suicidal tendencies. Could you relate to his feelings?

20. In the chapter titled The Quest, Haight details spending four days alone in the forest with no distractions. Have you ever spent an extended period of time alone for self reflection?

21. In the chapter titled The Amazon, Haight shares his experience of taking a psychedelic substance. What if anything did you find of value in that chapter?

22. In the Chapter titled The Wheel of Life, Haight describes the death process, afterlife, and reincarnation. What did you find of value in that topic, if anything?

23. What do you feel is the primary difference between mind and what Haight refers to as consciousness?

24. What do you think is the most important idea that Haight is trying to convey?

25. If you could ask Haight any question, what would it be?